ISBN: 9781290777926

Published by:
HardPress Publishing
8345 NW 66TH ST #2561
MIAMI FL 33166-2626

Email: info@hardpress.net
Web: http://www.hardpress.net

DULCE DOMUM

DULCE DOMUM

GEORGE MOBERLY

(D.C.L.; HEADMASTER OF WINCHESTER COLLEGE, 1835–1866
BISHOP OF SALISBURY, 1869–1885)

HIS FAMILY AND FRIENDS

BY HIS DAUGHTER
C. A. E. MOBERLY

WITH PORTRAITS AND ILLUSTRATIONS

Domum, domum, dulce domum
Domum, domum, dulce domum,
Dulce, dulce, dulce domum,
Dulce domum resonemus.

LONDON
JOHN MURRAY, ALBEMARLE STREET, W.
1911

PRINTED BY
HAZELL, WATSON AND VINEY, LD.,
LONDON AND AYLESBURY.

PREFACE

Now that the large majority of the persons mentioned in these pages are gone, and the record is of a generation that has passed, this book is published chiefly in the hope that it may come into the hands of those for whom it was originally written.

Thanks are due to all those who have kindly allowed letters to be published, and to the *Guardian* for leave to extract passages written after the deaths of my father and the Rev. John Keble. Much of the account of Bishop Moberly's early life has already appeared in "Six Great Head Masters," but the story is reproduced in his own words as told by himself to the writer.

C. A. E. M.

November, 1910.

CONTENTS

vii

ILLUSTRATIONS

CHRONOLOGY

George Moberly

DULCE DOMUM

INTRODUCTION

ONE of the reasons against writing family history is
that, unless material may be used which is unsuitable to more than a small audience, it is exceedingly
difficult to preserve any atmosphere of reality.   In
the following story journals, letters, and names are
used as could only be done in private, or semi-
private.   The company for which it is put together
can hardly be called small, though it is closely
related.   At this moment my father's and mother's
immediate descendants number eighty-one persons.
Bishop and Mrs. Moberly had fifteen children, all
of whom lived beyond childhood, and forty-one
grandchildren ; and they already have twenty-five
great-grandchildren.   Some   of   the   sons   and
daughters have passed behind the veil, but only
one of the younger generations is missing from
the family circle on earth.[1]   To my many nephews
and nieces this story is dedicated, in the belief that
they will be glad to make acquaintance with the
relations that they have never seen, and, as the

[1] Captain Ambrose John Awdry.

1

generations pass, with those they have never heard of.

It would be absurd to suppose that our love for the happy days of old exceeded that felt by other large and cheerful families; but there is one reason why our retrospect is interesting, and that is in its connection with the history of the Church in England after a critical moment. In our early days the English Church had only lately been reawakened · to realise fully its claim to be both Catholic and Apostolic. For some generations, whilst jealously guarding her apostolicity of doctrine, she had allowed the Church of Rome to monopolise the idea and the name of " Catholic." It had been the fashion to consider " Catholics " as meaning members of the Roman branch alone. The Oxford Movement helped to rectify this. Through good report and bad report, through great sorrows and great faithfulness the day was won, and now English churchmen know that the branches of the One Church can, and do, live side by side, each having much to correct, but each having a right to be considered true, in so far as the doctrines taught recognise the Church as being both Catholic and Apostolic. It is not yet known to what extent the future unity of the Church may depend on the faithfulness and purity of the Church of England.

The Oxford Movement is said to have arisen in great measure through the influence of John Keble's holy life, which arrested the attention of his friends.   In 1835 Mr. Keble came to Hursley, five miles from Winchester, as vicar of a country parish, where he lived in great quietness until his death in 1866.   In the same year in which Mr. Keble came to Hursley, my father became Headmaster of Winchester College.   He was no disciple of Mr. Keble's, yet he did most fully appreciate the newly recovered hold on Church doctrine won for England by the Oxford Movement, and in essentials they were agreed, as "The Great Forty Days" and, later, his Bampton Lectures, showed. For thirty-one years he taught Winchester boys the Church catechism, and by earnest work produced a tone of quiet, manly, intelligent church-manship in the school, not different in kind from what had been before, but marked in its results.

Four miles from Winchester, and linked to the parish of Hursley, was the village of Otterbourne. Here Miss Charlotte Yonge grew up under Mr. Keble's direct teaching, and through her gift of story-writing spread that teaching far and near. It is difficult for the present generation, which in these days has so much, to estimate the work accomplished by Miss Yonge.   Partly it judges of her and of her powers by the weaker work done in late middle life and old age ; partly it does not stop to think that when she began to write she had few rivals.   Miss Sewell was publishing, but George Eliot had not yet arisen.   Miss Yonge, through her popular stories, educated a host of good women writers, such as Miss Roberts, Miss

Peard, Miss Coleridge, and many others, who began their authorship through the medium of the *Monthly Packet.* Not only through her own prolific writings, but through the numbers of story-writers who have followed in her wake, she largely influenced the mothers of the next generation. The strenuous, intelligent, inquiring girls presented by her books were almost a new departure. The single heroines of Miss Austen's and Miss Ferrier's novels, the Emmas and Elizabeths, Annes and Marys, sensible, bright, and clever, did not stand alone in Miss Yonge's books, but had sisters and friends as charming as themselves; and the fathers of the next generation were also strongly interested and influenced by them. The high-minded tone of her young men and maidens delighted soldiers, statesmen, professional men, and countless lads who have loved, and still love, her historical stories, such as " The Little Duke " and " The Dove in the Eagle's Nest."

For thirty years Mr. Keble, Miss Yonge, and my father, each being, in differing degrees, centres of Church teaching and influence, lived in the closest intimacy and friendship; and it is difficult to overestimate the richness, fullness, and variety of living interests which they brought into the lives of one another. It is probable that each one had many more personally like-minded friends—friends corresponded with constantly and met occasionally —but for these three there was the exceedingly close bond of neighbourhood. It was an actual daily intercourse for so long (absolutely shared by Mrs. Keble, Mrs. Yonge, and my mother) which made the tie so binding. For twenty-seven years my father rented a farm in the woodlands close to Hursley, and we were in the habit (during the summer months) of seeing the vicar and his wife at least three times a week. On Wednesdays and Fridays, after the service, Mr. Keble and Dr. Moberly frequently spent the rest of the morning walking up and down the country road in uninterrupted conversation : even if not agreed on all points, they must have taken a great amount of counsel on many subjects from one another during those walks. During the other months in the year, whenever the Kebles and Yonges came into Winchester for Cathedral or for shopping, they, as a matter of course, made their headquarters in College Street. It is doubtful whether the Kebles had many acquaintances in the town beyond the College, where were Warden Barter, and, for a few years, Mr. Charles Wordsworth (afterwards Bishop of St. Andrews). So little was Mr. Keble known personally, that when he was living at Hursley, a clergyman's daughter residing in the Close was heard to affirm that " Keble had been one of the Reformation divines ! " A cart from our farm, carrying milk, butter, and bread to the school, every day throughout the year, passed through Otterbourne and St. Cross[1] and back. By

---

[1] Our grandfather, Mr. Thomas Crokat, with his son and daughter John and Tina Crokat, lived for some years at St. Cross.

this means letters, books, and parcels of all sizes from Otterbourne were answered from College Street, without the medium of the post, before noon on the same day. The Yonges were within a walk of the Kebles, and had their own possibilities of immediate communication.

Winchester was a smaller place then than it is now. There were no houses on St. Giles' hill, and no station at its foot. On the Romsey road the gaol (which was itself new) was the last building. The Training College for Schoolmasters and the Hospital were built outside the town while we were living at Winchester. Houses stopped at Culver's Close in Southgate Street, and with the Queen Inn in Kingsgate Street. The boys' boarding-houses in Culver's Close were not yet built. St. Cross was entirely divided from Winchester by fields, and beyond the church at St. Cross there was nothing but the little village of Compton between it and Otterbourne. Shawford Down had no house upon it, unless it was one lately built close to the railway, where there was then no station. Otterbourne hill, now altered in character by telegraph poles, water works, and the endless passing traffic of bicycles and motor cars, was a quiet country road, with the furzy common above, on which were a very few, deeply thatched, scattered cottages. Chandlers Ford was a country wayside station with no surrounding houses; the roads from it to Otterbourne and Hursley being delicious, silent, wooded lanes, where nightingales sang in abundance and little commons and deep fir woods alternated, and where a way-farer was scarcely .ever met. Our own lane (joining the two main roads from Winchester to Southampton) was cut out of pine and oak woods, within which foxgloves grew in forests. The lane and woods were entirely unfrequented save by birds, squirrels, rabbits, and glorious butterflies ; heather banks and bracken had it all their own way, and the wild strawberries and blackberries were untouched unless we took them. These woods—now, alas ! being cleared for small houses and villas in connection with Chandlers Ford—were the scenes of our picnics with the Kebles, Heathcotes, and Yonges, and are to us full of sacred memories.

Sacred memories : for though the life was full of so-called secular interests, the impression of the whole is of an atmosphere of holiness unparalleled by anything we have met with since. Reviews of Miss Yonge's life, and even of Mr. Keble's, speak as though their country lives must have been quiet to dullness, or at least that they produced no incidents useful for biographical purposes. To those who at that time were their nearest neighbours, their lives were wonderful examples of the self-controlled vivacity of high spiritual existence. The eyes of our elders were fixed on the holiest realities of Spirit, and in the services of the English Church they found the atmosphere in which they breathed most freely. Theology was to them a thrilling interest, and they moved and spoke and thought with unseen presences round them, not psychical or fancy-spiritual, but as realising the angels round about the Throne and the solemn awe of the Throne. In order to be able to think reverently, soberly, and highly about it, all their powers of culture, of insight, of common-sense, of religious obser-vance, and of social interest were to be fully trained and used for the purpose. Though no words about the Vision were suffered in our hearing out of church but with hushed voices and almost bated breath, yet the troops of children by whom they were surrounded did not miss the significance. The knowledge of the Centre round which their thoughts revolved was an open secret, and an infinite reverence for holy things was the first lesson burnt into us by the demeanour of our leaders.

Next in importance to the daily services (when-ever possible) the subject of Church Foreign Missions was nearest to their hearts. They were not so much a duty as a predominant interest. Missionaries needed no introduction ; even when not personal friends, their names were all known and honoured. Letters from New Zealand, Melanesia, Hawaii, and Africa were eagerly handed from one to another. Many missionaries asked for a service at Hursley Church before going out, and nothing could exceed the warmth of welcome to any who returned. It was the natural thing for Miss Yonge to give the proceeds of her books to foreign missions, and they were given with enthusiasm.

Our knowledge of Mr. Keble only included the later years of his life. We knew that he had lived through one of the most exciting controversial periods known to the English Church ; that the principal actors in it had been his dearest friends ; that the death of Hurrell Froude and the secession of Dr. Newman had wrung his heart with personal grief as well as sorrow for the Church of England ; and that the difficulty about his friend Isaac Williams concerned the filling up of his own vacated professorship of poetry at Oxford. We knew that he was in touch with every throb of the English Church, yet we saw him hardly ever leave home, or be away from the daily services, and a deep reserve and detachment of spirit, only to be explained by his living communion with heaven, was the chief impression we had of him : compatible as it was with the most kindly and bright interest in the details of our lives and of other lives.

Miss Yonge was comparatively young when we girls and boys first realised her, and the same interest in surroundings, yet detachment from them, was noticeable in her. Few persons living altogether in the country led a more intellectual life. Stars and moon, birds, flowers, and shells were eagerly studied. She read everything and forgot nothing. She had an enormous correspondence, including letters from admirers of her books all

the world over. Sometimes she would show us a
" round robin " addressed to her from a number
of ladies of rank in Holland, or letters from the
governess of Princess Margherita of Savoy about
" The Heir of Redclyffe," which the Princess was
reading, or from unknown Americans and bright
English girls who were desirous of writing themselves. Yet these most exciting and unusual
additions to a country life never seemed to matter
much. Intensely enjoyed as they were, such incidents only accentuated to her the need of living
the spiritual life more entirely. She was never
lost in her daily occupations. Her collections, her
botany, her astonishing knowledge of historical
persons, her clever stories, and village interests,
and duties of friendship, so delightful to her eager
mind, were always controlled to form material
for higher perception in spiritual realities. The
occupations of later life, such as editing *Mothers
in Council*, writing papers for the higher religious
education, and the festivities in her honour at the
Winchester High School for Girls, or the seventieth-
birthday present, were duties thoroughly done and
gratifications thoroughly appreciated, but to those
who knew her best they seemed strangely apart
from her. They were interesting to the extent to
which they might do service to Christ, on Whom
her whole heart was set ; otherwise they came and
went, and her life would have been as complete
without them.

Whether amongst her neighbours, or in stories

meant to influence a wider circle, the comprehensiveness of the spiritual combat inspired all Charlotte Yonge's undertakings. The idea embodied in La Motte Fouqué's "Sintram" gleamed through "The Heir of Redclyffe." A very fine engraving of Albert Dürer's picture of "The Knight and his Companions," which always hung over her writing-table, seemed to us to be the spiritual source to which many characters in her stories could be traced. The conception of natural weakness made strong by religious reality underlay such characters as Charles Edmonstone, Claude Mohun, Louis Fitzjocelyn, and Clement Underwood; whilst the charming weak person without religious effort, who gradually collapsed, was illustrated by Owen Sandbrook and Edgar Underwood. The same is traceable in the women's characters. Gentle Amabel Edmonstone, childlike Violet Martindale, and helpless Christina Sorel became, through faithful effort, the central persons around whom others could revolve. It was the discipline of their religion alone which steadied and made whole imperfect characters, such as Lilias Mohun, Theodora Martindale, Rachel Curtis, and Caroline Liddell; whilst the women without the inward discipline, as Laura Edmonstone, Lucy Kendal, and Lucilla Sandbrook never developed. Miss Yonge was fond of introducing as side characters quiet persons who, having gone through trials themselves, were interested to watch and encourage others in combat; and about them there is a faint reminiscence of Verena praying in her cloister: such are Ermine Williams, John Martindale, Alethea Weston, Margaret May, Mary Ross, and Edmund Arundel. There was an allusion to La Motte Fouqué's " Four Seasons" in Miss Yonge's suggestion that " Heartsease," " The Heir of Redclyffe," " Hopes and Fears," and " Dynevor Terrace " made a series of the seasons.

Whatever charm her early books had from the literary point of view, they were also permeated (so naturally that it was almost unconscious on her part) by her clear spiritual insight ; and it was the revelation of this which acted as a spiritual tonic in many and many a household, and was one secret of her popularity. She had a great message, and she was able to deliver it in a most persuasive form, exactly as it was needed at that moment. However much Guy Morville and Louis Fitzjocelyn were criticised as untrue to life, the possibility that a high standard of Christian holiness of life might supplement natural charm, and should in no way make merriment less bubbling and overflowing, had been suggested, and her audience welcomed the suggestion. Her own character of natural dependence and light-heartedness, converted by steadfast Christian endeavour into one of singular force and dignity, was often reflected in her early books, and illustrated Mr. Keble's thought :

" Why should we fear youth's draught of joy,
    If pure would sparkle less ?"

The world may now have many different ways of learning the lesson, or it may have become indifferent to it. Very few authors have messages for centuries other than their own, and Miss Yonge's books have been, in great measure, relegated to a back shelf; but her own personality remains as a study of peculiar attractiveness.

No one could accompany her twice daily to the Church services in the last years of her life and fail to realise that her life's work had consisted in learning to worship. The Psalms, Lessons, Creeds, and Prayers were the paramount interest. All her cultivation, and the experiences of an intensely-lived long life had been the means for entering more deeply into their meaning. The loud, thoughtful, joyous tone with which she was accustomed to repeat the Apostles' Creed, and especially the triumphant "The Life Everlasting. Amen," revealed the breadth and depth of her intellectual and spiritual life.

The last time the writer saw Miss Yonge was on an expedition to Winchester Cathedral to see the small statue of Mr. Keble placed by Dean Kitchen (as a companion to one of Bishop Ken) in one of the side niches of Bishop Fox's beautiful altar screen, lately restored. Before attending the afternoon service, we walked round and looked at the tablet to Jane Austen's memory. Now the reredos in the Lady Chapel has been restored in memory of Charlotte Yonge, whilst Mr. Keble, as the Winchester saint of the century, stands in

attendance on the great Central Figure, in company
with St. Swithun and St. Boniface, St. Alphege
and St. Ealswyth, Wykeham and Waynflete, on
the screen which replaced the one on which Canute
hung up his crown.

Winchester College has, in the last hundred
years, greatly developed, and has gained a special
place of regard among public schools.   The thirty-
one years of my father's Headmastership led up to
a critical and important period.   Ten years before
his resignation, the Oxford and Cambridge Commission, 1854–5 (which on account of the intimate
connection of New College and King's College with
Winchester and Eton caused these schools to be
included within it), marked an era when improvements of all kinds set in, vigorously carried out by
Dr. Ridding.[1]   It is one of his glories that the
spirit and tradition of the school were so carefully
adhered to that the splendid reorganisation of work
and buildings came, in some measure, as fulfilments
rather than as causing a painful rupture with
the past.   Some initial steps had already been
taken by his predecessor.   As far as a man with
seven sons and eight daughters could venture on
financial risks they had been made by Dr. Moberly.
With a view to ultimately emptying Commoners,
tutors' houses had been opened,[2] and the large
increase of numbers produced by the change caused

---

[1] Appointed Headmaster Sept. 1866.
[2] In 1859 Mr. Henry Wickham opened his house ; 1860, **Harry
Moberly's** house ; 1862, Mr. Du Boulay's house.

the removal of the partition wall between College meads and Commoner grass court.[1] This was done, under the greatest difficulties, before Dr. Ridding came even as Second master.[2] It will not detract from the greatness of what Dr. Ridding accomplished to remember that the presence of the late Headmaster among the body of Fellows greatly forwarded the schemes of his successor, though truly even then it was not always easy to carry reforms through.

The few domestic words written from Winchester during those years may impart some of the spirit of those ancient days. The chapters that touch on Winchester belong strictly to my father's tenure of office, though we take a personal pride in the developments which came later and are associated with the name of one indistinguishable from our own family circle.

Though my father and mother form the centre of interest in this story, it is not meant to be the biography of either. As such it would be quite inadequate. Very little is extracted from George Moberly's journals beyond notes on family affairs ; just so much about public matters is retained as to form a setting for the picture of daily life over a large number ∕of years. Chiefly from lack of material his public life as Headmaster of Winchester College is not specially dwelt upon, nor is there any attempt to make the picture other than

[1] In 1862.
[2] Appointed 1862 ; came to Winchester Jan. 1863.

domestic : to appraise, or even to mention, many of his writings and views on various important subjects, or to speak of his theories of education, or evidences of success.[1]   His work as Bishop of Salisbury is rather more prominent, because it is within the author's own recollection, and his note-books and charges afforded some aid ; but much of great importance to a really complete view of him and of his opinions, in both positions, is entirely passed over, as being outside the intention of the record.   The story of his school and Oxford careers was taken down at intervals from his lips.   My mother was surprised to find that what she had told us of her early years had been preserved in her own words, and she was shy of the old-fashioned stiff language of her journals, but on being asked, did not forbid use being made of them.   Miss Yonge saw the greater part of the book, and enhanced its value by adding, unasked, footnotes, as well as her own section of it.   Three of the sisters (Kitty, Emily, and Annie) wrote portions giving pictures of the home life at different stages of its develop-ment, whilst my eldest brother (George Herbert)

[1] For various reasons—partly from strong feeling as to the sacredness of correspondence—my father, on leaving Winchester, destroyed masses of letters from friends both in public and private life, including many most affectionate ones from parents and old pupils. Knowing something of the value of these letters (for his judgment being singularly independent, people of very different views wrote to him at moments of educational, political, and ecclesiastical anxiety), it was a grief to us to know that they were gone, and for purposes of biography the loss was irreparable. His journals were extremely bare of anything that could take the place of correspondence, and for ten years they were written in Latin.

added my father's views on Confirmation at Winchester.

The book is an attempt to sketch very lightly the picture of a home, and to realise afresh and from within the atmosphere surrounding a circle of friends through which they can, in some degree, speak for themselves. An unusually large family party grew up quietly amongst its own friends and in delightful circumstances. There is a perennial interest about Mr. and Mrs. Keble and Miss Charlotte Yonge ; and though the names of Dean Church, Bishop Patteson, Warden Barter, Bishop Ridding, Bishop Awdry, and my brothers Canon George Herbert, Dr. Robert Campbell, and Canon Walter Allan Moberly, occur in close connection with my father and mother, yet the story is addressed only to those who have a personal reason for desiring to know the outlines of a history rapidly becoming ancient.

CHAPTER I

GEORGE MOBERLY

There is a day in Spring
When under all the earth the secret germs
Begin to stir and glow before they bud ;
The wealth and festal pomps of Midsummer
Lie in the heart of that inglorious day,
Which no man names with blessing, though its work
Is blest by all the world. Such days there are
In the slow story of the growth of souls.

The Story of Queen Isabel by M. S.

GEORGE MOBERLY was born in St. Petersburg on October 10, 1803. His father, Edward Moberly, born at Knutsford in Cheshire, had married Sarah Cayley, daughter of John Cayley, English consul at St. Petersburg. They had a large family of eight sons and three daughters. These eleven persons have had between them the unusual number of 93 children and 256 grandchildren. George was a younger son ; his sisters Fanny, Harriet, and Emily became Mrs. Cattley, Mrs. Harvey, and Mrs. Bennett. The family had returned to England on account of the war when George's recollections first begin.

18

George Moberly's Story

"I cannot remember the life in St. Petersburg, but I remember an incident at Ham very clearly. One wet Sunday we could none of us go to church, and my father read the service to the household. I, being a small boy, was given a pencil and paper and told to keep quiet. I amused myself very happily for some time, trying to draw the opposite house, when I suddenly became interested in the Second Commandment which was being read aloud, and was greatly impressed to hear that it was wrong to make any likeness of anything in heaven above, or in the earth beneath. 'If that is the case,' I thought, 'of course it is wrong to draw,' and I left off; but after thinking it over a bright idea occurred to me, 'At any rate there can be no harm in my drawing, for it is not a bit like!' I took up my pencil again and went on quite comfortably.

"After a time my father took my youngest brother, Arthur, and me to Mr. Richards' school at Winchester, in Hyde Street. On our way we stopped at Romsey. After luncheon the waiter was asked whether there was anything to be seen in the place. He answered, 'Oh yes, there is an apple-tree growing at the top of the church tower.' So we marched through the Abbey and up the tower to see the apple-tree, and never looked, or thought of looking, at the church itself, which is the pride of the neighbourhood. How well I remember the first evening at school and our retiring together behind a tree to cry! There was a big boy there who wore 'baggy whites,' of the name of William Leeke. A few years later he carried the colours of the 52nd regiment at Waterloo.

"When my father went back to Russia in 1814, we were left (a whole heap of boys) over a mercer's shop in Fore Street, Cripplegate, under the charge of my aunt Margaret and my brother William, who was not twenty-one. Being a delicate boy, I had to lie on my back for a year and a half, and only got up to go upon crutches. During that time I read through Hume's History of England and Russell's Modern Europe. I was then sent to Southampton, of all places, for sea-bathing. Having five shillings of my own, I bought a book describing the antiquities of the town and wandered about alone hunting up the places. The bathing was very queer ; it was in a bath only full at high-water, with palings round it. There was generally some one there before me ; but if I was fortunate the guardian of the bath would touch his hat and say, ' Sir, the bath is void.'

" After a time my brothers all went into the mercantile line and mostly returned to Russia, with the exception of one sailor and one soldier. I should probably have done the same, but for the kindness of my mother's friend, Lady Pembroke, the daughter of Count Worontzoff. Count Simon Worontzoff was the Russian Ambassador in London, and his daughter being very young and without a mother, the wife of one of the attachés, Madame Poggenpol, used to take her out. Madame Poggenpol was sister to Mrs. Edward Moberly, and Lady Pembroke always preserved an attachment to the two sisters. She took a fancy to me, and managed to get me a nomination to Winchester College. From that time *my* centre of interest became Winchester, Oxford, and Winchester again, whilst the centre of interest to my family was in Russia, to which I only went twice. I was rather a lonely little boy in those days, and spent the holidays with any relation who would have me, until William married and settled at Whitchurch, near Pangbourne.

" I went to Winchester in 1816. They were

very rough days at Winchester; delicate boys
could not bear it, and I only managed to stand
the life by being excused 'Morning Hills' and
compulsory cricket. We had Chapel, School, and
'Morning Hills' before breakfast, which we rarely
got before 10 a.m. No boy had meat more than
once a week, owing to the horrid way in which it
was cut up. I was a small junior when College
was barricaded against the masters, and took my
part in the mutiny, being one of those who
watched all one night on Middle Gate, when we
frightened ourselves with ghost stories. If the
authorities had been wise they would have let
famine do its work,—we were all so very hungry.
The soup made by those boys who were told off as
cooks was not nice. It consisted of a mass of raw
potatoes at the bottom, then a layer of warm
water, and, lastly, two inches of bacon fat floating
at the top. The Warden (Bishop Huntingford)
and the masters held a parley with the boys from
a window, and directed us to write down our
grievances : this was done at once, the list unfortunately beginning with, 'that you are ugly.' We
were treacherously promised redress if we would
at once repair to our homes. In great delight we
all rushed up into the town ; but at the Slype, the
narrow passage at the west end of the Cathedral,
we were stopped by a row of soldiers with fixed
bayonets. The boys turned back, pursued by the
soldiers, and on reaching the College found the
gates shut and another row of soldiers drawn
across the road, so that we were enclosed. One
by one we were admitted into College, and the
rage of the boys was beyond all bounds. In our
burning indignation the great paving-stones from
the quadrangle were torn up, and every window
that could be reached was smashed.

" I was a boy of no mark whatever at Win-

chester. I never got the Books, and New College
was lost to me from the time I went. I was put
into Senior Part Fourth, but was sixth or seventh
of my year, and though I bettered my position
twice it gained me nothing ; for though I stood
fourth of my year, two founder's kin were put
first of all and so I was again sixth, and four were
elected. I entirely acquiesced in the verdict of
my masters and schoolfellows, and, so far as I ever
thought about it at all, never supposed myself
capable of anything. There was no special religious training. My father and mother were good,
God-fearing people, but there was no teaching on
such subjects. Then my preparation for Confirmation was nil. One day a lot of boys were sent
for to the master's study ; we had just come off
" Hills," and were hot and tired, and I was faint ;
thereupon the master sent me away, and I never
heard a word on the subject from that time to the
actual Confirmation.

"Lady Pembroke was disappointed that Winchester did not lead to New College ; but she
wished me to go to Oxford, and gave me a
hundred a year for three years. In what a
strangely casual way it was that I went to
Balliol ! William, who had the direction of me,
knew nothing at all about the University, and
being quite helpless, asked old Mr. Pigou, of
Whitchurch, what to do. Mr. Pigou applied to
Mr. Ellison at Balliol, and I heard nothing more
about it until, in the spring of 1822, I was sent
for to Balliol.

" I well remember the first afternoon at College,
and paying my first visit to my tutor, Mr. Ellison.
He took me across the staircase, and knocked at
the opposite door. 'Come in,' was called out, and
Mr. Ellison introduced me to Milne and left me
there. Milne himself was a very good fellow ; but

Ellison should have known his man better than to have introduced me only to him. He was in a set of fast men who were rather avoided. It was extremely difficult to know other sets, and impossible to leave the one into which I had been accidentally thrown by my tutor.

"It was everything to me not to go to New College. Had I done so it would have been just a repetition of old days. I should have had, and continued to have, my school reputation. I should not have gone into the Schools at all, and should probably have ended as the rector of a living in the country and an excellent player on the flute. I do not know how it was, but things entirely changed when I got to Balliol. From the first moment I could not but know that I was thought much of; my tutor told me so, and my companions, and I was gratified by hearing from my scout that some one had sworn at me for being clever. In the first few months I knew that I was looked upon as a probable Fellow. I was successful in examinations, and was fortunately able to get a first class and to take my degree early.[1] I also won the English Prize Essay. In 1826 I stood for a Fellowship of Oriel against Robert Wilberforce, who was elected, but in the same year I was elected Fellow of Balliol.

"As an undergraduate I was in a bad set, and being a good whist and billiard player, played a great deal too much, and went on in a very unsatisfactory way. I am not proud of those days. But on becoming a member of the senior common room all was changed. The atmosphere was de-

[1] G. Moberly fainted in the street before his *viva-voce*; but the next morning, after the ordeal was over, he confessed that he had never enjoyed a more interesting conversation, and the examiner, Mr. Longley (afterwards Archbishop of Canterbury), told him that it had been a real pleasure to examine a man who had so thoroughly grappled with his books.

lightful to me ; all sorts of subjects were topics
of conversation, literary and religious, for men's
minds were full of Church discussions in those
days.   I seemed to spring towards these higher
subjects, became immensely interested, read a great
deal, and began to have my opinions.

"How well I remember receiving my first £20
as a tutor!   I handled it and looked at it, and
sat down to write to my father that I hoped I
should never cost him another shilling, and I
never did.   When I was a young tutor of Balliol,
Manning was an undergraduate.   At one of my
first lectures (on the sixth book of Thucydides) I
told Mr. Manning to go on, which he did, nothing
loth, at railway speed.   After a little time I
stopped him, and said timidly that I did not think
he was right, upon which Mr. Manning looked up
innocently and said, 'I beg your pardon, but I
feel sure I am right.'   I held to it that he was
wrong, but he assured me that he had made no
mistake.   As I was modest and shy, and Manning
was not at all modest or shy, I gave in, and made
up my mind to look at the passage afterwards.
This I did, and sure enough it was just as I
thought,—I was perfectly right and he was perfectly
wrong.   One evening, when he was Fellow of
Merton and had become a great friend, he was
having tea with me, and I referred to my first
lecture and asked what he meant by it.   He said,
'Oh, didn't you understand?'   'Understand,' said
I, 'what was there to understand?'   'That I was
going on extempore, and hadn't looked at it at all!'
Two years ago, when our old friend Chapman died,
I received an affectionate letter from the Cardinal,
and on the blank sheet he wrote, 'How well I
remember your music and poetry and our metaphysics, and' (here he again misquoted the passage),
'and all your malice against me!'   I wrote back

that the words recalled a scene of long ago when a shy tutor was browbeaten by a most audacious undergraduate.

" Archbishop Tait was my pupil the whole time that he was an undergraduate at Balliol. I remember his coming up his first term as a shy young Scotchman; and wishing to do the best thing for him, I sent for Manning, introduced them to each other and made them have tea together in my room, and told Manning to look after him and see that he got into a good set. Years after, at my consecration as Bishop of Salisbury, as we walked in procession down Westminster Abbey, the Archbishop turned round and said to me, 'This is a strange reversal of the old order of things, is it not?'

" My ordination as deacon was in 1826. There was no previous examination; I called upon Bishop Lloyd in his rooms at Christ Church, and he took down a Greek Testament from a shelf and set me on; but it was merely formal, and he asked me no questions. My first sermon was preached at Long Wittenham on the afternoon after my ordination. It lasted just ten minutes, but, to my great delight, an old woman groaned deeply in the course of it, and I thought that I had made an impression!

" Being now independent, I could travel in the vacations, and, when not accompanied by pupils, stayed a good deal with my sister Emily, who had married the Rev. Henry Bennett and lived much abroad. One summer (1830) I went with my two pupils, Sidney Herbert (son of Lady Pembroke) and Charles Thornton, to Sandgate, and one fine day we thought we would make an expedition into France; so we put our horses on board the boat, and rode about Normandy for a month. We were quite independent, and groomed our own horses. When Sidney Herbert spoke we were taken for

Frenchmen, when either of us spoke we were *not* taken for Frenchmen.   One day there came on a heavy shower and one of the party provided himself with a red cotton umbrella.   This umbrella became a great nuisance, and we tried hard to get rid of it, but in vain.   We left it behind at each inn where we stopped, but sure enough, before we had got away, some one always ran after us with, ' M'sieur, M'sieur ! votre parapluie.'   At last, one day we had luncheon in a room where there was a high standing clock with a door and a key in it. At the last moment we opened the door, put the umbrella inside, threw the key out of window into the garden, and rode away.   We never saw the umbrella again !   In 1831 I went to the Pyrenees with my pupils, Salisbury Everard and Henry Usborn.   One beautiful morning, at Nice, I got up early and went out, first calling my companions, who assured me that they were just going to get up and would be up when I came back.   As I walked along I saw a travelling carriage standing at an inn door, and going up to it found, to my astonishment, that it belonged to my brother-in-law, Henry Bennett.   He persuaded me to go with them, so I went back to our lodgings and told my companions (who were both in bed) that I was going to leave them, at which they expressed much satisfaction.   I drove with the Bennetts to Genoa, Rome, Naples, and Leghorn.   Here it was that I missed seeing your mother, of whom I had heard so much.   My sister, Emily Bennett, had a great friend, Miss Crokat, who had been called the ' Beauty of Naples ' when she had spent a winter there with the Bennetts.   Emily was fond of talking of her to me, and I quite understood her reason and made up my mind that I would see Miss Crokat, if possible.

"On my return I drove by stages to Genoa,

Turin (in a burning sun), across the Mont Cenis by night, into France by Les Echelles, and at last, just a stage short of Lyons, knocked up.   I was tired out, and *how* ill I felt!   The Place was full of gendarmes drumming and trumpeting, the sun shone maliciously, and I ran into the nearest house, where a good woman took pity on me and made me lie down.   Afterwards I gave her a very fine cameo from Rome, to her infinite delight.   Then on to Lyons and Paris, where I remember getting into a tremendous argument with a party of medical students in the evening.   I was all for talking and arguing in those days, and talked all I knew, and a little more ; but they made sure that I was a medical student!   And so, at Boulogne, I got into another fierce argument with some Frenchmen about republicanism and monarchy.

" I did not know the leaders of the Tractarian party, excepting in the slight way that Fellows of different colleges may know one another ; the chief link that I had with them was Hurrell Froude. I knew him quite well ; he was a great friend. We stayed up in Oxford to read one long vacation, and walked out together every day.   I felt great sympathy with their views, but certainly did not agree with everything that they said.   They sometimes made use of me to write pamphlets, which I was supposed to do well.   Mr. Keble was at Oriel when I first went to Oxford, but I only came across him in my last years there.   He and I first made acquaintance at the dinner-table of an old maiden lady, and we had a little talk.   There I remember noticing what Southey called ' the pendulous motion of his eyes.'   The next time was when I met some of the professors, in order to select a poem in honour of the Duke of Wellington's installation as Chancellor.   Mr. Keble and I preferred one which the others did not.   Being at that

time secretary to the Philharmonic Society, I came
across some of the musicians of the day, and had
great difficulty in getting them to pronounce the
words of ' God Save the King ' so that they could
be understood.   Paganini was one of them.   One
singer declared that he was lodging at the 'Yannec
Ox'; no one knew where it was, but at last it
was discovered that under the name of the King's
Arms was written in small letters the name of the
proprietress, 'Jane Cox.'

" 'Twice I went in the vacations to Russia to
see my parents, and was at Moscow just twenty
years after the burning of that city.   After my
father's death, my mother tried to live on at
St. Petersburg ; but she did not like it, and came
to live in Broad Street at Oxford, in order to be
near me."

These few scattered reminiscences of George
Moberly's early life, told in old age to his daughter, end here.   Three letters written in 1885,
after his death, by contemporaries at Oxford, are
inserted, as they give an outside glimpse of him
at Balliol ; and an extract from an article in the
Guardian, written at the same date, is also added.

From CANON REGINALD SMITH

" Mr. Floyer[1] and I were both his pupils at
Balliol in (I think) the years 1830 and 1831.   The
ever-rolling wheels of time have not effaced from
our memories the new life and interest infused into
our studies when he became a Fellow and Tutor
of our College.   At a later period, when there was
a great gathering of old Balliol men at the rebuild-

[1] John Floyer, Esq., for many years M.P. for Dorset,

ing of the Chapel, I was one of those who listened with sympathetic admiration to the late excellent Primate, Archbishop Tait, when he declared in his speech that whatever he possessed of accuracy of thought, he owed to Dr. Moberly's admirable lectures on Aristotle." [1]

From MR. WILLIAM HUSSEY

" I wish you to know how deeply indebted I feel to one who did far more than any other single man to quicken into activity such powers as were given to me—not only in his direct lectures, but in remarks by the way on some collateral subject, or by a few friendly words to an early comer before the class had assembled ; he would throw out a shower of sparks, too often only to be quenched in apathetic dullness, but here and there to kindle a lasting flame. To a sermon of his on ' Things indifferent,' I think I owe the first awakening of an interest in St. Paul's Epistles ; and his comments and advice on the small matters of undergraduate life involved principles of far wider application, and his words in the well-remembered silvery tones have often come back to me with a meaning beyond what I saw in them at their first utterance."

From MR. M. W. MAYOW

" When I went up to Oxford in 1830, Mr. Moberly was recognised as one of the foremost men of his time. He was a Fellow and Tutor of his College (Balliol), and eminent among those who took the lead in University affairs ; a ripe scholar ; a successful tutor ; a word of power, not only in his College, but also in the University ; well known and marked among the men of his day. Who can

[1] His pupils called his horse " Aristotle."

forget the keen light of his dark eye? Whilst his
kindly nature and his never-failing courtesy, over
and above his academic distinction, gave him a
charm and an attractiveness which were a prophetic
forecast of his future greater eminence."

From LORD CARDWELL.

" December 1878.

" MY DEAR BISHOP,—
    " Let me express to you the satisfaction
with which I have read the expression of your
feelings with respect to my venerated friend
and tutor, Chapman. . . . And when I read
your affectionate and sympathetic words, I felt
myself drawn back into all the recollections of
those earlier days. You must ever be to me the
principal figure among the Fellows of Balliol. If
it had been for no other reason it would surely
have been for this, that to your encouragement I
owed the confidence which led me to offer myself
as a servant of the State, and to your special
assistance I was indebted for my preparation for
the Schools. I trust Mrs. Moberly will permit me
to refer to the special interest with which your
pupils regarded her advent at Oxford, in which I
cordially shared. . . ."

" With a distinguished Oxford reputation, Mr.
Moberly, soon after his degree and Fellowship,
became tutor of Balliol, just at the moment when
Balliol was beginning to take the place which
Oriel had once held in the University, and was
entering on that remarkable career which has never
been interrupted from that time to this. Few
tutors, few examiners had a higher name in Oxford
than the brilliant Fellow of Balliol, whose refined
taste and keen logical power and quick sympathies

threw life and interest into any subject before him, whether in the lecture-room or in conversation and debate. Great men, of the Balliol generation of that time, passed through his lecture-rooms ; among them Archbishop Tait and Cardinal Manning.[1] It was during this time that, invited to examine at Rugby in company with Dr. Christopher Words-worth, he made acquaintance with Dr. Arnold, and was deeply impressed with his boldness and his success in raising the tone, religious and moral, of a great public school. The experience bore fruit. Widely differing in many things from Dr. Arnold, he always spoke of that visit to Rugby as having opened to his own mind the necessities and the possibilities of the Public School reform, which he so vigorously carried out when he became Master at Winchester.

" During his residence in Oxford his position towards the leaders of the movement then be-ginning was distinctly an independent one, but also one of warm and friendly interest. He could not but be attracted by so much that there was to attract in the mixture of genius and religious depth and nobleness in the leaders, and in the earnestness with which they urged their cause. But his mind was a singularly keen and critical one, as well as one strongly influenced by what was lofty and imaginative ; and while in many things feeling with them and co-operating with them, he was from early days too much alive to mistakes of judgment and action, which have since become visible enough, to throw himself unreservedly into their ranks."

The same friend goes on to speak of—

" his inexhaustible vigour, the energy and resource and decision which he brought to all matters

---

[1] Dean Stanley was also his pupil.

before him, of government, or advice, or encouragement, or, it may be, of rebuke ; the charm of his
conversation, alarming sometimes, even in its bright
kindness, from his flashes of repartee, and the
terrors of his quick and unexpected wit.[1]   Much
too keen to be imposed upon, or to impose upon
himself, and dangerous to come near, even in
playful discussion or conversation, if a man's wits
were not in order and his brain puffed up with con-
ceit and confusion, he was in practice both nobly
and generously tolerant ; he was most sincerely and
unaffectedly humble.   No one with such formidable weapons of offence as were at his disposal
in his quick and polished word-play ever cared so
little to make himself formidable."

[1] Dean Church used to tell us, on Dr. Newman's authority, that when
of an evening Mr. Moberly entered the Oriel senior common room, the
Fellows would exclaim, " Now the lightning is going to coruscate."

CHAPTER II

MARY ANNE CROKAT

L' alba vinceva l' ora mattutina
Che fuggia inanzi, sì che di lontano
Conobbi il tremolar della marina.
Purgatorio, Canto 1.

JOHN CROKAT was born at Leith, near Edinburgh, in 1741. He was by profession a master slater, a fine-looking man of strong character and of a reflective cast of mind. He was much drawn towards the Church of England, but never actually left the Presbyterian Church, of which he was a member. He married Helen Robertson, who was so very quiet and reserved that even her children never felt very well acquainted with her. They had fourteen children, of whom six sons and four daughters lived to grow up. The sons Patrick, Thomas, John, James, and Charles became merchants, and William went into the army.[1] John Crokat would not allow his sons to have all the education which they ardently desired, lest too great love of literature should lead them away from their professional callings. His speech to his younger son

[1] Afterwards General Sir William Crokat.

3

William, on his becoming an ensign in the 22nd Regiment, was remembered : " Avoid duels—they are the pride of fools. Remember that death is better than disgrace." This soldier-son, who was at the battles of Vimiera and Vittoria, was the Captain Crokat in personal attendance on Napoleon at St. Helena. It was his unpleasant duty to see Napoleon twice a day. The Emperor tried so hard to prevent this that it could not have been done but for Count Montholon's assistance. William Crokat told the story of Napoleon's anger at Sir Hudson Lowe's entrance into the dining-room, and how the Emperor exclaimed, " Break every plate : Sir Hudson Lowe has looked at it." There is still in existence the little scrap of paper sent into the next room by Dr. Arnott, and on it the words, " Crokat, why don't you come in ? He is gone.—A. A."—suggesting that a feeling of delicacy prevented his entering the room until death had actually taken place.

Thomas was the second son of John Crokat. He went early as a merchant to Leghorn, and there fell in with his great friend Robert Campbell, also a merchant, whose sister, Elspeth Arbuthnot Campbell, he afterwards married. Robert Campbell's father, John Campbell of Smiddie Green in Fife, had married Mary Maclean. This marriage was considered a great experiment, for it took place shortly after the '45, which had reawakened the old feuds between the two clans ; and the story is told that on his honeymoon, when coasting along the Isle of Skye, Mr. Campbell's life was only spared by the boatmen fortunately discovering that he had married a Maclean of Treshnish. Their son Robert found it necessary during the war to become a naturalised American subject at Leghorn, and afterwards held the post of American Consul at Genoa. He was a remarkably handsome man, with elaborately gracious manners, and his little sister Arbuthnot was a very lovely person.

During a long sojourn at Palermo in charge of the Crokats' house of business, Thomas Crokat made the acquaintance of many of the Sicilian nobles, one of whom, the Marchese Spaccaforno (afterwards Prince Cassaro), was his great friend. This nobleman was very charming and refined, and Mr. Crokat taught him English and caused him to think deeply on many subjects in a way that a good deal affected his after life. He became the Neapolitan ambassador at Madrid, and was afterwards for a short time prime minister to King Bomba. He was a very good minister to that king, but had to resign before long, as affairs were not conducted according to methods sufficiently high-principled.

Thomas had not been able to remain abroad throughout the war, and on his return to England had been thrown a good deal with Robert Campbell's family, and especially with his cousin, Judge James Allan Park, who, finding Thomas greatly unsettled in matters of faith, persuaded him to be confirmed along with the Judge's two daughters

and Arbuthnot Campbell.   From that time Thomas
became a regular communicant in the English
Church, and in 1811, on her seventeenth birthday,
married Arbuthnot Campbell.   On the close of
the war, in 1817, Thomas Crokat took his wife
and little children back to Leghorn.   The eldest
child, Mary Anne Crokat, who inherited her
mother's beauty of face and character, was at
that time five years old.

MARY ANNE CROKAT'S STORY

" How beautiful my mother was !   She had soft
velvety eyes, such as delicate people have sometimes, with an upward look ; finely pencilled arched
eyebrows ; a sort of Madonna face with silky hair,
brown with a golden light on it.   I remember her
in the finest India muslin handkerchief crossed over
an open bodice fastened by a little coral cross ; and
a lace cap laid straight round her head, with its
little crown gathered in behind, and frills of very
fine lace round her face.   Her countenance was
very spiritual, and she seemed to live in the thought
and atmosphere of heavenly things.   Throughout
her lively Italian life she always found opportunities
for doing kind things for the invalids who came to
Italy for their health, and influenced for good all
whom she could reach.   When we went to Italy
Mr. and Mrs. Campbell found that they could not
part with their daughter, and so they came as well
and lived with us ; the eldest daughter, my Aunt
Christina, also came to us.   We were a large party
in the house, for my great-uncle, General Lachlan
Maclean, who used to croon Gaelic songs of an
evening and talk over all the Maclean clan with
my grandmother, joined us in Leghorn.

" We lived in the second story of the Palazzo

Bartolommei, the largest palace in Leghorn. We
had a flat which made a large house, including a
picture gallery filled with good paintings. There
was a beautiful large drawing-room with furniture
of chestnut wood and pale blue silk damask. The
sofas and chairs were elaborately carved with
dragons. The floor was of concrete, painted to
represent marble, uncovered in summer, and in
winter covered with a Persian carpet. We used
to see a great deal of company. There were not
many English residents, but many passed through
and had to be entertained ; and whenever a man-of-
war came into harbour, the officers were asked to
parties and dances, at which I expected to dance
as much as any one. When I was nine years old
I went to a day-school kept by Madame Meyer,
a stately lady with beautiful manners. My chief
school friend was Adelina Tobler, a German Swiss.
I also saw much of two Greek girls, Costanza
Rhodocanocchi and Anastasie Costacchi, and a
German, Ernestine Fehr. I was the only English
girl.

"I used to stay on Monte Nero with M. and
Madame Guigou. She was a lively young French-
woman who had married an old man. He was a
great gardener and had a lovely garden ; he kept
a large telescope in the drawing-room, through
which we looked over the sea and watched the
carriages winding up the road through the olive
trees. The hill was too steep for horses, so the
carriages were drawn up by oxen. How beautiful
the olive woods were at night, full of flitting fireflies
which seemed to light up the whole wood ! There
was a hedge of large yellow roses in front, and a
large white jessamine growing up the house, the
flowers of which used to drop with the heat, and
I often picked them up and threaded them. I have
loved the scent of jessamine ever since. There was

a terrace behind, but rather lower than the house, of green turf and a row of alternate pink and white oleander trees as large as birch trees. Here I used to come and say my prayers looking over the mountain side, it being rather shy work to say them in the house where Madame Guigou was accustomed to overlook my dressing. She took me to Mass once, but she never tried it again. I was a stubborn little person, and had strong opinions as to what was right—so when the bell rang and the congregation prostrated itself, I absolutely refused to bow; the bell kept on ringing, and Madame Guigou dragged me forcibly down. Sometimes she would take me on Sunday evenings to the Sens, a Swiss family, who were in the habit of dancing; again I resolutely refused, for conscience' sake, to do what seemed to me to be highly improper, for which I was much chaffed.

"When I was eleven we spent one summer at Lari, about sixteen miles from Leghorn, on one of the lower spurs of the Apennines. The house had a large hall hung round with pictures of the Pandolfini family. On one side of the house was a broad stone terrace, from which one saw almost sheer down into the Tuscan vale, wooded hills, valleys, vineyards, and fields of maize with their orange heads and long silk tassels. In the brown calyx of a head of maize, I once saw a green snake coiled up with its head hanging down the stalk as did the tassel. The green snake against the yellow heads was a beautiful sight. I remember the look of our servant, Carlo Jamini, wandering about the paths in the woods, playing the flute, in a broad straw hat with scarlet ribbon streamers. On this terrace my brothers and I used to act 'Peveril of the Peak' and have fine fun. What battles we had, and such arguments! Greeks and Trojans: Scotch and English: we worshipped Bruce and

Wallace. My father read Addison's papers from the *Spectator* aloud to us on Sundays.

" When I was thirteen, owing to the dishonesty of a cashier in the house at Genoa, the business engagements could not be kept, and all our business houses became insolvent. My mother failed from that time. Married at seventeen, she had had a large and difficult household to arrange for, and many different people to please ; she had been obliged to entertain and go out a great deal, and had superintended the education of her six children with most loving care and diligence. We could not go into the country as usual, and the heat of the summer was too great for her, as she would not allow herself any drives. After her baby's birth she never really recovered, and died in September 1825, aged thirty-two. Soon after, Judge Park's brother-in-law offered my father a large sum of money, and he began business again on his own account ; and by degrees it became more flourishing than ever.

" After my mother's death we went to live in the Villa Giamari, a mile south of Leghorn.` Across the road was the garden of the Capuchin Friars ; from my bedroom window I could hear all the bells and watch the brown monks walking about the garden reading ; and also I could see the lights on the islands of Gorgona and Capraja, and (on clear days) Elba. On the other side of the road a rich Jew and Jewess lived. At the top of their house was a Jewish synagogue, and we could see the Jews assembling on Saturdays and hear them singing the Psalms. On the occasion of their niece's wedding, we went to that most interesting service, a Jewish marriage, and then Signora Rachellina was resplendent in a dress of silk blonde, with head, neck, and arms one blaze of diamonds.

" I was confirmed by the Bishop of Ossory, who came to Leghorn in order to hold a confirmation.

" Mr. and Mrs. Church came several times to Leghorn from Florence, with their three sons, Richard,[1] Bromley, and Charles.[2]   Lady Church came with them ; she was in great anxiety about her husband, General Church, then fighting for Greece in the Greek War of Independence.   My brothers had a room with a carpenter's bench and tools, and Richard and Bromley Church often came and made ships and boats with them, and I had to hem the sails.   I went to my first formal ball when sixteen years old, and very shortly afterwards my grandmother died.   She was a great loss to me, for Aunt Christina and I did not get on at all well together ; she was cold and reserved, and because I thought she did not trust me, I was too proud to give her my confidence.   I became very independent, and went out whenever I could get my father or some friend to take me.   Baroness Decazes, wife of the French consul, often took me, and it was in their house that I was in a quadrille in the same set as the Prince de Joinville. I was dancing with a French officer who talked fiercely against the English, and when I told him that I was English he would not believe it.

" But now came a great change in my life, for Mr. Henry Bennett became English chaplain at Leghorn, and his wife was a young woman with several little children.[3]   She completely mothered me, and I know now that my father was delighted, and encouraged my being with her ; she went to all the parties with me.   In 1830, when I was just eighteen, Mr. Bennett took the chaplaincy at

[1] Afterwards Dean of St. Paul's.

[2] Afterwards Principal of the Theological College and Canon of Wells.

[3] Three of Mrs. Bennett's daughters became Mrs. Charles Crokat, Mrs. Richard Church, and Mrs. Charles Church.

Naples, and I spent two winters with them there.
The first winter we lived on the Chiatamone, close
to the shore; and I used to walk on the flat roof
and look over the bay to Capri, and was astonished
at the beauty of the colouring after Tuscany:
rose-colour, violet, gold, and then the translucent
air! Those were charming days, and how interesting everything was: Pompeii, Herculaneum,
Baiae, Pozzuoli! We went up Vesuvius, and the
cone was so hot that the soles of my shoes were
burnt, and Mr. Bennett tied them on with pocket-
handkerchiefs. And when there was a slight
eruption we drove to Castellamare to see it, and
on to Sorrento next day, riding back over the hills
on donkeys.

" There were two distinct societies in Naples.
One was called 'The Factory,' and consisted of
English merchants who paid for a chaplain; the
other included the nobility, the foreign ambas-
sadors, and the visitors. Each society was very
exclusive, but Mr. Bennett, as chaplain, mixed
with both. I, of course, much preferred the latter.
King Ferdinand had just died, and we were there
at the time of his funeral. Prince Cassaro (my
father's old friend) was still Prime Minister. He
was a grave man, immensely respected and looked
up to. He did not go out much, but sometimes
he was at the parties, where I remember him in
his broad blue ribbon. He was very kind to me,
and introduced me to his wife and daughter
(Princess Tricase), and sent messages to my father.
Lady Drummond (widow of the late ambassador)
was the queen of the society in Naples, as Mr. Hill
(the English minister) did not entertain at all.
She was rich and had a large house; and what
brilliant parties she gave! There we met the
cream of foreigners—Russians, Austrians, Italians,
etc. Her parties are mentioned in the ' Récit

d'une Sœur.'[1] The de la Ferronayes family were living that winter on the Chiaja, and I must have seen them without knowing it. Judging from the book, Alexandrine d'Alopeus came at the end of my second winter. The Court being there made Naples a very different place from what it is now. The King was constantly at the parties, and I used to dance with every one, from Prince Charles downwards. It is difficult to recall the names of my partners, but I remember Count Carlo d'Andrea, Prince Campofranco, and Count d'Arragon.

"It was at Naples that Mrs. Bennett told me that nice girls in England did not waltz, so I made up my mind that I must give it up; but it was a great trial. I always had waltzed—it was universally done abroad, it was delightful to me, and I had no lack of partners, who could not understand it at all. How I was laughed at and called 'sua altezza'!—but I never waltzed again.[2]

"After spending a fortnight in Genoa, I returned to Leghorn for the summer of 1831; and it was then that I missed seeing Mrs. Bennett's brother, Mr. Moberly. As she had told me a great deal about him, it was a disappointment. He called on Charles the very day my father and I came back, but was told that we were away.

"The winter of 1832 was also spent at Naples in the Palazzo Partanna; and it was in the following spring that I so nearly saw Sir Walter Scott. Two old Scotch ladies (the Miss Tullochs)

---

[1] By Madame Craven.

[2] The reason for this wonderful piece of self-denial was that Mary Crokat's dream was to marry an English clergyman, believing that parish work in a country living, with its monotony and poverty, represented the highest life of sacrifice possible to an educated gentleman. She never wavered in this hope (even when mixing with the most exclusive Italian society and being everywhere admired and sought out), and she would not sink below her own ideal of the "nice" English girl. Waltzing was not then the fashion in England as it is now.

were great friends of his, and they promised to
take me to tea with him ; but a day or two before,
I received the news of Aunt Christina's death and
was summoned to Leghorn by the first boat leaving
Naples.   It was a most bitter disappointment.

" After Aunt Christina's death quite a new life
began for me ; for I became housekeeper and had
the entire charge of my little sisters, Louisa and
Tina.   Tina was a child of seven years old, and
seemed like my own little girl.   The life suited me
and I was very happy in it.   My father went to
England the following summer, and sent me,
accompanied by my sisters and brother Charles,
and our maid Fortunata, to stay with Uncle Robert
Campbell at Genoa.

" That summer at Genoa was, even to us
accustomed to Italian life, like living in a poem.
Uncle Robert lived in the Palazzo Cambiaso, the
end palace in the Strada Nuova, looking into the
Post Office Square.   There was a central hall on
the first floor two stories high.   This was an
enormous place, with a fresco all round the walls
of a Roman sacrifice, with Roman men and women
leaning on the balustrade and looking over into
the hall.   The figures were life size, and strangers
constantly came in to see the fresco.   Below the
balustrade were panels ornamented with wreaths
of flowers in stucco and trophies of armour.   The
tables were heavy, inlaid with pietra-dura work and
jewels.   We used to draw the huge crimson arm-
chairs into a circle in the middle of the hall, and
put lighter chairs and tables inside, in order to feel
more comfortable.   On one side of the hall was
the drawing-room ; it was hung with crimson satin
brocade and crimson satin curtains over the door
openings.   The satin was so thick that the curtains
would stand by themselves.   On the other side of
the hall was the breakfast-room, with sea-green

satin hangings and curtains covered with wreaths of flowers and birds worked in natural colours. Next to the breakfast-room was the dining-room, hung with Chinese silk paper concealing panels, in one of which was a secret door leading to a stair-case and room built in the thickness of the wall. The drawing-room and dining-room windows opened on to a marble terrace encircling a court-yard below it. In this courtyard was a very large orange tree, reaching up to the first floor; it was covered with flowers and smelt most deliciously. A fountain was always playing on the terrace, and here Uncle Robert arranged a summer parlour for us, with stands of flowers and light tables and chairs.

" My mornings were spent upstairs in our sitting-room, teaching Louisa and Tina; we dined at three, and afterwards sat in the great hall. How cool and shady it was! I still seem to hear the rippling fountain and to smell the orange flowers! In the evenings we walked out, generally on the Acqua Sola, or sometimes in the gardens of Palazzo Andrea Doria: then we often went to the opera. Uncle Robert had his private box, and we just walked in for as long as we liked without having to change our dresses; and we thoroughly enjoyed the music. On gala nights the opera was a very grand affair and every one went in full evening dress.

" English tourists often come away with a very poor impression of Genoa. The town is built in the narrow space at the bottom of the hills encircling the bay, and the English hotel stands very low among the shipping and less pleasant parts. No one staying there for a day or two would be likely to realise how different it would be to live in the greatest luxury in one of the Palazzi, with daily walks and drives to villas and gardens high up on the hills, or driving to more distant gardens along the coast. Then we knew the best Genoese nobility and resident foreigners, and in Genoa, at that time (being the second capital town of the kingdom), the society was very choice. Uncle Robert, who was the American consul, and very handsome and dignified, was considered exceptional, and was admitted into the intimacy of all the neighbouring noble families, who rarely made the acquaintance of any English.

" His chief friend was the old Marchesa Pallavicini, whose husband had been ambassador at most of the European courts. She was a very grand old lady, and her country house was at Quinto, on the coast five miles from Genoa. Whenever, for part of the year, she and her son and her son's wife, came into Genoa my uncle often spent the evening with them, and I remember a great fête at Quinto to which we all went. I noticed a great contrast between the Piedmontese and Neapolitan nobles ; the former had much more stamina and strength of character, and were, I thought, less self-indulgent. Very few names come to mind now ; but there was the Marchese della Rovere, and Count Carlo Doria, and the two young Pallavicini at the Military College. Uncle Robert entertained largely, and I was expected to preside at his parties, being then about nineteen years old. How shy I was, and what lectures on manners I received ! The great thing I was told to avoid was behaving like an Englishwoman. The English ladies were said to spoil the parties; for either they would be provokingly silent, or would monopolise the conversation. I remember a grand ball, given on the occasion of an American frigate coming into the harbour, when many of the nobles were present. It was a great surprise to me when several of them told me that they had already heard of me ; the reason must have been that my friend Count Carlo d'Andrea had been to Genoa and had spoken kindly of me.   He was a naval officer on board a Neapolitan frigate.[1]

"Our friend Mrs. Church had for some time been a widow, and was living in England ; and, though we were all very fond of her, it was a great shock to me to hear, in 1833, that she and my father were to be married.   Probably it was settled that summer when he was in England, but I was not told of it for some time.   We all went to England for the wedding, but, meaning to return to Italy, we left most of our possessions behind, as well as old Betty, who had lived with us since my mother's marriage.   Charles remained at Genoa, where he lived with Uncle Robert, and later on became consul.   We drove in a vetturino from Genoa to Paris.   Such a beautiful drive it was through Savoy, but it took a month, and we stopped at picturesque little inns.   It was beautiful weather on our arrival in England, so we saw it as favourably as possible ; but I remember going one day to Ascot with Mrs. Bastard (Judge Park's daughter), and hearing every one say what a beautiful day it was, and thinking that it was not at all beautiful, for the sun did not seem to be really shining, but coming through a mist.

"Mrs. Church lived with her mother, Mrs. Metzener, at 3, Lansdowne Crescent, Bath, and we all went to live there, but I was not at all happy ; the change of circumstances was too great, for my sisters were no longer in my charge, and the climate was so dull.   I was taken to a hunt ball, and I thought it very shabby and paltry after the balls

[1] A lady who mixed in the Genoese society at the time has since told us that Mary Crokat's fame as the " Beauty of Naples " was spread in Genoa before she came there ; and that at a party there would be a pause when she and her brother entered the room, for they were both so beautiful.

in the great houses in Italy; the gentlemen had
not the polish of Italians, and danced so shockingly.
I enjoyed the Long Vacation when Richard Church
was at home.   He was a great comfort to me, for,
having been so much abroad, Italy was as much to
him as to me.   He was very kind and brotherly,
and told me a great deal about Oxford, to which
he had just gone as an undergraduate, and taught
me to appreciate the Christian Year.   Richard
Church wanted me to see a pretty English seaside
place, so we both went on a visit to Lynmouth
with Miss Harwood and her brother Philip,[1] whom
we had known well as a little boy in Leghorn.   I
was delighted with the prospect of being near the
sea again, as I often used to cry and think that
I had lost all feeling for poetry and beauty.
Visions of the blue Mediterranean, by the side of
which I had spent all my life, rose up before me.
It was dark when we arrived at Lynmouth, and
next morning I sprang out of bed and lifted the
blind.   It was a dreary, foggy morning, and through
the grey fog a dull leaden-coloured sea was rolling
in.   I could not help crying.

"I was a great deal away among friends,
especially with Judge Park, my godfather, at
Merton Grove, Wimbledon.   It was a delightful
place to stay in, for they were such kind, merry
people.   The three daughters, Mrs. Bastard, Mrs.
Dickens, and Mrs. Robert Eden, were all equally
kind to me, and the wife of the eldest son (Alick
Park) became a good friend.   I spent a long time
with them all at the Judge's house in Bedford
Square.   At that time several judges lived in
Bedford and Russell Squares.   Next door to us
was Sir John Coleridge, on the other side of
the Square lived Sir John Patteson and Sir John
Richardson.   Miss Richardson[2] was a pretty and

[1] Afterwards editor of the *Saturday Review*.
[2] Afterwards Mrs. George Augustus Selwyn.

very lively young lady, whose parents were in such bad health that she had to go out by herself; she was like a sister to the Parks, and she and I made great friends.   On Sunday evenings Judge Park used to assemble those whom he called his apprentices; amongst others I remember Mr. Robert Kenyon, Sir James Riddell, and Mr. Patrick Shaw Stewart.   All this was very pleasant and amusing; the conversation amongst the lawyers was clever and witty, and very different from what I had been accustomed to.   Several other gentlemen were a great deal in the house: Sir Michael Shaw Stewart, and Admiral Houston Stewart; and Sir Fitzroy Maclean of Duart was also much there.

"Mr. Bastard was chaplain at Hampton Court Palace, and we used to go over to service and luncheon.   Mr. Robert Eden was the vicar of Peldon, in Essex,[1] and I loved being with him and his wife.   He was like the dearest of elder brothers to me.

"The Bennetts came back from Italy in the autumn after our return, and took a house at Sydney Place, Bath.   It was there that I first met Mr. Moberly.   He came to stay with his sister, and I went to spend the day.   Richard came to fetch me in the evening, and was most horribly shy at having to speak to an Oxford don; we have often laughed over it since.   Later on, Mr. Bennett was given the living of South Cadbury, in Somerset-shire; and for a time they lived at Woolston, whilst their house at Sparkford was being built."

MARY ANNE CROKAT'S JOURNAL

"*Sept.* 27, 1833; *Lansdowne Crescent.*— . . . Went to see Mrs. Bennett, who detained me to dinner.   Mr. Bennett was there, and *her* brother,

[1] Afterwards Bishop of Moray and Ross, Primus of Scotland.

the Rev. George Moberly, whom I had so long
wished to see, and now became acquainted with
for the first time. Liked him very much. Papa
and Richard came for me in the evening.

"*Sept.* 28.—A pouring, dismal, regular English
day, such as we may expect for weeks together
in the winter. . . . I am vexed to find how much
money I spend in dress, and yet I appear never to
dress expensively, and try to do with as little of
every kind as I possibly can. Papa tells me that
I have had £24 since I came to England, and yet
I have only had two common gowns, one cotton
and one muslin, besides the two silks I have just
had made. How can this be? It requires reflection
and attention, for this is no trifling subject where
there is no money to throw away. N.B.—To have
everything *good* at first, and to *fit*, and to make
it last as long as it is at all presentable ; especially
to have nothing gaudy, or flimsy, or fanciful ; to
be *quite* sure that I want a thing, before I have it,
and reflect how it would suit me best, without
precipitation ; and above all, never to buy anything
merely because some one else has it, and fancy that
it looks pretty or fashionable. . . .

"*Sept.* 29.—This day I complete my 21st year.
This is a serious consideration. I hope I feel
impressed by the idea that so much of my life
has rolled away, and that my words and actions
during that time are never to be recalled. I can
only trust to God for strength for the future.
When I came down this morning I was presented
by Mamma with a beautiful little edition of Ossian's
poems. The children gave me Baxter's 'Saint's
Rest,' and Taylor's 'Holy Living.' On the table
I found a splendid edition of Bowdler's Family
Shakespeare ; this was an offering from Richard,
who was ashamed to present it, so I was obliged
to guess who it was from.

4

" *Sept.* 30.—The anniversary of the passage to glory of my angel mother. I know not whether any one remembered it besides myself; at all events it was not mentioned. . . .

" *Oct.* 2.—The first thick fog I have witnessed in England. It actually entered the room when I opened the window. . . . The subject of elections seems to be almost as engrossing and interesting here as that of church politics in Leghorn. We were entertained with it all dinner-time.

" *Oct.* 11, *Woolston.*—Mr. Moberly is acquainted with Keble, the author of ' The Christian Year.' . . . He particularly recommends Taylor's ' Holy Living ' to me. . . . Mr. Moberly is full of information, anecdote, and good sense ; his conversation is both amusing and instructive. We sat up talking nearly an hour after prayers.

" *Nov.* 14, *Hanworth.*—Saw a hoar frost for the first time ; the lawn was perfectly white, and long icicles hanging to the windows. The day bright and cold ; most *joyous* and invigorating weather. We walked seven miles ; but such an unusually long walk tired me. . . . Went to see an English Court of Justice at Kingston ; Judge Gaselee and Baron Vaughan.

" *Dec.* 24, 1833.—Last Christmas Eve, at this time, I was sitting alone in our own little drawing-room at Leghorn very happy, little dreaming that I should be in England the next Christmas. I was not then aware of the important change in our family that was to take place. Perhaps I might have looked forward to it with dread ; I now look back upon it with pleasure. I regard the conduct of my dearest Father with the sincerest admiration ; I feel that he will ever be entitled to deep respect and the warmest affection from his children, as he has been actuated by the highest motives of anxiety for their welfare. . . . I now retire to rest on Christmas morning in a happy and peaceful frame of mind.

"*Feb.* 4, 1834.—We went to see the opening of the House of Lords. Jane Falconer went with us, and arrived at 11 o'clock decked in her plumes. Alick Park went to the door of the House with us, and then we were obliged to take care of ourselves. As we were early we got good places. I was extremely struck with the beauty of the young Marquis of Abercorn. . . . Lord Sefton in his robes looked exactly like Riquet with the Tuft. . . . Talleyrand . . . Prince Esterhazy . . . the Duke of Sussex. . . . The Judges were on the woolsack with Lord Chancellor Brougham. At 2 o'clock the guns sounded announcing the King's arrival. The crown appeared to be far too heavy for him, it sank over his eyes like a nightcap ; his robes were so heavy that they were obliged to support them on the back of the chair of state. After the Commons had come in, Lord Brougham, kneeling on the lowest step of the throne, presented the speech to the King, who took it, and putting on his spectacles, read it aloud. Afterwards he walked out in procession, as he had come in. The Judge called us to the woolsack, and made us sit down on it by him. All at once every one stood up, and I perceived that the Bishop of Hereford was going to read prayers.

"*Peldon.*—The time I spend here is delightful. Every hour I feel that I am learning something new and useful. Mr. Eden's conversation is ever-varying, lively, full of information, and deeply imbued with the spirit of religion. He is a delicate man, yet thinks that he can never be sufficiently active in the performance of his duties. Emma is a model of what a clergyman's wife ought to be, and makes herself as useful as he does. We had a very interesting conversation on the joys of the righteous after ˙ death, and I thought that one of the sweetest pleasures would be meeting those two dear friends in glory. I admire their manner to their children particularly; it is always polite to the last degree, and as gentle and considerate as if they were visitors of great importance, without allowing it to interfere with proper enforcement of discipline. Everything here breathes love and happiness. After the bustle of London this is just what I needed. I thank God for having sent me such precious friends.

" *Connaught Square.*—I find fasting clears the intellect and makes the mind more vigorous to perform devotional duties; but it must be done in moderation—overdoing it produced a violent headache, which unfitted me for everything. On Saturday we went to Mr. Wilkie's [1] and saw the paintings which are to be at the exhibition this year. He paid me a compliment which I must be so vain as to record : he said, ' I wish I had had you to sit for my Spanish lady.'

" *April 6, Bedford Square.*—The Judge's 71st birthday. All his children assembled. At church one of the Psalms sung was four verses of the 116th, beginning at the 9th verse. At luncheon we were an immense party, including Sir John and Lady Richardson, Mr., Master, and Miss Richardson, Sir Walter Riddell, and Mr. Baddeley. Afterwards we went to St. James's for afternoon service. Sir W. Riddell waited for Emma, Waldegrave, and myself, and we four squeezed into a pew that certainly was never meant to contain so many. The scene after dinner was most affecting ; the dear old Judge's health was drunk in a bumper. He then proposed the health of Waldegrave (his second son) and Eliza, and made his darling son a little speech which he could hardly get through,

---

[1] Sir David Wilkie, a cousin of Mr. Crokat's.

hoping that he would live to see his children's children, as he had done. Waldegrave could not answer distinctly, and all the family were in tears. He then drank the health of the " 32 " (children and grandchildren) and the three gentlemen present ; which produced a small expression of his regard for me, which I treasure up in my heart. Alick reminded him that by this arrangement he had left me out ; upon which he coloured, his eyes filled with tears, and he said in a choking voice, ' My dear Mary, though last, not least, believe me : your health, my love.'[1]

" *April* 14.—To-day it is beautifully bright, but still cold. The wind always in the east seems to make everybody cross. . . . Funeral of a *Unionist*, at which were assembled 7,000 of them *to show their strength.* Last Sunday met the O'Connells and Dr. Bramston, Roman Catholic Bishop of London, at Mr. Kiernan's. O'Connell a heavy, farmer-like, good-looking man. Mrs. O'Connell very plain and quiet. Mr. and Mrs. Maurice O'Connell sat together opposite to me at dinner, and took away my appetite—they never once opened their lips to speak. . . ."

George Moberly's account of an expedition to Stourhead in the summer of 1834, taken with the Bennetts whilst Miss Crokat was staying with them at Sparkford :

" One day it was arranged that we were all to spend the day at Stourhead. The ladies were to drive by one road and the gentlemen to ride by the other. When we had started, I at once boldly said that it was very stupid to divide the party, and proposed going by the other road ; this was

---

[1] He had greatly desired Mary Crokat's engagement to his son.

agreed to, but——we never saw the carriage, though we met our friends at Stourhead when we arrived. Mrs. Bennett greeted us with laughter, and would only say that it had been pronounced a foolish plan, and that the carriage party had been persuaded (by whose influence I cannot surmise) to try the other road ; this they had accordingly done."

MARY ANNE CROKAT'S STORY

" I stayed that summer with the Bennetts at Weymouth, and my father and sisters were there too. Mrs. Bennett was expecting her mother, Mrs. Edward Moberly. I remember coming into a room where she was having luncheon, and being introduced. I was quite frightened at the magnificent dark *flash* of her eyes, that seemed to look through one, with a sort of concentrated light in them. It was the same flash as Mr. Moberly's, only his eyes were small and hers were large. I said to my father, ' I daresay she is very nice, but what dreadfully bright eyes she has ! ' He answered, ' Oh, bother her eyes—they won't hurt you.' He was probably not over-pleased with my critical tone just then, for no doubt Mrs. Moberly was particularly anxious to study me, and I was especially sensitive, as I became engaged to be married to Mr. Moberly the next day.

" We were married at South Cadbury on December 22, 1834, on a bitterly cold day with snow on the ground. My dress was of creamy white figured silk poplin, with a cape of the same, rounded at the back just below the waist, with long points in front ; it was deeply trimmed with white swansdown. The bonnet was of flowered satin, coming well over the face, with orange flowers made on wires which shook when I moved, and a long veil of white French blonde. My two sisters, Louisa and Tina, were dressed alike in pale blue silk. To go away in, I had a dark green silk poplin pelisse trimmed with dark green velvet, and a large sable muff.

" We drove to Salisbury, where we put up at the Antelope Hotel in Catherine Street, and the next day drove on to Pear Tree Green, near Southampton. We then settled at 25, New Inn Hall Street, Oxford,[1] where we lived for the short year before going to Winchester. It was a very small society at Oxford then. Eight married ladies used to meet one another at all the parties, and were, of course, pretty intimate. The wife of a tutor was an innovation ; I was the first, and had no others to make friends with, and being entirely foreign in my manners and upbringing, I felt extremely shy and uncomfortable amongst the eight older ladies. But Mrs. Hawkins, of Oriel, took pity on me, and was very kind indeed, causing me to look upon her quite as a friend. I also knew Mrs. Gaisford, wife of the Dean of Christ Church, and Mrs. Burton, and Mrs. Pusey pretty well ; the others I saw little of."

GEORGE MOBERLY'S STORY

" In 1835 the Headmastership of Winchester College became vacant. Though not yet thirty-two years old (at that time considered very young for such a post), I was persuaded to stand for it. The three candidates were Dr. Christopher Wordsworth, Dr. William Sewell, and myself. I had not the least chance against Dr. Wordsworth, who would certainly have been elected, but that his brother Charles, a most distinguished tutor of Christ Church, wished to be married ; and they agreed that Charles

---

[1] Now St. Michael's Street. The small house adjoining the grounds of the Oxford Union Society.

should stand for the Second-mastership at Winchester, and that Dr. Christopher Wordsworth should withdraw from being a candidate for the Headmastership, and so I was elected.

" We were at Sea View in the Isle of Wight, with Mr. Patrick Muirhead, Mr. Charles Marriott, and Richard Church, when the news of my election came. That was the time when the long walks and talks with Richard began, which established our lasting and intimate friendship. Our constant and brotherly correspondence continued through all the most anxious years of English Church controversy.

In 1853, on his marriage to my niece, Helen Bennett, he left Oriel and took a country living at Whatley, in Somersetshire."

CHAPTER III

THE NURSERY

Downs, joyous downs, where the wind sweeps free
O'er long, long waves of a grassy sea :—
Streams—brighter than glass—thro' the green that glide,
While the grey trout lies still in the hurrying tide :
Three sisterly towers of the days of yore
For mercy, and praise, and churchly lore—
Long aisles, where the pealing organ streams,
Bright storied panes that stain the moonbeams,
Dim cloisters pale, where 'mid wreathéd stone
Sleep in their several chambers lone
The young and the fair, 'neath the grassy sod,
Their "bodies are dust, but their souls are with God,"
The music of bells 'mid the tall plane trees
And the bright tones of boyhood borne high on the breeze.
Such is my home : and a hearth is there,
Where sit a sweet Mother and children fair :
From each bright little face of girl or boy
Come rays like a prism of love and joy ;
Various and sweet as the colours at even,
The hues are many, but all of Heaven.

G. MOBERLY.

MARY A. MOBERLY'S STORY

"It was on a bitterly cold day in November 1835, when the baby Alice[1] was six weeks old, that we arrived in Winchester, driving from Clifton through Romsey and Hursley. We were in Mrs. Davis's lodgings (in the house afterwards occupied by La Croix, the pastrycook), Dr. Williams not

---

[1] Alice Arbuthnot Moberly.

57

having vacated · the Headmaster's house. Old Mrs. Moberly was living with us.

" At that time Dean Rennell was an old man, very infirm and weak, but still capable of talking scholarship with his friends. He was fond of giving little parties, and it was on these occasions that I made great friends with his daughter, who was in charge of his house.

" There were, I think, then twelve Canons of the Cathedral : Canon Pretyman, Dr. Nott, Hon. Gerard Noel, Canon Vaux, Dr. Wilson, Canon Harrison, Dr. Dealtry, Canon Garnier, Canon James, Archdeacon Hoare, Dr. Williams, and Canon Jacob, who was a very young man. Canon Pretyman was also Canon of Lincoln. He and his wife were rich, grand people. We knew Dr. Williams the best, who was the late Headmaster of the College, and afterwards Warden of New College. He had a large family, and the youngest daughter, Anna (afterwards wife of Bishop Edmund Hobhouse), was about twelve years old, and made close friends with my sister Tina. Living in what was afterwards Canon Carus's house was an old Mrs. Poulter, quite a relic of old times, whose husband had been a Canon. Mrs. Jacob was Canon Noel's daughter, and had only been lately married ; she was a great friend of mine. Bishop Charles Sumner had not long been Bishop of Winchester. He and almost all the clergy of Winchester and of the diocese were of the Evangelical school. He had entirely made up his mind that Mr. Keble would go over to Rome, and was dreadfully afraid of him. The Oxford movement was just beginning, and the new Headmaster had the reputation of being connected with it and being full of Romish tendencies, so for many years he had a hard time of it in Winchester. Canon Jacob was in the forefront of the Bishop's party, but we could not help getting on with him, he was so truly sweet-tempered and kindly. The ladies all got on very well together, but the gentlemen were always in difficulties and sparring.

" Of other friends in Winchester with whom we were specially intimate, there were Mrs. Gilbert Heathcote (widow of a naval officer), living with her daughters Maria and Marianne at the Abbey ; her sister Miss Lyell, and Miss Short, sister of the Bishop of St. Asaph.

" It was at the end of our first winter in Winchester that the Kebles came to Hursley, five miles away. We called first, and found them at home, with wedding-cake and wine set out on the table. Without being really pretty, Mrs. Keble was most sweet-looking. She had beautiful brown eyes and hair, a delicate complexion like porcelain, and an air of extreme refinement.

Sir William Heathcote, afterwards member for the University of Oxford, was lord of the manor at Hursley. At that time he was a widower with three little boys, William, Gilbert, and George, and one little girl, Caroline.[1] His mother, the widow of a former Canon of Winchester, and his aunt, Miss Bigg, lived with him. Mr. Keble's curate at Hursley was Mr. Robert Wilson. He became a dear friend, as did his future wife. She was Miss Maria Trench, a niece of Sir William Heathcote's first wife. When Mr. Wilson moved to Ampfield to take charge of a district of Hursley, Mr. Peter Young became Mr. Keble's curate ; he married Miss Coxwell, a cousin of Mrs. Keble's and brought up by her ; she was, at this time, living at the vicarage.

" I well remember the first call that the William Yonges made on us when we were still in lodgings

---

[1] Afterwards Mrs. Cooke Trench.

in College Street. They lived at Otterbourne, a village four miles out. Charlotte Yonge, then a girl of twelve with a very shrill voice, came with them. This was about the time when, according to her own account, she was in the habit of relieving the weariness of a formal call by imagining it to be another period of history, and that every one was discussing (for instance) the prospect of invasion by the Spanish Armada ![1]

" Robert Speckott Barter was Warden of the College. He was a tall man, with a fine, open, benevolent countenance, large well-opened blue eyes, and silvery hair. His character was singularly sympathetic, sunny, and warmhearted. There are several stories of the wonderful strength of the Warden and his brothers. He was once travelling on the top of a coach. A man sitting at his right hand was using very profane language, and after a time the Warden could bear it no longer; so he lifted the man from his seat and held him over the road by the collar of his coat, until he promised not to speak another word before reaching the next stopping-place. The Warden then quietly returned the man to his place. The Warden, his brother William (Rector of Burghclere), and a friend went for a walking tour in Wales. They covered forty miles each day, and on the last day walked eighty miles back into Devonshire. Every day they ordered a loin and two legs of Welsh mutton for dinner. The Warden was one day walking from Oxford to see his brother Charles at Sarsden, a distance of eighteen miles; at Woodstock he passed the Bishop of Oxford's carriage. The Bishop called to him to ask him where he was going. ' To Sarsden, my lord.' ' I am going there too : can I give you a lift ? ' ' No, thank you, I

[1] I remember that first call, and that I wrote to my godmother, Mrs. Jones, of Exeter College, that Mrs. Moberly was just like a Madonna in a picture.—C. M. YONGE.

am rather in a hurry ' ; and he arrived some time
before the Bishop.   He once walked fifty miles
from Winchester to Oxford to vote at an election,
and back the next day.

" The Warden inspired strangers with confidence.
On one occasion he was walking to a dinner-party
many miles off, and finding himself late asked a
man who passed him on horseback to lend him his
horse.   The man looked at him for a minute and
then said, ' Yes, sir, I will ; I like the look of you.
Leave the horse at ——, and I will call for it.'   He
had a very great love for children, and would invite
whole families to stay with him.   Every one could
reckon on his readiness to help in taking services
and sermons for others in sickness and trouble.[1]
He was exceedingly hospitable, especially to
Wykehamists, and made a point of looking up any
young officers at the barracks who had lately left
Public Schools ; he had a party of them to dinner
every Sunday evening, often first bringing them
with him to 5-o'clock Chapel.   Mr. Keble used to
talk of his ' royal ways,' and to say that he was so
loved and admired that if the King were elected by
vote, the Warden would be king.   When old Mr.
Barter, vicar of Cornworthy, died, Mrs. Barter came
to live in College with her son.   She was a very
old lady, and was bedridden for many years.[2]   Her
granddaughters from Sarsden were constantly with

[1] Whatever happened to him was " the best possible," even being
laid up with gout at an inn on progress.   He never went home but
" his father and mother were better than ever."   It was like sunshine
to see his face, and for him to think ill of a person was so rare that it
was the greatest condemnation.—C. M. YONGE.

[2] The beauty and cheerfulness of her nature always showed itself.
She could see a corner of the Cathedral tower and a fragment of tree
and sky from her bed ; and once she said, " I see so much beauty there
that I am sometimes quite overcome by it."   Nor should it be forgotten
what were almost the last words to her son when he hoped she would
have a good night : " O yes, I shall be thinking of my joyful
resurrection ! "—C. M. Y.

her, especially Kate and Lizzie Barter, clever, eager people, who made great friends with us.   Warden Barter was a staunch churchman of the old school, and had his fears of the effect of the Oxford movement, as indeed few had not.   So all shades of opinion were represented in the circle into which we stepped."

Mary Anne Moberly's Journal

" *Nov.* 13, 1836.—This day my sweet Alice is 13 months old.   She is the joy of our hearts.   My dear George is writing his first lecture on confirmation, to preach this evening in the College Chapel, as the Bishop is to hold a confirmation for the boys this month.   Poor Richard is now undergoing his examination.[1]   His tutor, Mr. Griffiths, says he has never felt so much interested in any young man for many years.

" *Nov.* 29.—At 11 a.m., just after George had returned from School, I was sitting with him in the study, when I was alarmed by hearing a crack and seeing the branches of the great trees in the court flying about.   We both ran to the window. The wind was blowing furiously, and to our great astonishment the ground in the court, the paved pathway, was heaving to the height of two or three feet; the largest tree was coming down, apparently to fall upon ' Wickhams.'   Our first thought was for our child.   George ran upstairs and quickly removed her and the nurse to my room, but when he got there the three largest trees had all fallen—most providentially in another direction.   The Warden's stables were cut open by the blow, but no harm was done besides.   Another great tree soon followed, and only one was left standing ; about 1 p.m. the

[1] R. W. Church : afterwards Dean of St. Paul's.

fearful storm was lulled and the sun shone out brightly."

From Mrs. Arnold

" Fox How, Ambleside, *January* 1837.

" My dear Mrs. Moberly,

" You will not perhaps expect to hear from me before my boys return to Winchester,[1] but I cannot feel satisfied without thanking you at once for the kindness of the letter which I lately received from you, so fully meeting the feeling of confidence which in the first place encouraged me to write to you. Your writing too under the circumstances, when you had been grieved so deeply[2] and were yourself in expectation of your confinement, make me feel your kindness the more strongly, for I know what it is to feel my bodily powers entirely unequal to the exertions I might wish to make. Now I am happy to know by the newspapers that I may congratulate you on your expected trial being over, and on the birth of your infant.[3] In this Dr. Arnold wishes to join me both to yourself and Dr. Moberly. You are probably feeling, as we are, that the holidays are much too short, and that the length of the next half-year is formidable in prospect ; but the rest when it comes is so complete, and the responsibility so entirely shaken off, that nothing can be more delightful than the refreshment we are now enjoying. While I write this, however, of the labours of the half-year, I must not let you understand that I mean any individual exertions of my own, but simply the natural feeling that one's husband's cares are one's own. The interior of

---

[1] Matthew and Thomas Arnold were at Winchester at this time.
[2] Louisa Crokat died November 1836.
[3] George Herbert Moberly.

our large family, with the aid of faithful servants,
and still more with the valuable assistance of the
head of our house—answering, I suppose, to your
senior prefect—makes at present all go easily ; but
the general responsibility is a feeling of care and
anxiety that time will not, and perhaps ought not,
to lessen.   We can well understand what you say
of the difficulties arising from old abuses and
perquisites.   We found many of those which could
only be broken off by incurring additional expenses
ourselves, and very often exciting discontent also ;
but I should say also that many of the internal
arrangements which we found were very judicious
and good.   For instance, the plan of requiring a
boy to have a note signed with your name before
a tradesman lets him have anything which is
entered in the bills and sent home to the parents.
This very much checks expense, for these notes
are not sent up to me, till one of the confidential
servants has seen a line from home, authorising
them to have sent what they wish.   Of course
this extended to their books as well as their
clothing, and in this way Dr. Arnold sees whether
they buy books over again, or those things they
do not require.   Your numbers would make this
general check rather more laborious, but we have
felt it very important to check as much as we could
early habits of carelessness and expense.   I mention
this without being sure that you have not some
corresponding plan ; but you encourage me to
suggest anything which eight years' experience had
taught me, and if in this, or in any other respect,
I could be of the least help to you, it would give
me the sincerest pleasure.   Our dear boys tell us
that the elder must be at Winchester on the 9th.
My paper is so nearly finished that I cannot tell
you of all my dear children's happiness in being
united again, which I was half inclined to do from

MARY ANNE MOBERLY.
By Sir David Wilkie.

p. 64]

the kind tone of your letter, and the feeling that you as a mother could extend your sympathy.

" With our united compliments and kind regards, believe me, dear Mrs. Moberly, yours very sincerely,

"MARY ARNOLD."

MARY ANNE MOBERLY'S JOURNAL

" *July* 1837.—Summer is come at last. Our good King William died on the 20th of last month, and the young Queen is an object of great interest. We received the news while Mr. Muirhead was with us. This day is Founder's commemoration, and George dines in College. I shall feast on the 'British Poets,' which he has just made me a present of. I am now reading Bishop Hall's 'Contemplations on the New Testament' in the mornings, and enjoy them very much.

" *July* 8.—This day the King was interred. The tolling of the Cathedral bells, muffled, from 9 to 10 in the evening was very melancholy and impressive.

" *July* 14.—The day of the Domum. The Domum very fatiguing and very hot; the room crowded to excess. I felt it painful and awkward to be in a chair of state, while Mrs. Williams was seated below. Went to the ball in the evening for half an hour, while George went to bed: did not enjoy it at all, especially being dressed out in the hat and feathers which I should never have possessed had not Sir David Wilkie set his heart upon painting them.

" *July* 30, *Sea View.*—Very happy to be here. My darlings very well; little Georgie has quite *come out* since his travels, growing a regular scold. We had a pleasant drive from Winchester to Portsmouth in lovely weather. Mr. Anthony Froude is with us. An interesting letter this morning from Mr. Manning after his wife's death.

5

"*May* 11, 1838.—How much has happened
since I last wrote! One of our family circle has
joined the Saints above.[1] A sweet little baby was
born to us on March 28[2]; she was christened last
Tuesday, and Miss Short and Mrs. Wordsworth
went to church with us. It was a happy day and
I had a most lovely drive through Avington Park
with Julia and Helen Bennett.[3] The weather was
quite Italian; there has not been a cloud in the
sky for five days, a circumstance which I never
remember to have noticed before since I have been
in England.

"*May* 12.—These last two days I am glad to
have been in Commoners, and have spent my
mornings actively. After luncheon walked in the
meadows with George, and sat down by the clear
stream watching the bright sunlight on the pebbles
in the water.

"*May* 18.—Mr. and Mrs. Keble joined us in the
garden. Mr. Keble's attention to the children
quite wins my heart; he was so desirous of seeing
the baby that I brought her up to him. He took
her in his arms and said, 'Those who christen little
children have a right to love them.'

"*May* 23.—We had a large dinner party on
Monday. The George Ryders and Henry Wilberforces were with us. It is the night of the
theological meeting, and Mr. C. Baring, Mr. H.
Wilberforce, Mr. G. Ryder, and the Warden dined
here and had a long discussion upon Wordsworth
and English poetry. Mr. Keble and Mr. Wilson
joined them, and they are now all gone down to the
meeting.[4]

[1] Old Mrs. Moberly had died.
[2] Mary Louisa Moberly, afterwards Mrs. George Ridding
[3] Afterwards Mrs. Richard Church.
[4] There was a clerical book club which met occasionally for debate.
The members were Mr. Garnier (Dean of Winchester), Dr. Williams
(Warden of New College); Canon Wilson; Mr. G. Deane of Bighton;

" *June* 28.—This has been a day of great public rejoicing : the Queen's coronation ; in all probability it is a cause for rejoicing that will not soon be repeated. This day is one likely to be remembered for many years by those among the lower classes who have partaken of its gaieties. From 12 to 1600 children were dined on the parade ground behind the barracks ; the higher classes partook of a cold collation at 3 o'clock in a pavilion of green boughs, and the Mayor presided in a chair covered with garden flowers. In the evening there were various amusements—jumping in sacks, climbing soaped poles, etc., ending with fireworks. To me, individually, it was not a happy day, as my dear husband was engaged from morning till night in arrangements for the Church Building Society, it being his one free day. Thus I was prevented from seeing anything but the children's dinner, and then I wandered out alone. It has been a most glorious day. Let us trust that Queen Victoria may bring peace and happiness to this nation ; one cannot help feeling a doubt about it.

" *Christmas Eve.*—How can I suffer a day to me so solemn to pass without notice ? I must acknowledge my deep sense of the blessings with which I have been loaded during the last twelve months ; my cup of happiness filled to the brim, though the loss of friends has here and there cast

Canon Beadon of Stoneham ; Archdeacon Wilberforce (Bishop of Oxford and Winchester) ; Warden Barter ; Mr. C. Wordsworth (Bishop of St. Andrews) ; Dr. Moberly (Bishop of Salisbury); Mr. Baring (Bishop of Durham) ; Mr. Keble ; Mr. R. Wilson ; Mr. G. Ryder. In the summer they met at Bishopstoke, Bighton, or Stoneham. Regularly at the end of each meeting a vote of censure was passed on the host for preparing too good a dinner, and a fine exacted if parliament gingerbread had not been provided for dessert. One other little fact has been remembered : that Warden Barter undertook to read a paper on " Unfulfilled Prophecy " ; this paper was called for after each meeting, and the subject was completely and exactly illustrated by the non-fulfilment of his promise.

a shade over its bright sunshine. But their age had taught us to expect their summons to reap the reward of a long and well-spent life. Such have been dear Mrs. Moberly, the good Judge Park, and my aunt Marion. My sweet little Mary Louisa has this year been added to our family party and is healthy and merry; we call her our little fairy. Let me try to set an example of cheerfulness and good temper to my dear little children. Let me endeavour to keep in view the spiritual welfare of our servants. Let me strive to make my dear George's home a happy one, by affectionate interest in his pursuits, cheerfulness when he has time to be with me, unrepining when he has not. Let me always have some useful occupation at hand, that I may not waste so many precious minutes in thinking what I had better do.

"*Jan.* 12, 1839.—In consequence of the unhealthy condition of 'Commoners' it has been decided to rebuild it entirely, so we have to move out of our house for two years. We are now in Kingsgate Street.[1] Here I was interrupted by a very kind visit from the Kebles, who came to ask us to go to Hursley for a few days these holidays, and stayed some time. My first visit in my new drawing-room was thus a very propitious one.

"*Good Friday.*—I am happy in being able to go to church every morning this week. The last three years I have been prevented by being on the sofa at this time. I am truly thankful for the privilege. The matter of fasting is still denied me to any extent, but I must make up my mind that God has appointed other duties for me. I sigh to be able to resume my duties in 'Commoners.'

"*June.*—Another little girl was added to our

---

[1] In the house occupied long after by the widow of Bishop Harold Browne.

store on May 5th ;[1] and on the 10th we received
a great shock in the death of Mrs. Charles
Wordsworth at a time when we were all looking
forward to her becoming a mother for the first time.
She was so young, so lovely, that the thought of
her death seemed to be far from the minds of her
friends. Her little baby (Charlotte Emmeline) is
doing well."

MARY ANNE MOBERLY'S STORY

" We were looking for a house in which we could
spend the summer holidays in country air. Sir
William Heathcote offered to build us one at
Hursley, and he, Mr. Yonge, and the Head master
rode about " Cuckoo bushes" and " Malabar " looking for a site. Just then the owner of a farm
called Fieldhouse wished to leave, and Sir William
bought the farm and proposed that we should rent
it of him. We were charmed with the approach
to it through woodland lanes and the look of it,
and Sir William's offer was accepted. It was in
the parish of Hursley, but two miles farther into
the woodlands, at the beginning of the New Forest
country. Our quickest way of reaching it from
Winchester was through the village of Otterbourne,
separated from the farm by Cranbury Park. The
house was old, with oak rafters and floors, and
had primitive latches to the doors. On one of the
chimneys was the date 1500. We built a verandah
to the front south rooms and covered it with vines,
roses, and clematis. From our bedroom latticed
windows, embowered in banksia roses and vines,
we looked over the pleasant garden, divided from
a meadow of thirteen acres by a rail hidden in
a sweetbriar hedge. The meadow sloped down to
the south, and beyond it rose a hillside of woods.

[1] Edith Emily Moberly.

Rick-yards, farm buildings, and a well-stocked farm-yard surrounded the house on the other sides. For twenty-seven years we spent the summer months at this pleasant place, and dearly have we all loved it. The farmyard with its manifold life was a never-ending delight to the children, who from their nursery window would watch for hours the manœuvres of the cocks and hens, the ducks coming in slow procession from the pond, the pigs, the horses and cows, without ever seeming to tire. A more completely country home could not be found. There were copses and woods all round us, yet it stood high, and the air was free and sweet, whilst the silence was absolute. From a steep pitch (called Ladwell) between Fieldhouse and the village of Hursley the Isle of Wight was softly visible on clear days, and even, occasionally, the smoke of steamers in the Southampton Water ; whilst to the north Hursley spire nestled amongst its trees under the chalk downs. It was a farm of 160 acres, and there the bread was grown and baked which was eaten in ' Commoners,' and a herd of thirteen cows supplied the school and our own house with milk and butter."[1]

From A Friend

"1840.

" . . . Every feeling of pain and ease, of delight or anxiety, the last few weeks has made me turn to you with a fellow-feeling which the being a mother oneself alone enables one to realise. I should like extremely to compare babies : to show you my nursery party and to see your

---

[1] The house is now altered. The verandah and the old porch under the oriel-windowed " glory hole " have been removed ; and the absence of creepers makes the house look bare and commonplace. The garden has been divided and partly turned into rough ground.

little Arthur. I am so sorry to hear that Georgy is so delicate. Is he pleased with his little brother? and what does Edith say to this baby usurper? I often long to ask you many mother's questions of health and dress, how to check fretting and obtain immediate obedience,[1] but I must not wish the bounds of my habitation changed. Being a mother has unlocked the beauty and meaning of many a passage in poetry and Scripture where God is spoken of as a Parent."

MARY ANNE MOBERLY'S STORY

" One day I was walking down Kingsgate Street to our house when I saw the little children with their nurses on the opposite side of the street coming back from their walk. Little George, about 4 or 5 years old, caught sight of me and ran across the road to meet me. At the same moment Lady Rivers' large carriage with two horses dashed up and caught him. It was a terrible instant. Both the nurses and I saw him amongst the horses' legs, and it seemed impossible that anything could save him, when to our surprise he was seen standing by his nurse on the pavement. The carriage did not stop, the driver having apparently not seen him. I hurried across the road, and in reply to our question the little boy said, ' An angel came and took me out.'[2]

[1] My father used to say that by the time a child is three years old it ought to have learnt by experience that if it chooses to be disobedient, it is entering on what will certainly be a losing game.

[2] This little boy was afterwards a scholar of Winchester College and Corpus Christi, Oxford ; he won the Stanhope, Arnold, and Ellerton prizes. After many years of clerical work, he became Principal of the Lichfield Theological College, and died in 1895. To the end of his life George said that he remembered the incident perfectly, and that he had been lifted up and put back on the pavement by some one in white.

In July 1907, Alice Moberly, George's senior by a year, wrote : " I

" In 1841, though our party was large, we offered to take in two little Indian nieces, who were with us for many years; their elder brother, Harry Moberly, had already been received as a child of the house, and the three (Harry, Louisa, and Rosa) were looked upon as brother and sisters by their cousins."

" Commoner Buildings " being finished in 1841, the family moved into the Headmaster's new house in College Street. The buildings were arranged to hold a hundred boarders; they were of brick, entirely unornamented, and certainly far from beautiful. Miss Kate Barter wrote the following lines on the occasion:

> " 'Tis true our walls are unadorned,
>   Though strongly built and fair;
> But mark their deep foundations laid
>   With curious art and care.
>
> " E'en such the pride of Wykeham's race,
>   Not in vain wit displayed;
> But solid learning on the base
>   Of true religion laid."

From A Friend

" . . . I do truly and heartily rejoice for and with you in the good promise of your children,

distinctly remember seeing George entangled amongst the horses' feet and knowing that he could not get out. In the horror of the moment I shut my eyes. I also remember our all meeting in the drawing-room immediately after; there were a good many people in the room, but I don't know who, and I was conscious of the hushed awe that fell upon all, and that my knees were still trembling.—ALICE ARBUTHNOT MOBERLY," almost the greatest and sweetest of all earthly blessings ; and I trust that each child may ' go on from strength to strength,' and that each may be a bright crown of rejoicing to its dear anxious parents.' The words ' for all women labouring of child ' unite us, I hope, in that House and Presence where of all others we would most desire to be united ; and to-morrow's service, though we cannot join in it with the same feelings of recent happy recovery that we could last year, still, I trust, may be a help and a comfort to us both. . . ."

It was when " Dora Frances "[1] was a year and a half old, and " Elspeth Catherine "[2] had taken her place as " the baby," that the incident mentioned in " Children's Thankfulness "[3] took place. One day Mr. Keble came to call at Fieldhouse, and found only the children, who were playing in the garden. Little Dora presented him with some flowers, and on his making no audible response, said to him in a reproving, yet questioning, voice, " Ta-a ? "

> " Why so stately, Maiden fair,
>   Rising in thy nurse's arms
> With that condescending air ;
>   Gathering up thy queenly charms,
> Like some gorgeous Indian bird,
> Which, when at eve the balmy copse is stirred,
>   Turns the glowing neck, to chide
> Th' irreverent footfall, then makes haste to hide
>   Again its lustre deep
> Under the purple wing, best home of downy sleep ?

[1] Afterwards Mrs. Charles Martin.
[2] Afterwards Mrs. Henry Barter.
[3] *Lyra Innocentium.*

"Not as yet she comprehends
　　How the tongues of men reprove,
But a spirit o'er her bends
　　Trained in Heaven to courteous love,
　　And with wondering, grave rebuke
Tempers, to-day, shy tone and bashful look.—
　　Graceless one, 'tis all of thee,
Who for her maiden bounty, full and free,
　　The violet from her gay
And guileless bosom, didst no word of thanks repay.

"Therefore, lo! she opens wide
　　Both her blue and wistful eyes—
Breathes her grateful chant, to chide
　　Our too tardy sympathies.
　　Little Babes and Angels bright—
They muse, be sure, and wonder, day and night,
　　How th' all-holy Hand should give,
The sinner's hand in thanklessness receive.
　　We see it and we hear,
But wonder not: for why? we feel it all too near."

When George was staying by himself at Hursley as a child, Mrs. Keble found him one evening in bed, frightened at being in a room alone. She offered to read him a story, but he said, "No; let it be something true." She at once read a Psalm. This incident found its way into the *Lyra Innocentium,* under the title of "Loneliness." "Repeating the Creed" was also written during one of George's visits to Hursley.

From MRS. KEBLE

"HURSLEY VICARAGE.

"MY DEAR MRS. MOBERLY,

　　"I send you a copy of verses which I think will be acceptable to you, because you will find in them a very true picture of your dear little George as he used to look here. The happiest thought one could have about him would be that this earliest picture might be an emblem of all his future life. John says the poem wants more explanation, but I daresay *you* will understand it."

G. Moberly's Journal

"*Jan.* 22, 1843, *Colchester.*—A Sunday away from home brings to my thoughts my dear wife and little children, and with them the *soft heart* in which men are fit for journalising. I am come hither to see Round, and have been holding a long theological argument with him. . . . I believe that, after all, he and I would be found to rally round precisely the same standard—the standard of the English Church, as maintained by Andrewes and Hammond—with only such differences of statement which must always subsist between different men, however closely agreed in the main. . . .

"*July, Winchester.*—The end of the half-year, and how much to think of! Scarlet fever, with the dispersion of the boys, and no death in the house, nor infection to my own. Poor Hooper died after he went home. Election passed quietly and satisfactorily. The school promises to be very full. . . . I expect near 140 boys, and have refused more. Now we are on the wing for Scotland, having sent the little Indians to Sparkford.

"*April* 2, 1844.—Since last July how many mercies! The awful scarlet fever in our house, in which every child and two servants were ill. Dear Alice's five delirious nights of, as it seemed, hopeless illness;[1] George, Mary, Edith, Arthur, Dora,

---

[1] Dr. Harris told us that the habit of instantaneous obedience to "Now, Alice!" when swallowing was agony to her, was what saved her life.—C. M. Yonge.

and Kitty all woefully and long ill ; and the terrible illness in the school."

After our return to College Street the christenings took place in the College Chapel. For " Frances Emily's " [1] christening, Mrs. Yonge brought a miniature stone font.[2] Afterwards the Head-master presented the large stone font now in the Chapel, and the first child baptized in it was " Robert Campbell." [3] The christenings of the eight youngest children in the College Chapel became occasions of annual meetings of the special circle of friends for prayer and intercession for the children of the house and of the school. All former sponsors within reach, including of course the Kebles, the Yonges, Warden Barter and his nieces, and many other likeminded friends, were invited as a matter of course, and a long procession formed in which each of the unconfirmed children was escorted across the ancient quadrangle to the Baptistery by his, or her, Godparents.[4] Robert's baptism took place at a moment of great anxiety, and but a month or six weeks before Mr. Newman's secession to Rome. It is not difficult to realise the time of heavy strain that it was to the elders of the party, or the

[1] Afterwards Mrs. William Awdry.

[2] This little font has since been used for both infant and adult baptisms in Japan.

[3] Afterwards Vicar of Great Budworth, Cheshire ; Regius Professor of Pastoral Theology at Oxford, and Canon of Christ Church.   Died 1903.

[4] And it was the custom to take the infant from the Chapel to the bedside of the Warden's aged mother to be blessed.—C. M. YONGE.

urgency of their prayers that the unconscious infant should be led by the " Kindly Light " into all Truth and become a strength to the Church of England.

It was no restful position to be Mr. Keble's next-door neighbour for thirty years, and especially such years for the Church of England as from 1836 to 1866, for every phase of Church politics was watched, discussed, and prayed over at Hursley. Mr. Keble took up every point of State policy which affected the Church and of religious controversy with keen anxiety. An article in the *Guardian* describes him admirably :

" Homely plainness, in manner, in speech, in the external aspect and practice of his religious life, went along in singular combination with rich and delicate cultivation, with fire of imagination, with the loftiest thoughts and an ever-present consciousness of the unseen. His horror was—it was almost morbid, but that it was so genuine and consistent—to allow the consciousness to come into his mind of his gifts and success, or to do anything which looked like setting them to advantage. He absolutely revolted at the least thought of display. And so in intercourse with strangers, or in his writings, in his preaching, the first feeling was of disappointment ; he seemed dry, hard, awkward even—a contrast to all that had perhaps been suggested by ' The Christian Year ' ; there was indeed something more, not to be missed, of strange sweetness, of refined considerateness, of curious downright force and strength, which somehow mingled, one knew not how, with what seemed unattractive, or flashed up and drove it at once out of sight : but the evidence of the power, the grace and beauty of soul, the deep and living religion was not on the outside, and for the superficial and unreal might not be found at all. The plain, retiring, shy, country-bred Englishman, jealous of everything brilliant and on his guard against anything hollow, masked to common eyes at once the poet and the saint. He had that which has found partial expression in Dr. Newman's lines on the greatest of preachers :

> " ' Courteous he was and grave—so meek in mien,
>   It seemed untrue, or told a purpose weak ;
>   Yet in the mood, he could with aptness speak,
>   Or with stern force, or show of feelings keen,
>   Marking deep craft, methought, or hidden pride ;—
>   Then came a voice—" St. Paul is at thy side." ' "

" He was eminently one of those persons who remind the world, by the way in which, in spite of themselves, they become the object of its deep interest, and by the contrast between that interest and what there is producible to account for it, that there is a greatness greater than the highest of this world."

Mr. Keble's sensitive shrinking from anything like praise and observation has perhaps been the cause for the idea gaining ground that he was rather a gentle, holy man than a strong living force in Church matters. His friends, on the contrary, remember chiefly the fiery eagerness, the indignant remonstrances poured out, and the sternness of his judgment when he thought Church doctrine was being endangered. Eagle-eyed to detect danger, he allowed no one to be idle if things could be bettered by letters or protests.

His long and more careful letters were probably
written to those friends upon whose sympathy on
all points he could reckon ; but Dr. Moberly was
the recipient of his first impressions and hurried
utterances—scraps of half-sheets of paper full of
impetuous desire to be up and doing.   Mr. Keble
was in the habit of forwarding to College Street
letters and papers to be criticised before sending
them out, and George Moberly used to say, " Mr.
Keble constantly asks my advice, and *sometimes*
does me the honour of taking it."   One little
letter opens with, " Will this do ?   Something of
the sort I really think I *must* write, for fear of
bursting."   Another begins : " The Archdeacon
having done his best to extinguish us at the
Visitation, I suppose we must lose no time in
flaring up as well as we can.   Peter Young and
I have therefore passed an unanimous Resolution
to . . . send . . . some resolutions . . . to all the
clergy of Hampshire, as soon as the Visitation is
over. . . ."

It is not always clear what these letters refer
to, but the following probably concerns the proposal to bring out a commentary on the Bible.

From MR. KEBLE

"HURSLEY, *January* 20, 1847.

" MY DEAR MOBERLY,

"Will you cast your eye over the Pro-
spectus, which I enclose with this ?   And could
you take an ostensible part if you were asked ?

Besides other reasons which you know of, I cannot help fearing that our undertaking will be damaged, generally speaking, by having the initials the same as the Library of the Fathers. If you cannot give your own name, can you recommend any one who perhaps would? It will much sweeten the pill which I have to send to Pusey (many thanks to you for making it up) if I can say that you cordially approve this new scheme. Did I ask you if you knew any one who might do for that forlorn hope, St. Saviour's? He must be as near a self-contradiction as possible : for he ought (1) to sympathise with Pusey, yet (2) not to be mistrusted by Hook. If both these cannot be had, I advise P. to give up the first as far as is necessary for the second. Am I right? . . . .

"I never thanked you for a turkey which you sent us at Christmas, nor ever half enough for any of your great kindness.

"Your ever affectionate and grateful
"J. KEBLE."

Occasionally a longer letter appears, but it is evident that, living so close to one another all the year round, and within two miles of each other during the summer holidays, long and carefully expressed letters were, as a rule, unnecessary.

From MR. KEBLE

"H. V., *March* 6, 1848.

"MY DEAR MOBERLY,
"I can scarcely understand a person laying such extreme stress on the issue of this one controversy, unless he had been in serious perplexity before, and had come to that state of mind which causes men to lay hold of the first 'sign' that occurs as decisive. I trust that this

is not the case ; but if it were, is not the true way
of meeting it to show that it is altogether a
delusive, and, at the bottom, really a profane and
heathenish state of mind ? And is it not a fair
presumption of its bad origin, when quiet, simple,
devout persons, *aware of the circumstances*, find no
such difficulty in them ? But granting that a
sign might be innocently looked for, is *this* such
a sign ? I mean, if persons have thought it their
duty to bear with the Puritans and Latitudi-
narians of times past, so far as not to give up
the Church of England to them, nor to acquiesce
in their interpretation of its formularies, what
is there in this case to make them take a different view? We are not bound in any measure to
express approbation of Hampden's notions ; we
are not at all committed by them ; we have pro-
tested against them as far as we were able, on
the ground that they are contrary to the Prayer
Book ; yet were we to retire from the Church of
England because of them, must it not be on the
very ground that his was the right interpretation
of the Prayer Book ? It would be another thing,
were we called on as a condition of Communion to
subscribe to his views, or to refrain from holding
and teaching our own. As I understand it, so far
from retiring on account of the mistaken toleration
of such views, it is an additional reason for every
one of us to keep his post and do his best, as I
understand St. Basil and others to have done with
the semi-Arian Bishops of their time. As long as
the formularies continue unchanged, I cannot see
how the toleration even of heresy in this or that
Bishop, or even in the whole Bench, can be other
than a question of *discipline*, not of *doctrine* ; and
I thought it had been ruled ever since the days
of Donatus that questions of discipline affect the
well-being, not the being, of the Church ; and

6

therefore can never be of themselves a sufficient ground for separation. All this goes upon the worst supposition; but it should be considered that many good persons really do not think the B. L.[1] so evidently bad: *e.g.* C. Marriott, and the main body of those who stand up for him do it on the ground, not that his doctrines, being heretical, are tolerable, but that they are not really heretical. Then as to Erastianism: the more I think it over, the more I seem to see that we are on better ground than we have been at least since the Revolution; and if people will now be patient and persevering, we have every chance of making that ground good. The one thing to ruin us would be impatience. Does not the general admission of Toleration make a good deal of difference as to the need of separation from corrupt bodies? To separate, *i.e.* to act so as to be cut off, might be formerly a duty; now that for the very same act people do not cut us off, are we to cut ourselves off? . . . ."

There was a story that when the Anglo-Catholic Library was being discussed, Mr. Keble said to Dr. Moberly, "Well, *you* shall undertake the Anglo part and *I* the Catholic, and we will fight over the hyphen." When occasionally upbraided for not putting himself more forward in Church affairs, the Headmaster defended himself by saying that he did a more useful part in teaching Wykehamists the catechism and sound Church principles than in posing as a more extreme man than he was. To teach the catechism and churchmanship meant a good deal in those days, and, to his great discomfort, made him a marked

[1] Bampton Lectures by Dr. Hampden.

man in the diocese.   For thirty years he was
never asked to preach in any but one of the
many parish churches in Winchester, neither were
his wife or daughters allowed to join in any
parochial or district works until 1864.   A letter
to Sir John Awdry and another to Mr. Keble
show his mind very fairly on the principal subject
of controversy in 1847 and 1848.

From Dr. Moberly

"Winchester College, *Jan.* 21, 1847.

"My dear Sir John Awdry,
        "I feel extremely obliged to you for your
kind letter, and not a little flattered to find that
my book[1] has attracted so much of your consideration and thought.   It is indeed most true,
I think, that the claim of Infallibility, ever present
in the Church, and capable of being elicited in
answer to difficulties, is destructive altogether of
the virtue of Christian *Faith*, whether regarded
objectively in respect of its credenda, or subject-
ively as the inner rule and direction of life.   And
what you further say seems to me most important
as well as most entirely clear and certain—*i.e.* that
not only the same natural and feeble craving leads
men to the apparently opposite conclusions of
resting on their own personal presumptions, and
the presumptions of Rome, but also that it is a
craving which in the nature of things, and according to the history of opinion, never has been nor
can be satisfied.   It is a perpetual struggling to
endeavour *to be* and *not to be* together; to relinquish
choice by choosing ; to wriggle, as it were, out of
freedom of will by an intense act of wilfulness.
        "The moral opposite to all this is what our

[1] "The Great Forty Days."

friend Keble seems to me in every part of his writings and speakings to put forward most beautifully. You refer to the 6th Sunday after Epiphany, where it is admirably given. It is that which he is now *living on*; and which seems day by day to make him happier and more contented, in the midst of much to bear, in his position.

" He has recently been drawing up an argument (which I hope he designs to print) on the predicted Unity of the Church: showing, as I think with much force and justice, that the analogy of the fulfilment of all older general Prophecies would lead us *almost to expect* (certainly not to be so much distressed at seeing) a sort of Unity unlike what the *primâ-facie* aspect of the Predictions would have suggested: that it is a kind of carnal fulfilment which the Roman Catholic Church claims to show: that such a fulfilment as Christendom in general now shows may probably be very much more consistent with *Faith*, in its essential element of *uncertainty* (in which seems to lie all its peculiar power both of leavening the character and being acceptable with God), than such visible, clear, unquestionable unity as is by many demanded. I am not sure that I report his view quite rightly; but this was my impression of it on a hasty reading.

" May I add one word about my own Preface?[1] It is strictly a casual and therefore most incomplete argument. It is very far from pretending either to answer Newman fully, or to give a digested theory. And therefore I declined Rivington's advice of publishing it separately; hoping that it might be understood simply as an endeavour to relieve one portion of my connected argument from the pressure of his new theory. Strange to say, I find myself obliged sometimes to

[1] Third edition of " The Great Forty Days."

defend it against attacks grounded on the omission
of matters with which it would have been quite
impertinent to my point to have burdened it.

   " Yours most faithfully,
      " GEORGE MOBERLY."

The pressing anxiety of the time was as to
whether Mr. Manning would go over to Rome or
not. The following little note from Mr. Keble is
inserted for the sake of the answer to it, in which
my father speaks with care of his own position
in regard to some of the vexed questions before
the Church of England at the time.

       " H. V., *April* 3, 1848.

" MY DEAR MOBERLY,
  " This letter is a great relief as to H. E. M.,
but it gives one some grave thoughts as to whether
J. K. has been doing rightly. But I must talk to
you of this at leisure.

  " It is, indeed, an awful time. . . .
    " Ever yours affectionately,
      " J. K."

     " WINCHESTER COLLEGE, *April* 1848.

" MY DEAR KEBLE,
  " I send back Manning's letter ; pray do not
be surprised or less pleased that I write a few lines.
I find it easier to write to you ; for I know not
why I have always felt unable to say fully what
I have meant to you. And now I cannot help
writing a few words—partly to explain myself, and
partly to express my opinion, fearing, however,
painfully, that you will hardly agree with it.

  " I fear Manning's view is in many ways
true. Hook has gone back, others have gone
back, some have gone forward. Hook is an

historical Church of England man. There comes a collision : and of those who have advanced, a stratum will very likely be wedged off to Rome. It was the inner consciousness of this fear which led me to write as I did a day or two ago. That Hook has gone back I see, and greatly lament : and differ from his new view utterly. Had Hook retained his old mind (I only speak of the particular point now at issue) I believe that I should have felt very much with him about it.

"For it seems to me that it was our wisdom, considering where we were after the Reformation, and our last century and a half of coldness, to hold fast by our Prayer Book. We acknowledged that it gave us opportunity and direction for living in a holy and Catholic way ; and if it was less perfect than it might have been,—why, the great struggles and tempests which we had gone through not only accounted for such imperfections very amply ; but also made it our duty, as I think, to acquiesce thankfully,—wishing for better things, and ready to help wherever it might be practicable ; but meanwhile lifting up ourselves, our parishes, and our country to the level of the Prayer Book, which was, at least, a much higher level than that which we occupied.

"And, up to the time of the appearance of Oakley's and Ward's articles in the *British Critic*, we seemed to be going on so. But then came a change which we have not yet nearly seen to the end of.

"I will not vex you by a long story. I own I have been distressed by all things which went beyond the Prayer Book—feeling perfectly sure in my own mind, that the result, humanly speaking, of all such movements (even though some of them might be Primitive, and *per se*, good) must needs be the alienation of the masses and with them of the rulers in Church and State, and the consequent triumph of Puritanism in the Church of England, the probable secession to Rome of some, and the total helplessness of such other teachers of Church Principles as stayed where they were baptised.

" Now I suppose many would agree with me in what I have said as far as regarded things of *small consequence* ; and would say that to produce such effects in order to carry preaching in the surplice, or flowers in churches, or lights on the altar, was plainly undesirable.   But they would say that the case is different with such essential matters as confession and absolution.

" But I should feel that the Prayer Book which quite recognised the priestly powers, had given two directions for using them privately, in sickness and in distress of mind—that very great and good men had lived and died in the Church of England under this restricted use of these divine powers, and that it would be a very great thing to bring the Church of England generally up to the recognition and use of them thus far, and that it would be a still greater thing, wisely, peacefully, and generally, to reinstitute the more primitive practice of discipline ; but that such introduction was the duty of the Church of England in her rulers, not of individuals, and that, meanwhile, dutifully-minded men ought to abide by the restricted use of these powers, thanking God for them, and praying for the restoration in His good time of the more perfect system.

" Is not this what you do ?   What your brother does ?   Cornish, Prevost, Wilson : what Hook did do ?   What H. Wilberforce and, I suppose, Dodsworth does ?

" When I said (I forget exactly what) about my fearing that there was some weight in some of Hook's remarks, I meant to signify that I feared that St. Saviour's had practically been a hindrance rather than a help to him : that in Leeds, and in the West Riding, the cause of the Church and Church principles had lost rather than gained since it had been built, and in consequence of what had been done there. I fear that what Leeds and the West Riding had suffered was precisely what Church principles were suffering all England over from similar causes,—that every isolated movement *beyond the Prayer Book*, reacted in the triumph of opponents, the discouragement of friends, and the alienation of the indifferent.

" I have no right to say anything on the patronage of St. Saviour's, which Hort speaks of : certainly if it had been in the Bishop's hands it might have led to good.

" I had no particular reference in what I said about this Diocese except to the triumphant state of Puritanism,—witnessed in the division, the other day, about the Training School,—the Bishop's opinion, the way people have been speaking about the Propagation Society, and the great success of the Church Missionary operations under the new Archbishop, which has given spirits and hope to that party to a very great degree. . . .

" I wish I could feel sure that I shall not lose some of your good opinion by my writing, and yet I seem to feel that I ought to write it ; but I feel sure that you will read it kindly, so I will not scruple to send it.

" Believe me, dear Keble, yours affectionately,
　　　　　　　　　　　" GEORGE MOBERLY."

GEORGE MOBERLY'S JOURNAL

" *January* 1848.—Another day very characteristic of the holidays. Church service : interviews : a page or two of my Preface : boy's lessons. I am asked for a subscription for the Hampden proceedings.   Have had a long talk with Hickley and William Yonge about Oxford debts.   I am very much convinced that the University ought and could do a great deal more to check them.   My article in the *Christian Remembrancer* is out.

" *February.*—Since my last entry in this book the Archbishop is gone from us, leaving his sacred post to be filled up by the Whigs.   I must look forward to further and more decisive declension in the School.   Whilst in former times the inner life of the School was fearfully severe and outrageously impure, all was profoundly secret, and Winchester flourished with a reality and depth of inward baseness which is fearful to think of.   Now it is otherwise.   There is the utmost disposition to make much of, and to publish everything that takes place.   Thus, though the improvement is immense, I might say wonderful, at least in all the better boys in the School, the outcry out of doors is raging louder and louder, and day by day something occurs.

" *March.*—To-day the Holy Communion, to which I take 70 boys.   I have seen all the Commoners, but one : and my interviews with them make me cheerful as to the soundness of the inner heart of the School.   I alone of mankind see and know anything of this, so that I alone have a right to correct external impressions on the ground of better and deeper knowledge.   I believe the School was never, in the main points, better, more united, more gentlemanlike, or more religious than it is now—at least for 32 years back.   But the numbers dwindle ; will the College support me ? They sympathise with my theories, I think, but care nothing for me.

" Meanwhile Louis Philippe and his dynasty are gone to the winds, and half a dozen enthusiastic men are trying to keep their seats in a temporary castle on the Wild Elephant's back, following his gallop, in the hope that they may some day control it. But financial and other difficulties gather round them in such multitudes and force that it seems difficult to foresee any other—— But the bell begins. May God Almighty bless me, my dear wife, and children, and house : my pupils of all ages : my brothers, sisters, kindred, friends, god-children, penitents, His Church, our governors, those who labour for His truth in all lands, and His sufferers of all kinds for Christ's sake. Amen.

" *Easter Eve.*—Eventful times ! Since I wrote last France has been whirling round and round and drawing nearer day by day to the inevitable maelstrom of perdition. London attempted by Chartists amid the anxious watching of all Europe : and the design frustrated by the most noble, unanimous, and complete rising of the whole upper, middle, and many of the lower, classes in defence of the Queen and the Constitution.

" And this afternoon, a fourth sweet son was born.[1] Most deeply do I feel what all our friends say, how admirably their mother brings up our children, steadily, tenderly, sensibly, and equably, so that they are most perfectly happy and under complete control."

From Mr. Keble

" Bisley, *2nd S. after Easter*, 1848.

"'My very dear kind Friend,

" I cannot say what I feel, or rather ought to feel, at your trusting me with anything so precious as the care of your little boy. You know the sort of reason why I ought to shrink from such a trust, and have done so before, but you do not, alas ! at all know the degree of it. Yet, if you still wish me, I will most thankfully

---

[1] John Cornelius Moberly

undertake the charge. Even in respect of my godchildren, I seem to know reason enough why I ought not to be trusted. But perhaps this ought not to make one withdraw, but rather to stir up one's diligence. . . . Many thanks for your kind congratulation. Tuesday was a happy but trying day : it is a special joy to see how entirely my brother seems to be his old self again, and how thoroughly he accepts and enjoys his new son and future daughter : as indeed it would be a wonder if he did not. How glad I am that dear Mrs. Moberly was able to write so long a letter : we have had very refreshing ones from Maria Wilson and Charlotte Yonge. I send you letters from Mozley. . . ."

GEORGE MOBERLY'S JOURNAL

" *Christmas Day*, 1848.—We have had a good deal of trouble in the School ; an extravagant evening of bonfire and fireworks on Saturday. I told the boys they could not go home on Monday : turbulent disquieted feeling all Sunday ; passive rebellion on Monday, which we effectually put down ; but indications reach my ears of a growing disaffection for some time. Certainly such an interpretation falls in with the bad performance of the Commoners in the Goddard examination. I dismiss three boys, and have received a very proper apology from the Senior Prefect.

" *Dec.* 30.—Church. Arthur's lessons ; he has begun Greek. I have seen the *Independent's* account of our row ; which makes me the aggressor, the violent, the unforgiving, the defeated, and the revengeful of the transaction, and visits the whole on the head of poor " Fagging " and me its unfortunate advocate.

" *Feb.* 25, 1849. — The half-year has begun well. I never saw the boys so much disposed for

quietness, order, and content. Also I have several
taking very good pains.   I have also begun, and
I think with obviously good effect, prayers every
morning and evening, and full Church service on
Sundays in the Continent room, and prayers with
the Commoner servants every evening.   Also we
are beginning a Continent room library. . . .

   "*Easter Sunday.*—My boys go from School
with wonderful rapidity, yet were we never in such
a state of moral, religious, and intellectual growth,
as I verily believe, since I have known the School.
. . . I have to preach at St. Mary's, Oxford, on
Whitsunday.   I rejoice at the appointment, for I
like speaking to my old pupils, and delight to think
that the ban is removed.

   "*June.*—I preached in Oxford to a large congregation, and I have offered a sort of peace
offering in the shape of an inoffensive sermon.
George has got one of Bishop Maltby's prizes, and
Arthur is so confirmed a schoolboy that he seems
to prefer school to home—a real ground for
uneasiness.

From REV. J. ROBERTS

"TWYFORD, 1849.

   " Nothing can have been more satisfactory than
Arthur's general conduct and progress since he
has come back to work.   I have found him more
diligent, more active, and more smiling than before.
He seems to have such a very clear comprehension
of things ; and I have been more than once very
much pleased and surprised with the intelligence
and accuracy of his work.   I think I can see
clearly that my grand point with him will be not
only to keep alive his attention and interest, but
to make the constant and assiduous and accurate
getting up of all his lessons *the* condition of
happiness and comfort.   He seems always happy

and contented when his mark is β. or *Opt.*, but there is always the downcast head and almost inaudible voice when it is *Male*. It has always been our custom at Morning Prayers to read a few verses from the Bible, and from them I catechise the boys generally for a few moments. Arthur does answer so very nicely and thoughtfully that I feel sure that he has been attentive and interested during the reading. I mention this as one out of many nice points about him, and as one of those points which make me feel that I can safely say to you that you have another very hopeful and very promising boy."

From ARTHUR

" TWYFORD.

" DEAR MAMMA,

" I hope you are quite well, and my marks for gatherings are ; B, Opt., B, at least my marks for gatherings for last week. This week is quarter week, so there is no gathering to-day, which is Saturday. My Entomology is not getting on at all well ; I have not got one caterpillar, or moth, or butterfly, or chrysalis yet. I hope to find a burnished gold moth. I caught one on the downs the other day, which I gave to another entomologist in the School, and a great one too. I shall also find an Argus moth on the downs, I hope. I have kept my place very well against Baker or Sterry. I have not lost or gained any place.

" Your affectionate son,

" ARTHUR MOBERLY."

GEORGE MOBERLY'S JOURNAL

" *Dec.* 7.—I think it will be well to write lectures for Confirmation, but my work is so great and oppressive that it is difficult to know how to manage it. An occasional sermon is not so hard,

for there is generally some compact thing to say—
a corner—a strong necessity—and lo ! a sermon.

"*July* 1850.—I have refused the Wardenship of
the College at Canterbury, New Zealand ; my age
and many children compelling. . . . Rather more
comfort about Manning.   But Allies and his wife
and Mrs. H. Wilberforce are gone, and Mr. Dodsworth is, I fear, resolved.   It is unspeakably melancholy.   Edmund Bastard urges the visible Unity
of Rome.   I reply : (*a*) By the parallel case of
sanctity ; (*β*) by the fact that unity as a duty
involves *two*, and that one can only keep it by
holding the Apostolical descent, and love, and
readiness of unity ; (*γ*) by the question, Who
broke unity ? (*δ*) is Rome more one than the
Eastern Church ? (*ε*) by the reflection of God's
continuing to be with the corrupt Jewish Church ;
(*ζ*) by the cost of 100 millions alive (and ten times
as many dead) at which Rome purchased her apparent Unity.   Again, as to the Ark, Tree, etc.
A boat broken by the waves into three swimming
portions : no need to change though one may have
the mainmast aboard ; so a tree may throw up
stems.

"*Jan.* 1851.—Never did so dark a year break
upon the Reformed Church of England.   The
Government, the vast majority of lay people, and
a considerable portion of the clergy are bent on
banishing the Catholic element from the Church
of England.   Meanwhile secessions take away our
very heart : Bastard, Manning, Anderson, Lapri-
maudaye, Dodsworth. . . ."

KITTY'S STORY

" After George's great illness and paralytic stroke
when he was ten years old, he became the brother
for whom everything was to be made as happy and
bright as possible, and for whom we had a very

reverential affection.   Arthur was nearer to us in age ; he was not strong, and was inclined to be indolent, and we used to ward off scrapes, and get him ready in time for things, so that he might not have a scolding.   Robert was a great character in our nursery days on account of his strong opinions, quaintly expressed.   His power of passive resistance was so great that it might have caused difficulties, but for his other as strongly marked power of self-control.   This was the result of definite effort (unusual in one so young) to see things as others saw them ; and all the funny childish and boyish stories related of him illustrate the one characteristic keeping the other in abeyance, or at least making the resistance perfectly courteous (as he thought) and disarming opposition.   He had inherited a good deal from our mother, and he and George were both like her in face and features. Robert had early an eye for beauty, and (in his baby days) thought that the rainbow had sucked up the colours of the flowers, and that the painted windows in Hursley church were angels' wings. Johnnie and Edward [1] were too young at this time to take much part in our nursery lives.

"One Christmas Eve (1850) my father walked home from the Cathedral service with Major Wilbraham of the 7th Fusiliers,[2] then quartered at Winchester.   Major Wilbraham was sad, having just lost his young wife.   With some hesitation he was asked to come in, though warned that he would find a family tea of the homeliest description and an evening that might jar with its merriment.   The invitation was at once accepted, and he spent the evening helping us to dress the house with holly ; most useful to us children on account of his height.   He became an intimate friend, and caused us to know Mr. Watson, a lieutenant in the

[1] Edward Hugh Moberly.
[2] Afterwards General Sir Richard Wilbraham.

same regiment, almost as well as himself.[1]   They
constantly brought other officers to the house, walking over to the farm in summer, and adding much
to the general merriment.   Major Wilbraham's
sisters came to stay with us, and one of them
became my mother's great friend ; their knowledge
of Italy and love for Dante and the Italian poets
being a special attraction.

" For several years Miss Charlotte Yonge wrote
plays for us to act at Christmas.[2]   The learning
the parts and rehearsing took weeks beforehand,
and Miss Yonge liked to act herself sometimes.
She was Queen Philippa in ' St. Barthelemy's Fair.'[3]
Mary made a lovely Cinderella, and was small
enough to be pushed into one of the cupboards of
the carved oak sideboard when the prince came to
try on the shoe.   She was dressed in my mother's
dark green silk, and under it a dress of white net
with all her most glittering ornaments sewn on
to it, which was displayed when the fairy (Dora)
touched her with her wand tipped with a silver
star.   When ' The Pigeon Pie ' was acted, Mrs.
Yonge made a lay figure to represent a soldier,
which went by the name of Zedekias Dunderhead,
and George gave much trouble by resolutely re-
fusing to act the part of the Roundhead colonel,
so Mrs. Yonge had to take it herself."

[1] Afterwards Colonel Watson.
[2] The reason was this.   One day we were calling in College Street,
and the children announced that they were just going to act Miss
Edgeworth's play of "The Knapsack."   Rather against Mrs. Moberly's
wish, I think, we stayed to see what this private joke of the children's
would be like.   Presently George, in the character of the captain,
called out in a grand manner, "Now I will show you the remains of
the once magnificent Swedish regiment," and in hopped three little
girls in red cloaks.   We all burst out laughing, and Dr. Moberly
exclaimed, "They have indeed degenerated in *quality* as well as in
quantity."   This set me thinking of writing a play.—C. M. YONGE.
[3] This came out in *The Magnet Stories* by the name of "The Mice at
Play."

From Miss Yonge

"My dear Alice,

"I am glad you think 'St. Barthelemy's Fair' practicable. I shall very much enjoy doing what I can in the preparations, and I will try and grow as fat and dignified as I can in honour of her Majesty, Queen Philippa. I was almost afraid that there were too many characters, though I could not see how to manage with less. We can furnish a real sword and spinning-wheel. My notion of the King is in a long blue cloak, which we have here, and a fur tippet. The object of this letter is to ask you and Miss Cowing, and as many of the schoolroom party as the carriage will carry, to come in the afternoon and look at the illuminated illustrations in Froissart and talk it over and see what can be done. You cannot think how I shall enjoy the fun of the rehearsals, and it will give me such a good opportunity for correcting any part of the play that may not have the right effect."

Another

"My dear Alice,

"Would George mind being the Colonel? He is never on the stage with Edmund, and a cloak and blue scarf would turn him into a Roundhead. I do not see what else is to be done, for altering the part now would spoil the dinner scene. I am glad you are not more perfect in your parts. I say mine every evening when I am going to bed, but I cannot leave off laughing in the wrong places, especially when I have to congratulate Edmund on his alteration since I saw him six years ago. Mr. Dunderhead lives in the little dressing-room, to the amazement of all beholders who come suddenly upon him in the twilight."

7

Another

" My dear Alice,

"Herewith is the 'Bridge of Cramond' finished. I hope George will not think too much sentiment falls to his share; and that we shall soon fall in with that important actor, the hawk. You and your two gipsies (Emily and Annie) will make courtiers, and Zedekias will help; indeed six, besides the other actors, is nearly as much as the stage will hold. Pray be grateful to me for bringing in a rat and the old lark. As to the Scotch, I believe it is shocking; but if you can get it corrected it will be a good thing. My boast of no scratches was futile; I had to make them afterwards. We were glad to hear of Kate Barter."

G. Moberly's Journal

" *May* 21, 1852.—My sweet little maiden is above a week old,[1] and most thankful am I to say that she and her mother are going on well. . . . The Oxford Commission Report is out: sweeping confiscation and revolution are what it means in plain English."

From Miss Yonge

"*Ascension Day*, 1852.

" My dear Dr. Moberly,

"Of all days in the year this is one that I should specially have chosen for receiving the note Mamma sent on this morning. Indeed, I do thank you and Mrs. Moberly very much for giving me a Pearl to think of every day. How I shall look forward to the christening day and to having a possession of my own in your house! I wonder what you will think of my venturing, since you

---

[1] Margaret Helen Moberly, afterwards Mrs. Charles Awdry.

said nothing about a second name, to say how much I should like, if you have no other view, for her to be Margaret Helen; though, as it is for the sake of nothing but some fancies of my own, it does not deserve to be twice thought about, and I hope you will forgive my mentioning it. I am very glad to hear such a comfortable account of Mrs. Moberly. I am sure this is weather to recover in and Daisies to thrive in." [1]

EMILY'S STORY

" My earliest recollections of Fieldhouse begin with the delightful excitement of packing and of having the house turned upside down with the removal of furniture. How well we knew what pieces of furniture went to the farm! and what joy was in the excited announcement ' The waggon has come!' I think one of the chief delights was the white dimity curtains in the bedrooms; they in their first freshness always contained a good deal of the essence of the first evening in the country, when we children roamed from room to room, terribly in the way of our elders, no doubt, to watch all the arrangements within, and then out again to the garden wild with happiness, and resting in the knowledge that it was to last a whole summer. Then there were the animals in the

[1] After " Margaret Helen's " christening, Miss Yonge carried back the baby to our mother, who was lying on her sofa, and said that she thought of writing a story about a good Margaret, as she had as yet only invented a rather unpleasant person of that name in "The Heir of Redclyffe." The family in " The Daisy Chain " was given the name of " May " in honour of our baby, and the words " Dedicated and named after the May Daisy, M. H. M.," were written in the first copy sent to College Street. Miss Yonge told us that the large family of the book had been suggested by the party of her cousins at Puslinch, whose ages corresponded more to her own than ours did. As far as the personality of " Dr. May " was a reproduction at all, her uncle was probably in her mind. Winchester may have suggested the old town and school of Stoneborough.

farmyard to visit, and the dairy, and baby must be persuaded to run on the lawn or in "the nook"; till at last, weary with happiness, we were summoned to rest in the clean little white beds. There is but little detail that fixes itself in my mind as belonging to those earliest days. The little gardens came into them, though, as far as I can remember, we never had any plants in them but the centre rose-tree in each. As far as I remember it was a continual process of weeding, and that child was the most successful who most effectually cleared everything out of his garden. I set great store by my rose-tree, which bore red and white roses, having been grafted. Kitty's was a blush rose, and we always considered it exactly like her. The ditch by the barn which shut in our gardens was full of stiff yellow clay, and wonderful were the specimens of pottery and the early attempts at art that we constructed out of that ditch! I remember especially a figure of Sir William Wallace on horseback, whose horse's legs were not strong enough to support the weight on them, even when strengthened with sticks. On the rare occasions on which I now hear the musical sound of the mowers whetting their scythes, it brings back in all its freshness the rapture with which we woke to it on a bright summer's morning. And the pleasure was not all in the happy prospect of collecting the grass and carrying it away to the farmyard in George's little waggon; the actual music of the sound was a great part of the enjoyment.

"In the spring, before the year was far enough on to allow of our living at the farm, we used to be occasionally driven over for the afternoon. I doubt if any child living constantly in the country could delight in the wild flowers so much as we did on those occasions, when we were let loose among the primroses. How we gazed up at the blue sky, and down again at the crimson tassels and plumes of the budding larches, and so to the mosses underfoot and the uncurling ferns ; and then paused to listen for the note of a nightingale, while the fragrant smell of the moist ground rose round us ; and we could have cried for joy. And so back to Winchester again through the scent of the fir woods, silent and dreamy, and feeling inclined to make poetry which never came."

KITTY'S STORY

" The Warden's beautiful garden, with the clear trout stream running through it, the great plane-trees, and the east window of the College Chapel looking towards the stream, was the delight of our childhood, as we were made free of it. Warden Barter liked nothing better than to see plenty of friends in the garden and to come down and welcome them. The scent of sweet woodruff leaves dried in our best prayer books, which are still sweet, recall feelings and associations never to be forgotten ; whilst the scent of violets and lemon geranium reminds us of the Warden's drawing-room and of the sound of the running stream with its little waterfall. The engravings from Raphael's Vatican pictures on the dark oak-panelled walls, the large roomy sofa, the grand piano, and the solid writing-table in the window were the most noticeable points in the room. The Warden started an 11-o'clock service in the Chapel on Wednesdays and Fridays for the College servants and any one who could attend, when he would shut his eyes and say the Litany by heart.

" The walk to St. Cross, about a mile and a half out of Winchester, was a favourite one, and we liked to rest in the quadrangle on a warm spring afternoon, when the old almoner's gardens were full of sweet-smelling, old-fashioned flowers ; or in summer, when the honeysuckle was in full bloom over their porches ; or in autumn, to see the Virginia creeper hanging in crimson wreaths over the entrance to the ancient Hall.   Grandpapa's house was at St. Cross, where he lived with Aunt Tina and Uncle John Crokat.

" We grew up amidst historical remains, and imbibed our elders' bright interest in everything, and a most enthusiastic reverence for our Cathedral, where so much had happened.   We knew the chests in which were the bones of the Saxon kings and queens ; admired the delicately carved stone altar-screen which replaced the one on which Canute had hung up his crown.   There, in the Lady Chapel, was the chair in which Queen Mary sat at her wedding with Philip of Spain, and (what was then supposed to be) William Rufus's tomb, on which the College boys placed their hats at Sunday morning service ; and William of Wyke-ham's shrine.   There was a story that he walked in the nave of the Cathedral at night, which made Warden Barter exclaim that if he could only believe it to be true he should certainly spend the night there, as he could imagine nothing more delightful than half an hour's chat with William of Wykeham !

" I think it must have been in the summer of 1853 that Dora, Emily, and I spent some time at Otterbourne.   We used to have long walks by the river gathering water flowers, with Rover the brown water spaniel jumping into the river, swimming and barking at the moorhens.   Mrs. Yonge was very fond of natural history, and taught us to care for flowers and birds and to notice their habits.   Miss Yonge began to teach us something about shells, and used to show us the beautiful collection she had.   She set us on collecting snail shells—almost the only possible thing to collect in our limited walks near Winchester,

THE WARDEN'S GARDEN.

p. 102]

"The earliest childish recollections I have of Hursley Vicarage are of playing on the lawn in the Vicarage garden, which was very steep in one part. The fun was to be put into a little wooden cart at the top of the hill and given a shove, when down we went at a furious pace and always overturned at the bottom on the grass. This was the amusement of the pupils of the successive curates, Mr. Robert Wilson and Mr. Peter Young. The long tool-house under the terrace was a capital hiding-place, dark and mysterious. I remember a good deal about the *Hursley Magazine*, and as I was very fond of reading and also eager to know what the elders were talking about, I wished to hear the stories and see the illustrations, which were by Mr. Newbolt and very amusing. I believe Lady Heathcote edited and bound it, and Miss Yonge and others contributed to it. Of course we used to go to the school feasts at Hursley, in which the Otterbourne and Ampfield children joined. The children carried garlands to church ; then they had tea on the lawn, going afterwards into the Park for games. As twilight came on they trooped back to the Vicarage lawn and sang, whilst we all stood on the terrace to listen. Those were lovely days in our lives ; and the scent of the crimson scabious, called at Hursley 'gipsy roses,' always reminds one of them.

"We greatly admired Mrs. Keble, with her beautiful gentle brown eyes ; she drew very well, and was fond of music. Then there was fragile, delicate Miss Elizabeth Keble (Mr. Keble's sister), who walked with a crutch and lay on the drawing-room sofa. Mr. Keble used to have many jokes and funny speeches for us children, and this sort of playfellow feeling was the earliest idea we had of him. Later on came the knowledge that he was great and clever. I used to wonder at the distress with which in preaching or speaking he would mention the troubles of the Church, and hope that I should some day understand why he spoke so much of the Church.   I remember his christening Annie and Selwyn in the College Chapel, and the many christenings at Hursley, when he used to wipe the water from the baby's head with his surplice and kiss it before giving it back to the nurse.   He catechised the schoolchildren on Sunday afternoons after the second Lesson.   He had them all taught carefully beforehand, and so caused it to be a lesson for the congregation as well. We know now how intensely reverent his manner was ; never allowing it to be forgotten for a moment that it took place in church and in the course of the service ; it was always, ' What then must *we* do ? ' his humility making the teaching so impressive. Afterwards he preached on the same subject.   His constant mention of the Love of God in his sermons was striking, and also the way in which he pulled himself together and spoke of *sin* with a tone of awed horror and with a degree of fierceness which could never be forgotten.

" The church had a dark oak roof, carved angels supporting the rafters, and white pointed arches. Before the clerestory windows were opened it was very dark, which we found most refreshing after our long hot walk from the farm.   We had names for all the parts of the road : there was the ' baking bit,' and the ' roasting bit,' and the ' frying bit,' before we reached the lych-gate and the cool church.   The doors used to stand open, and I remember the sound of the summer wind in the lime-trees in the churchyard and the delicious scent of the blossom." [1]

---

[1] A woman at Hursley told Mrs. Keble : " They Mulberries was so many that when they came into church the foremost had to look and see where the hendermost was."—C. M. YONGE.

Annie's Story

" Our seats in Hursley church were under the tower, where we could study the Cromwell tablet ; for Richard Cromwell with his children and grandchildren had lived at the old house in Hursley park, the foundations of which could sometimes be seen on the bowling green. The walk home after Sunday afternoon service was delicious, with its sense of leisure and comparative coolness. Our mother and the little ones drove ; but our father and a mighty army of girls and boys strolled slowly home, first along the length of the village, then a mile of gradually rising sandy road crossed by long shadows from the trees, till we climbed to the top of Ladwell hill. Here we felt the air, and had a wide view of woodlands with the Isle of Wight in the blue distance beyond them ; and we sat down to rest among the pink and white convolvuluses on the edge of the cornfields before going down the less steep descent to the farm, which lay below us ensconced in its nest of trees.

" Very soon after reaching the garden Mrs. and Miss Yonge joined us, for (after Mr. Yonge's death) it was their habit, for twelve years, to spend the latter part of Sunday with us. We greatly enjoyed the animated talks that took place on those summer evenings between them and our parents. We cannot remember the time when we did not sit by and listen to the eager talk on every kind of subject. It was a great education ; all the more, because it was so constant, merry, and unconstrained. The information on all sides was considerable and the enthusiasm great, exciting interest on a thousand topics. Miss Yonge loved to discuss the Peninsular War and every detail of the battle of Waterloo as she had heard of it through her uncle. Lord Seaton was Mrs. Yonge's step-brother ; he had been the Colonel Colborne of

the 52nd regimént at Waterloo, and it was his flank
movement which finally won the battle. The
Yonges were extremely proud of him.

" Military subjects naturally had a great attraction for us, living in a garrison town. From our
earliest years we had stood on the railings above
the parade ground and watched the soldiers at drill,
and (thanks to the nursemaids) had attended a
large number of soldiers' funerals. Our hearts
were stirred to their depths by the strains of the
Dead March, the roll of the kettledrums, and
the wild sound of the shots over the grave. The
sight of the long procession of soldiers marching
with arms reversed affected us greatly ; but perhaps
the part which produced the worst lump in our
throats was the incongruous jig played as they
walked quickly back to the barracks. Well do
I remember the pathos of the contrast, which was
associated in my mind with the look of the large
floating white clouds making passing shadows over
St. Cross in the Itchen valley. Not till we were
grown up did we realise that our mother was
ignorant of the nurses' habit of taking us regularly
to these funerals ; she would never have allowed it.
Certainly, even as little children, we were far more
moved by the grand beauty and poetry of the
scene than the nurses had any idea of."

From Miss Yonge

" My dear Alice,
      " The *Times* was quite right, Lucien was
at the camp, though I cannot remember him.
Montebello told Lord Seaton that he is very sorry
to see our troops in such excellent order. The
Queen looked in great good-humour, and was
determined to see the men have their dinner.
She came to Virginia Water with Prince Albert,

who was sneezing and looking as if he had the
measles. Lord and Lady Seaton are at the Palace
again to-night. They have a great luncheon in
marquees to-morrow. So much for camp news.
. . . We have had a famous party from Fieldhouse;
you should have seen Robert, Johnnie, Emily, and
Rover all at tea at the little round table. I wish
you could have been at Hursley yesterday. We
had a nice sight of the Bishop[1] and Mrs. Gray in
the Vicarage after service, and Mrs. Gray brought
down some beautiful drawings of the Table
Mountain . . . ."

GEORGE MOBERLY'S JOURNAL

" *Christmas Day*, 1853.—A bright and cheerful
morning ushers in Christmas Day ; and a company
of little carollers at my dressing-room door, including Edward, Walter,[2] and Maggie, made it sweet
as well as bright. I cannot be thankful enough
for the kind Providence which makes my home so
smiling and happy. Little Emsie said yesterday
she was so happy, she could not *clasp* all her
happiness. Lessons. George with his next year's
Goddard. Arthur saying ' Standing up.' Robert
with his little Latin, and a class of arithmeticians
daily. The Ministry is still rather at sixes and
sevens, but no apparent change. War with Russia
towards.

" *Feb.* 1854.—Little indeed did I think when
I wrote last that in the next entry I should have
to mourn for our good friend William Yonge. He
parted from his son Julian on Wednesday, and
had a fit of apoplexy at night. Julian sailed on

---

[1] Bishop of Cape Town.

[2] Walter Allan Moberly, afterwards Vicar of St. Philip's, Sydenham ;
the Church of the Ascension, Blackheath ; St. Bartholomew's, Sydenham ; Hon. Canon of Rochester (changed to Southwark) ; Rural Dean
of Lewisham. Died Dec. 1905.

Saturday for the Crimea, and his father died on Sunday. I cannot at all realise the loss yet, and that his vigorous, manly step and voice will no longer be heard in my house again.

"*March* 7.—The Warden came to tell me of the death of Bishop Denison : a heavy loss to the Church.

"*March* 21.—The Dean tells me that the See of Salisbury is given to Walter Hamilton : a good appointment. Discussions with the Warden and Sir William Heathcote on the Wykehamical aspect of the University Reform Bill. . . .

" Dear Robert wins my heart with his courageous, affectionate, industrious ways. . . .

" The 7th Fusiliers sail for Gallipoli from Southampton on Wednesday ; we will try and shake hands with our friends there.[1] My brother Edward and his family have left Odessa ; my brother Tom and the Cattleys stay at St. Petersburgh. Cholera beginning to appear."

George Moberly's Story

" In July I went to my brother William's house in London, and whilst there a cab covered with luggage drove up. I exclaimed, ' Whom have we here ? ' It was our nephew, Charles Cattley, who had been vice-consul at Kertch, and was living in Odessa. The Russian Government had sent him away at a moment's notice, made him go round by St. Petersburgh, and here he was with nothing to do. ' Surely,' I said, ' you must have a great deal to tell us.' He said that he had much local information ; he knew every inch of the Crimea—the depths of the waters round it, etc. He could speak Russian and Italian, and got on perfectly with the Tartars. I sat down at once and wrote to Mr. Sidney Herbert (then Minister for War),

---

[1] The Crimean War was just beginning.

and asked whether he had any use for such a man. In the course of the same evening a summons came to Charles from the Admiralty; he was sent from one office to another, closely examined, and finally desired to start instantly and go out as fast as steam could carry him to put himself under the command of Lord Raglan. In May 1855, when the Government was accused of beginning the war without adequate information, Sir James Graham, before Mr. Roebuck's Committee, denied the accusation on the ground that they had with them a man intimately acquainted with the Crimea and knowing every necessary detail; that every piece of information he gave them was found perfectly accurate, and that he had joined them in July.[1] Charles Cattley died

[1] Pp. 284–5. (Examined by Mr. Layard.) ". . . Instead of an opinion I will give you a fact. In the last week in July I saw a Crimean authority . . . who had left the Crimea in the month of June. I saw him at the Admiralty, and I myself examined him; and an officer of the Admiralty was in attendance on me, and took down his statement in writing. It was most circumstantial and full, giving a complete account of the Crimea, its localities, its harbours, its roads, its productions, and supply of water; and, what was most important of all, a statement of the force, which was estimated by him at 70,000 men, 8,000 of whom were cavalry, 40,000 of which constituted the garrison of Sebastopol, and the remaining 30,000 dispersed throughout the Crimea. . . . The person I have alluded to was an Englishman, and a most intelligent man, and I had at the time the utmost reliance on his statement; and subsequent events have proved that his estimate of the force at that time, such as, I believe, we encountered at the period of the battle of the Alma, was accurate, within a few thousand men; and, more than that, the individual himself followed the information which I sent, and had a personal communication with Lord Raglan. . . ."

21240. (Examined by General Peel.) ". . . The only information the Government has obtained has been here: all the information on which any reliance could be safely placed has been transmitted from hence, such as this particular information which at the time I relied upon. My deep conviction was that it was accurate, and subsequent experience and knowledge confirm me in its accuracy. It was received by the officers commanding the Army and the Navy before the expedition left Varna. . . ."

of cholera at headquarters not many months after."

The early "fifties" were anxious years; not only on account of the war, but also on account of the pressure of Church questions. On the one hand, in 1854, Churchmen had the great satisfaction of the renewal of the meetings of the Convocations, which had long been earnestly desired; on the other hand, the University Reform Act, admitting dissenters to the University, destroying clerical monopoly of Fellowships, and gradually leading on to the abolition of all religious tests, greatly divided opinion. Where Mr. Keble was apt to take the gloomiest view of such changes, as wrong because disloyal to the Church, Dr. Moberly was hopeful as to the general movement of things, and also as to the ultimate religious feeling of England. The elder man belonged more entirely to the older conditions; the younger one to the time of transition, though it was difficult enough for him, at that date, to see the trend of events. Meanwhile their differences of temperament, of political leaning, and of general outlook, increased the interest of discussion.

The children surrounding them saw the reflection of controversial anxieties on the faces of their elders without knowing more; and a dim recognition that important subjects, involving great principles, were exciting the keenest interest, and were capable of being looked at from different points of view without dividing friendship, formed a background to the thoughts of the younger generation from the first.

George and Arthur were Winchester scholars at opposite ends of the school, and Robert had gone to his first school at Twyford, near Winchester, when in 1854 the nursery received its full complement of children, and the seventh son and fifteenth child was born.

From Mr. Roberts

"Twyford, Winchester, *April* 29, 1854.

"You will like to have a line about Robert. I never saw such a nice little boy. I have made up my mind not to keep him in the fourth class. It is below his mark in everything. I doubt greatly whether the third is at all above him, excepting in Greek. At any rate I am bound to work every boy up to his capacity ; and so I have no choice about Robert. Hitherto he has been everything that we could desire."

From Mrs. Yonge

"*May* 1854.

"My dear Alice,

"I wrote instantly to thank Dr. Moberly for his good news, but the cart was missed on Sunday morning. Tell us if Margaret has seen the brother, and what she said of him, and tell us who the boy is like and whether he is large or small, dark or fair. Three days of well-doing make us think you will soon be ready for ' Heartsease '; there will be plenty for you to begin upon. I am bent upon Charlotte seeing all she can of Bishop Selwyn,[1] and trust to Dr. Moberly to manage it for her, and must have her see Mrs. Selwyn somehow."

From BISHOP G. A. SELWYN OF NEW ZEALAND

" MY DEAR DR. MOBERLY,

" As I might at this time have been one of your suffragans, if the counsels of the Church had been guided by impartial judgment, I cannot refuse you the allegiance which you are virtually entitled to ; and will endeavour to be at your meeting on June 8th.   You will excuse a tardy answer, as I have only now been able to see my clear way through the engagements made for me by Coleridge and others."

From MRS. YONGE

"OTTERBOURNE, *June* 1854.

" MY DEAR ALICE,

" The Warden has asked Charlotte and Anne[2] to dine there to be ready for the evening meeting ;[3] but at all events they will come to you first, about 10 o'clock, to go with you to the Cathedral.   You would have enjoyed a walk with

[1] Bishop George Augustus Selwyn became Bishop of New Zealand in 1841.   His work there brought him into great prominence, and he was recognised by English Churchmen as "*the* great missionary Bishop." At this time he was anxious to collect funds for the Melanesian mission already begun by him, and it was during this visit, in August 1854, that Coleridge Patteson (afterwards the first Bishop of Melanesia) decided to offer himself as a missionary.   Mrs. Selwyn had been Miss Richardson, a friend of my mother's before either of them was married.   One of the sons, John Selwyn, who succeeded the martyred Bishop Patteson as Bishop of Melanesia, was at this time a schoolboy in England, and often stayed with the Kebles at Hursley.

[2] Miss Anne Yonge of Puslinch.

[3] The Bishop of New Zealand and Mrs. Selwyn came to Hursley in June 1854, and held meetings which were largely attended both at Winchester and Hursley.   On the day of the Winchester meeting we children were running about the Warden's garden in the late afternoon.   Miss Yonge was with us.   We saw Bishop Selwyn coming with the Warden

us last evening in a part of Cranbury quite unknown to us, where we found some beautiful lady-fern and a dragon-fly surpassing in beauty. And so the dear people did come to us, Mary, Dora, Emily, and Annie, and we are only just come from walking to meet Miss Cowing and the rest. Charlotte sends all that is finished of ' Heartsease,' and has no doubt there will be more by the time you are ready for it ; she is numbering the pages with red, in case they get wrong. I do think Mrs. Moberly will enjoy little John Martindale, even more this time than before. Miss Keble is very fond of him."

GEORGE MOBERLY'S JOURNAL

" *July* 9.—Yesterday we happily christened our little ' Selwyn William,' Sir William Heathcote, Dr. Merriman, Miss Wilbraham and little Arthur the sponsors. Seventeen former sponsors were present. And so I have fifteen little Christians of my own to guard and guide as a father may. I thank God for their health, present goodness, and promise ; also for their many good friends. ' It *is* joy to think when I am dead ' my children will have some of the good among men for their friends.

and Mr. Keble over the bridge. As they came down the garden towards us a packet was put into little Maggie's hand, and she was told to give it to the Bishop. She obediently put it into the hand of " Man " as she called him. It was the proceeds of " The Heir of Redclyffe," with which the missionary ship *The Southern Cross* was afterwards built. The College for Melanesian boys at Kohimarama, New Zealand, was built with the proceeds of " The Daisy Chain," 1859, and was at first named St. Andrew's College, in allusion to St. Andrew's Church at Cocksmoor in " The Daisy Chain " ; but afterwards it was changed from a feeling that it was better not to have the connection with a work of fiction. For many years Miss Yonge wore a pendant, given her by her mother, of a gold St. Andrew's cross having an enamelled daisy in the centre, at the back of which was a tuft of little Maggie's hair under glass with the date June 1854 and Maggie's initials engraved on the cross. The proceeds of " The Daisy Chain " were afterwards entirely made over to the Melanesian Mission.

8

Keble is quite dispirited about the admission of dissenters, which is a *fait accompli*, and the Warden is, not without reason, indignant and unhappy at the ejection of Charles Wordsworth from Glenalmond."

"Recollections of Hursley," by Frances M. Wilbraham

"'Children's sports' and 'children's troubles' were studies of deep interest to Mr. and Mrs. Keble; they showed an almost parental love for their godchildren, looking upon the tie as lifelong, not, as so many think, dissolved at confirmation. On the occasion of this christening they were doubly interested, having stood sponsors to two of the older children who were both present. The gathering took place at Winchester on a sultry July day. There had been drenching thunder showers all the morning, but clear shining after rain had followed, and now lighted up trees and red-tiled roofs, and the grey length of the Cathedral. I saw Mr. Keble's face assume a careworn expression as he talked with one of the sponsors who was fresh from Town, and had sat up till 3.30 that morning listening to a debate in the House of Lords on the University Reform Bill. It did not seem to be progressing well, and the lukewarmness of one or two, in whose championship Mr. Keble put faith, was a chilling disappointment to him.

" We walked to the College Chapel, and in the porch Mr. Keble was beckoned away, the grand old Warden having expressed a desire that he should officiate at the christening, in his room. " It will make the event historical," he said afterwards. After a little friendly contest Mr. Keble yielded and took his place before the font. It was beautifully decorated with roses in all stages, from the early bud to the expanded flower. The service was most impressive: in those parts which immediately concern the sponsors, Mr. Keble turned and addressed us so personally, with such an earnest look and distinct voice, as carried the words straight home. After signing with the sign of the Cross, he seemed loth to part with the child, and there was a pause of a minute or two before he replaced him in my arms. On our return home Mr. Keble stooped to kiss the forehead still 'glistening with baptismal dew,' and spoke simply, but earnestly, in an undertone, of the grace given in baptism, and said that to his mind the water, the outward sign of that grace, ought to be shed as freely as prudence would permit over the infant and the little head always bared to receive it.

"He took up and narrowly examined an 'Apostle's spoon' of which the handle was a robed figure holding an anchor. This led his thoughts by a natural transition to the Church's work in New Zealand, respecting which he had gleaned many particulars from the Bishop and Mrs. Selwyn in their recent visit to Hursley. An allusion to a private letter from Turkey, written on a reconnoitring expedition within hearing of the cannon of Silistria, now changed the subject, and conjectures were hazarded as to the probable scene of the struggle with Russia, then a subject of anxious surmise. A few words which dropped from Mr. Keble respecting the 'mercy' and guidance which could bring light out of this perilous and dim uncertainty were very comforting. To the parents of the newly baptised one, Mr. Keble's parting expression of feeling was, 'Thanks, thanks, for this kindness,' and to the sponsors he said, 'We belong to the same corps now, do not we?' The sayings and doings of that day seemed to furnish a practical illustration of many exquisite passages of the *Lyra Innocentium*."

CHAPTER IV

THE SCHOOLROOM

O household blithe, whose epochs all
    Are chronicles of gladness,
Few shades thy sunny dates recall
    E'en of reflected sadness.

With chastened joy and pensive fears
    Thou numberest o'er thy treasures,
Lest time should change the smile to tears,
    The reckoning for thy pleasures.

Nay thankful Love gives mirth the beams
    That can illumine sorrow,
For what are earth's best lights but gleams
    From the eternal morrow?

                    C. M. YONGE.

KITTY'S STORY

"THE elder brothers were very fond of poetry, and in their schoolboy days Scott and Southey were special favourites. We used to work ourselves up into great states of excitement over 'Marmion' and 'Thalaba.' 'Hiawatha' we knew by heart. We delighted in the Waverley novels from the time when Alice and George, as small children, rushed out into the street to greet their father, who was just alighting from the omnibus, with the excited announcement, 'Such good news, such good news : the black knight has got into the castle!' to the time when Annie entreated Emily

116

and me to say nothing against the Vehme Gericht, whilst undressing at night, lest our beds should be drawn down by pulleys into the larder below. From the time we could read we were made free of La Motte Fouqué's books, and knew 'Sintram,' 'Undine,' and 'The Magic Ring' almost by heart. Books lined every wall of every room in the house at Otterbourne, and others were perpetually pouring in, and the Yonges kept us supplied with any number, to suit all ages. Miss Yonge's own books were, of course, very familiar to us, and she helped Mary to illustrate 'The Heir of Redclyffe' and drew a picture to show us what 'Phyllis Mohun'[1] was like.

"From early days Alice had been a favourite at Otterbourne and paid long visits to the Yonges. Mrs. Yonge taught her to illuminate. Alice remembers how, of a morning, when sitting opposite to one another painting, Charlotte, who was writing, would burst out with some indignant opinion ; and how her mother would drily remark that a gentler sentiment was likely to be more appropriate. The reproof constantly made was always taken in good part. We used to recognise personal traits in Miss Yonge's books. She had a remarkable reverence for the judgment of her elders, and when 'Elizabeth Woodbourne'[2] and 'Rachel Curtis'[3] allowed their impetuosity to carry them into predicaments quite opposite to their real intentions, they were made to confess that the opinions of others had been more correct than their own. When 'Honora Charlecote'[4] walked over the fields with her silent cousin Humphrey, discoursing long and eagerly over her favourite characters in history or fiction with-

[1] In " Scenes and Characters."
[2] In " Abbey Church."
[3] In "The Clever Woman of the Family."
[4] In " Hopes and Fears."

out expecting an answer, we remembered Miss Yonge's bright talk poured out to any intimate friend who would listen, or only appear to be listening.

"As we were kept very strictly for the nine months of the year spent in Winchester under the eye of the governess, no wonder we enjoyed the summer holidays. We were entirely with our parents, and they gave us great liberty. We might get up in the mornings as early as we liked and wander freely about the woods—we could not get beyond the woods—and except for a few lessons as an excuse for keeping us indoors during the hottest hours of the day, we lived completely out of doors, drinking in an infinite love for the natural objects round us. The rambles in the woods for hours, there being no limit but hunger or our powers of walking, gave us the impression of living with the birds, butterflies, and flowers. How delicious it was to sit down in the middle of a fir wood to listen to the silence, with only the light wind *soughing* in the tops of the trees—the solemn hush and dimness of the fir woods with their grey-blue distances and the soft ground matted with fir needles and crossed by ant roads : the paths were edged with heather—long straight paths where our younger brothers loved to act trains, whistling in the distance, where they were almost invisible, then coming nearer and nearer and passing one another ! And then how delightful to change into an oak copse with its thick bright greens, the paths full of ruts with occasional bogs covered with yellow. tormentil : its birds and rustlings : the sound of the 'midsummer hum': the distant cough of a pheasant and the laugh of a woodpecker; whilst nothing was pleasanter than to skirt round a cornfield with its hedges covered with sheets of wild roses and honeysuckle. There were thirteen different kinds of ferns to be found in the neighbourhood, and we were keen to collect them all.

" Open-air singing was a very special characteristic of those days. Dr. Samuel Sebastian Wesley was the organist of the Cathedral and College, and for ten years he came regularly twice a week and taught each one of us when old enough to join the singing class. We were all musical, and had good voices, and were so many that we possessed not only a first and a second quartet, but a chorus as well, and reading music became no difficulty to any of us. Dr. Wesley could be fierce occasionally, and charming at other times, and would come of an evening to accompany our home singing. He once made us sing all through Rossini's opera of the ' Cenerentola ' at sight, and sometimes brought his own compositions to try over. Arthur was very musical, and had a soft sweet tenor voice, and could accompany himself a little on the piano, and later on Johnnie, Edward, and Walter had really beautiful choristers' voices. My father kept his high tenor voice all these years, and sang to us, and with us, a great deal. Sunday evenings at Winchester were given up to sacred music ; beginning with the evening hymn, we went on to motets and oratorios, which became perfectly familiar to us ; whilst on summer days at the farm, glees or trios would be started at a moment's notice in the garden and woods.

" In the spring of 1855, Alice and Mary were invited to stay in London with an old Leghorn friend of our mother's for music lessons. Mary had singing lessons from Signor Manuel Garcia. She had a high, flexible, soprano voice, and after these lessons her singing was really beautiful. Garcia wished her to become a public singer. Quite a new era in our knowledge of music began ; for we all reaped the benefit."

From MARY ANNE MOBERLY

" DEAREST HUSBAND,

". . . The first evening was very pleasant ; they were all so kind—such real old friends. The girls are delighted and a little fatigued with pleasure. I am not able to sleep at night from the noise and excitement. I hope to go to the Exhibition and to the Opera this evening. Mrs. Christie has got a box, I am afraid at great expense, for it is the first night of the ' Trovatore,' a new opera, and Viardot and all the best singers are to perform. Garcia's first visit was very satisfactory. He talks good Italian, and was glad to get an Italian answer from me. He took pains with Mary, and went at once to the bottom of the little defect in her way of producing her voice. He was exceedingly pleased with her voice and way of singing ' Di piacer ' ; they say he seldom praises, but he commended her voice repeatedly as he tried it in all ways ; he often said ' La voce è buona, buona,' and said that she would have more voice than we should require. . . ."

From GEORGE MOBERLY

" MY DEAREST GIRLS,

" It has been a great delight to me to find that you have been so kindly received and so well amused in Town, yet we are puzzled to know why Alice leaves out so many words in her letters, and Mary always writes *Exhition* instead of Exhibition. I told Dr. Wesley that Mary was taking lessons from Garcia ; Edith was quite frightened of his hearing it, however he bore the intelligence very amiably. Robert was here on Sunday ; he did not like going back to school, though he took a precious bat with him, which had slept for two nights in his bedroom. Maggie got several presents on her birthday, with which she was highly delighted, particularly with a little thimble : she declared that she *would* dream of it ; but, poor little soul, she could only say ' My pimble on my fum.' "

Hardly was this London visit over, when a great anxiety arose. George had been a cripple, with one arm and leg contracted, ever since 1846, but this had not prevented his going into College. At Winchester he had won a Maltby prize for Greek Iambics and the Goddard Scholarship, after being for two years *proxime accessit* ; he had also gained two silver medals for English and Latin speeches, and a Scholarship at Corpus in Oxford. He had scarcely been there a month when he became seriously ill, and our mother and Alice hurried to Oxford to nurse him through a long, tedious illness.

From MISS YONGE

"OTTERBOURNE, *June* 1855.

" MY DEAR ALICE,
        " I hope George is feeling the freshness of these nice cool days, and Mrs. Moberly is contented and happy without the babies, who by Mary and Edith's account must be very funny, especially Edward. What a pleasure it will be to see George at Winchester again, and to hear of all your doings, by which I hope ' The Daisy Chain ' will profit, as it has a Commemoration in it. ' Cleve Hall ' I like very much, I think the best of Miss Sewell's stories. . . . We had a nice visit from Dora, Kitty, Annie, and Johnnie last week, and we all joined Mr. Bigg-Wither and the Miss Yards and walked to Brambridge Gardens ; there was a very hot sun and a thunderstorm—not quite enough to satisfy

you, but enough to flatter the children with the hope of being rained up at Otterbourne, in which case I think Miss Cowing would have been in a tolerable state of alarm. I should have liked to have heard that Sea-King lecture."

ANOTHER

" It is a great relief to-day to hear of the operation being over. I am so glad Dr. Moberly was able to be there. I have been wishing to see Mr. Keble to hear how you were all looking in Oxford, but we have not been able to go to Hursley. Johnnie's wig is very shaggy, but we agree that he is growing very handsome. . . ."

From MARY ANNE MOBERLY

"FIELDHOUSE, *September* 1855.

" DEAR ALICE,
" The children went down to church this morning, and found Johnnie saying his Delectus to Mr. Keble. He and Annie were very happy, and Mrs. Keble has asked to keep them to go with them to Southampton and have a sail. The Hursley bells rang yesterday for the taking of Sevastopol, but Mr. Keble did not like it at all.[1] It was almost a relief not to have the fatal list with the *names* sent out yesterday, one feels so afraid of seeing them."

From MISS YONGE

" *October*.

" MY DEAR ALICE,
" With all our best birthday—20-year-old—wishes, we send a peculiar assortment of presents. 1. Eau de Cologne from the most genuine-looking place in Cologne. 2. 'The Lances of Lynwood,'

[1] Mr. Keble did not at all like our fighting on the side of the Turks against Christians.

hoping the Black Cats will not frighten Edward. 3. I doubt whether it is in your special line, but Mamma's heart was so grieved by hearing of the bereaved canary sitting disconsolate—and as she is sure you would desire everybody's happiness on your birthday, she begs to present him with another wife, hoping that in honour of Otterbourne you will call her 'Lady Percy' after Hotspur's wife. Last touches are being given to the Daisies,[1] and the Spider has devoured Sir Thomas." [2]

ANOTHER

" December 1855.

" Here are the last three chapters ; I think the others had better come by post. When it comes back, it is to be added that Margaret gave her pearl ring to be worked into the chalice. I have gone into correspondence with College Street about Miss Bracy. I realised that it was necessary to be careful what was said, but did not suspect danger in that quarter. I know two good women together can argue each other nearly to death if they will not stop themselves, and I wanted to give a hint. Tom Thumb's last proof goes by to-day's post, and in the 'Landmarks' I killed Louis XIV. this morning. A great weight off my mind the old gentleman seems."

From MARY ANNE MOBERLY TO ALICE.

"WINCHESTER, 1856.

" . . . I went to Otterbourne and met Miss Keble, getting back in time to hear Robert read before dressing to dine at the Warden's to meet the Merrimans. Mary and Edith went too, and as no one else was there we dined in the study, quite a cosy party, and sat round the fire in the evening

[1] " The Daisy Chain."
[2] " History of Sir Thomas Thumb."

without candles. I have been reading Italian with Edith ; we do several pages of Tasso every day. Papa had a party of schoolmasters yesterday, and did not appear until bedtime. To-night he is deep in Helps' ' Mexico ' and can hardly look up, but he cannot resist baby's sweetness when he comes and asks his father to play ' Dum, dum, Funeral.' Mary very much dislikes walking out with the children, but she is learning to give up her own way. On the whole our schoolroom matters prosper, but sometimes I feel as if I could not possibly do both upstairs and downstairs satisfactorily. Edward has begun Latin, and does the exercises very steadily, and enjoys them. Arthur received his first Communion to-day in Chapel, and seemed very much impressed ; he has been reading to me ' The Christian Year ' for the day and for ' Holy Communion.' We all went to the Confirmation, down to Katie ; the Chapel looked beautiful by candle-light, and the boys' white surplices so suitable to the service."

George H. Moberly's Story

" 'That my father's convictions upon the subject of Confirmation remained the same all through his Winchester career, is plain from the similarity of the language he uses in the Preface to the First Series of ' School Sermons ' which he published in 1844, to that used in Letter IV of the ' Five Short Letters to Sir W. Heathcote,' published in 1861. In both places he pleads for the recognition of Confirmation as the *Strength of Boyhood*, and for the administration of it, as a general rule, between fourteen and fifteen. Confirmation, he urges, administered at this age becomes the hinge upon which the whole life of a boy, from the beginning to the end of his schooldays, turns.

" Before Confirmation, he used to assemble all

WINCHESTER COLLEGE CHAPEL
(Before the alterations).

p. 124]

the unconfirmed boys in the school into a large Catechism Class, every Monday morning for half an hour. He used by this means 'to hear the Catechism said through every week, and in the course of three half-years to go, more or less completely, over the explanation of the Creed, the Ten Commandments, and the Lord's Prayer, in the way of catechising.'

"Confirmation was administered by the Bishop of Winchester's kindness every other Advent in the College Chapel. This was settled at my father's special request, and in order that all the boys might be confirmed before they left school. At the beginning of the half-year in which a Confirmation would fall, he called all who would be fourteen before Advent into a Confirmation class. In the first years he at first simply retraced with more fullness the ground of the more general Catechism lessons by the aid of the Manuals of others on the Catechism. But about 1848 he tried a new plan, and one that (he thought) succeeded better. He went with these boys 'most carefully and minutely through the three services of Baptism, Confirmation, and Holy Communion, with the Rubrics as contained in the Prayer Book, examining and interpreting' (he says), 'as far as we can, every word in them. . . . The total number of this Confirmation class has of late years been from sixty to eighty before weeding'; and of course it did not follow from his beginning in this class that a boy would be confirmed at the end of the half-year.

"'The next step has been to call them one by one to a private conversation in my own study.' Here he urged them to the practice of self-examination : suggesting that they should employ a time on the three next Sundays to examine their whole life. Their home life before going to school—their life at the preparatory school, to which most boys have been before they came to Winchester—and their life since they had been public school boys. ' Let him not trouble himself to try and recollect a multitude of things which he has necessarily forgotten, but let him be sure that he *intends* to be honest, and to confess such things as he does remember. Then in the evening, when he says his prayers, let him say, not think only, " O God, I confess before Thee that I sinned against Thee by doing and saying such things and such words," definitely and in plain words saying what they were, and asking forgiveness for Christ's sake, and the strength of the Holy Ghost to refrain from all such things in the future. The only point on which I have ever allowed myself to ask any definite questions as to a boy's conduct or conscience is that of his using bad language or swearing. I have always taken care to explain that I ask this, not as thinking this sort of sin a more serious or worse one than many others : on the contrary, I am well aware that there may possibly be others much more considerable than this ; I only meant to suggest to the boys the way in which they ought to inquire of themselves on other points, and to put it to them seriously whether this one sin, to the extent to which they may be guilty of it, begun perhaps in childishness rather than in intentional evil, ought not, if Confirmation be anything real, to be absolutely relinquished and conquered in the course of this very half-year.

" ' When the whole number of my boys has been gone through in this way, it is my practice to begin the list again, and in a second interview to ask each whether he has been doing what I recommended him before. Does he know what he is going to do in being confirmed ? Is it his own serious and personal wish to be confirmed ? Has it the full approbation and consent of his parents ? Is he intending to join us at Holy Communion ? I must honestly and thankfully say that I have found, in this course of preparation for Confirmation, and Confirmation itself, by far the greatest and most powerful instrument for good that I have been able to use. I think that the boys feel that there is no kind of attempt or wish to take them one step beyond the honest teaching of the Prayer Book : that we are not setting up any personal views, or wishing to obtain any personal influence with them either for ourselves or for our own opinions, but that we are teaching what the Church bids us teach—teaching which we have inherited from those who have been before us, and which we hope to hand on to our successors.'

" There is no doubt that the boys did so feel, and that Confirmation time was generally regarded with affectionate personal remembrances towards him who had prepared them for it, as very many of them have since testified.

" As to my father's ordinary school teaching on religious subjects, I quote again from his Letters to Sir W. Heathcote, for his practice never varied. ' My own practice has been to begin every week-day, except Monday, with a school lesson of half an hour on this subject. At these times, and in our lesson of three-quarters of an hour on Sunday afternoon, we have read carefully and regularly through the four Gospels and the Acts of the Apostles in the Greek, studying them with such a degree of attention as we could ; and if the seniors of any generation have been found to have gone through all these during their stay in my classes, we have read one or two of the easier Epistles, or employed a quarter of an hour in going through part of the Prayer Book and its history.   All the boys in my own classes (amounting to about eighty) go through this course ; and I think I may venture to say this—that the effect has been very good.   Many of the boys have at various times surprised me in the fullness and carefulness with which they have drawn up volumes of notes upon the parts of Holy Scripture which they have read with me.' "

From ARTHUR

" COLLEGE, *Oct.* 1856.

" MY DEAR ALICE,

"I am sorry not to have answered your letter before, and am afraid that I have not any excuse to offer ; but I will try and make amends by giving you every scrap of news that I can put together.   The other day I found out how to construe a passage in 'Hermann und Dorothea' which had baffled Major Watson, so I wrote to tell him, and he answered by return of post in French.   I am meditating answering him in Greek.

"The night of the eclipse here, at about 7 o'clock, it clouded over, and we feared that we should see nothing ; but about 9.20 the clouds (which were of a light scud driving along at a great rate) suddenly cleared away, and we saw that the eclipse had just begun.   We watched the moon growing less and less until half of it was gone.   The clouds then drove over it again, and we were lamenting that we should have had such good hopes and then be disappointed of seeing the best part.   However, just at the right time the clouds cleared away again, and we saw it once more.   The eclipse was nearly total.   Mamma and Mr. Keble both say that it was the most beautiful eclipse they ever saw.   I have drawn the moon with about the right proportion of light and darkness.   That little rim of deep black represents the bright bit of the moon; all the rest was an 'awful' lurid red colour. This was about 10.58. All prefects turned out into court to look at it. From that time it began decreasing (by 'it' I mean the earth's shadow) till about a quarter to 12, when the dark and light parts of the moon were exactly equal. The increase and decrease were much alike, but they had this peculiar difference—that whereas in the increase of the shadow the moon looked just like a half, or crescent, or gibbous moon (I mean that you could not see the dark part of it), during the decrease of the shadow you could always see the whole of the moon.

" We are beginning to sing glees in College again. While I was looking at the moon a shooting star shot across just above the moon like a fiery spark. It must have been very bright to have been visible so near the moon. Also on Mamma's birthday, about 10 o'clock, as I was talking to a boy out of my chamber window my attention was attracted, and looking up I saw a star fall over the Chapel tower, seemingly quite in front of the other stars, about twice the size of Jupiter, and looking just like a Roman candle, its light was so white. Also the other evening, as I was standing at the school door, a splendid meteor shot across from the east to the west, scattering sparks of fire in its trail.

" I am going to learn about shells and minerals with Emsie, which makes her very happy. My Goddard work gets on; I am now reading up Hume. I am learning to play ' As Pants the Hart.' Give my love to Aunt Tina; I hope she is better. . . ."

ANNIE'S STORY

" It is time to describe the annual festival of ' Domum,' the celebration of the last day of the summer half. For some time before there was apt to be an influx of old Wykehamists towards Winchester, and to those of us who were old enough to be in Winchester then, it was the crowning day of a very gay time. To us younger ones, who were already established at the farm, it came by itself as a treat of treats. We were up at any time in the morning to see if the scarlet pimpernels were out in the ditch of the gully—a sure sign of a fine day. What excitement we had in putting on our very best muslin frocks; and how we enjoyed the six-mile drive to Winchester in stuffy flys! In College Street we found every one gaily dressed, and determined to enjoy themselves. The lime-tree walk in the Close was in its full glory of scent, and resounding with bees; and the festoons of jessamine growing on the old Close wall opposite our windows were in perfection of bloom and sweetness.

" After luncheon came Medal Speaking in school, when, even if a brother was not going to distinguish himself, one of our many schoolboy friends was bound to make himself a hero that day in our eyes. Medal Speaking was not then at all like what it is now. We remember the time when no outsiders were present; and when the Headmaster took with him one of the younger children (Robert), it was considered an extraordinary innovation. Then gradually we were all allowed to go, and for years and years my mother, we sisters, and Mrs. Frederick Wickham (the wife of the Second master) were the only ladies present. As the fashion grew for crowds of ladies to attend, the boys went less and less, and instead of the whole school being there to clap the successful speakers, now, I believe, it is the exception for any schoolboy besides the medallists to be in the building.

" In older days, as soon as the College boys left

Hall after the great dinner, the rest of the guests
repaired to the Warden's gallery for dessert ; and
we, in order to hear the speeches, sat on the
steps outside the gallery—a far pleasanter place
than it was later, when the gentlemen remained in
Hall, and we could only stand on the top of the
flight of stone steps amongst the choristers hurrying backwards and forwards with plates and dishes.
By the time this was over distant strains of the
band in Meads were heard, and every one went to
Domum proper.   In the days now described the
system of tickets for Meads was strictly maintained, so that the company was select and all of
one mind.   It consisted of old Wykehamists ; the
whole school staff ; the friends and families of boys
who had been, or were, at the school ; the College
tradespeople ; the servants ; and a certain proportion of the recognised society of the town, who
obtained tickets either by courtesy (such as the
Mayor and magistrates and the Commandant at
the Barracks), or from a private friend in the
school.   These made up the by no means overwhelming number of guests.

" It would sound like a very uninteresting ceremony to say that every one promenaded about
Meads till it was dark and the grass was wet with
dew, singing ' Domum ' at intervals ; and in truth
Domum cannot well be described, for the charm
lay in the enthusiasm evoked and passed from one
to another.   No stranger could ever thoroughly
enter into the proper feeling at all.   To a real
Wykehamist the mere sound of that particular tune
made him realise afresh his deep love and loyalty
to his school ; and this could only be demonstrated
at the moment by shouting the beloved song at
the top of his voice, in company with those of the
same mind.   It was often the occasion of delightful
meetings of Wykehamists who had not seen one

another for years. We heard of others far away who kept the day by singing 'Domum' as a solo; there was one who sang it at intervals all day in the Australian bush. All this joyous, wholesome enthusiasm was worked up to fever-pitch on this one day of the year, and became identified in our minds with the loveliness of a summer evening: the sunset lights over the meadows; St. Catherine's Hill fading in the twilight; until the deepening darkness compelled the company to adjourn into Chamber Court for another and last singing of 'Domum,' followed by the always-touching strains of 'Auld Lang Syne.' Gravely the outlines of the Chapel and tower and old buildings stood out against the evening sky with its twinkling stars, and no one with the least poetry about them could fail to be touched by the depth of feeling shown for the historic school. Another side of Domum was the inevitable fun, which could not be absent where the company was largely composed of boys of all ages just going home for the holidays. Probably we felt more enthusiasm than even the ordinary Wykehamist; for whereas it was only connected with one phase of his existence, it was to us a great family festival as well, from which no one of us was willingly absent until necessity compelled. Nothing puzzled us more than to be asked by a visitor beforehand what happened at Domum; there was but little *event* in it, but the genuine enthusiasm of the older Wykehamists awoke the same in the younger ones, and made the gatherings notable occasions of a unity of feeling, happy at the time and valuable in memory.[1] Of

[1] There is no forgetting the wandering in the twilight or moonlight; the meeting old friends; the keeping with some seldom-seen friend as it grew darker and darker; the enthusiastic cheers in Chamber Court; the singing louder and hoarser each time; the hats waved; the losing all one's companions, and their all turning up again in the drawing-room, full of fun and anecdote.—C. M. YONGE.

course there were occasional wet Domums—complete failures—but on looking back, the chief impression is of the many successful ones.

"Tired, excited, and happy, the party from the country was dismissed about 10.30 for the drive to the farm. However tired and sleepy we might be, there was one more pleasure in prospect, and that was the chance of seeing to perfection the soft green light of innumerable glow-worms in the banks on either side of the dark wooded lane which led down the steep hill into our own fields; and very striking the sight often was.

"The Domum ball followed on the next evening, and it was in order that the house in College Street might be filled with guests for the two evenings that the schoolroom party could not stay in Winchester. Before 1858 the ball had been on Domum evening, and our elders assured us that we could not imagine the loss to the dance by moving it to the next night; but even they allowed that Domum gained by the change, and we always found the ball as charming as we could desire. It was the merriest ball ever invented : at which the prefects were the stewards, and their sisters came to enjoy it with them. As to most of the boys present it was their first public dance, the amusing unconventionalities which took place at it can be imagined: for instance, when a College prefect remarked to his partner (our pretty Edith), 'I hope you are not heavy, for I am not strong.' It was a public ball, so that the boy element was only one amongst others."

Kitty's Story

"At Christmas 1857 we came to the great event which broke up the quiet routine of our childish lives. Mary was engaged to be married. Mr.

George Ridding was a distinguished old Wykehamist and Fellow and Tutor of Exeter College ;[1]
he had often stayed with us when examining for
the Goddard Scholarship, and constantly came
for Domums. Mary had soft brown hair and
blue eyes, with a neat, pretty figure. She always
dressed herself very becomingly and well, and her
dresses and laces had a charming freshness and
crispness special to herself. She was a beautiful
needlewoman, and made her own dainty dresses.
She had a very clear head and was fond of arith-
metic, and was clever with her fingers, painting
and playing the piano ; besides singing quite deliciously. She was so keen and enthusiastic about
everything as to be quite a romance to the younger
ones ; but her especial love was for Maggie, whom
she taught entirely."

From EDITH

" DEAR ALICE,
        " We were all turned out of the drawing-
room the whole afternoon after you went, in order
that Mary and Mr. Ridding might have it to
themselves ; which was rather a long time, I really
do think. Dr. Wesley came unexpectedly this
morning, and Kitty was in a dreadful fright because she had not practised her fugues ; but Mary
sang with them, and they went on with that much
longer than usual. Arthur came up in the middle
with the news of the taking of Lucknow, upon
which Dr. Wesley remarked that he did not see
why the English should want to take Lucknow at

[1] Balliol College : Craven Scholar 1851 ; 1st Class and 2nd Math.
B.A. 1851 ; Fellow of Exeter College 1851 ; Latin Essay 1853 ; Second
Master of Winchester College 1863 ; Headmaster 1867–84 ; Bishop of
Southwell 1884 ; died 1904.

all! 'How should *we* like an enemy to come and take one of our towns in that way?'—showing that he had heard nothing at all about the circumstances! . . ."

KITTY'S STORY

"It was a fine dry spring, but with insufficient rain; and on Ascension Day I remember Arthur standing by the drawing-room window looking at the soft warm rain which was soaking the trees and making their leaves drip, and saying that they were "wagging their tails with pleasure." There was an eclipse of the sun that spring which was sufficiently total to alter the colour of everything and to silence the birds, and when the sun shone again they began to chirp and sing as though it were morning. After Bishop and Mrs. Eden's merry visit to us to bring their youngest son to school, the junior part of the family went as usual to Fieldhouse, coming in for the day when the cricket match with Eton was played for the second time at Winchester. This annual match had, for many years, been played at Lord's cricket ground, but the authorities of the two schools decreed that for the future it should be played at Eton and Winchester on alternate years. This change was greatly disliked by many old Wykehamists, and as strongly preferred by those responsible for the boys.

"During the long summer afternoons Arthur, Robert, and Johnnie managed to get an immense amount of interest out of fancy elevens, personated by themselves, which were supposed to play each other in the great meadow. The unconscious humour and jumble of the dramatis personæ of these elevens was a perpetual amusement to our elders, such as;

Agamemnon	.	b. Copleston
Ajax	. .	b. Julius Cæsar
Mozart	. .	c. Beethoven
Kwasind	. .	c. A. Moberly, b. Havelock
Handel	. .	c. Beethoven
Galileo	. .	b. Kepler
Sir Galahad	.	c. Achilles, b. Julius Cæsar
Nana Sahib	.	c. Gen. Nicholson, b. Havelock
Sir Gawayne	.	c. R. C. Moberly, b. Marsham
King Arthur	.	not out.

After early tea the whole family swept through the cornfields single file (the corn standing over the heads of the little children) to escort the parents to see the sunset from Halsted common. On returning the elder ones were expected to join in some game in the garden until the babies' bedtime. On a fine evening the signal for that event was the first faint appearance of stars. As soon as Vega, Altair, Arcturus, the Cross, and the Crown had been identified there was a move inside for the evening Waverley. The second batch of children was afterwards dismissed to bed, whilst the elder section turned out again to enjoy the sound of the purring of the nightjars in the woods and to set up Arthur's beautiful telescope on the lawn and to see, under his direction, whatever of interest we learnt from the newspapers there was to be seen. In winter this telescope could only be utilised out of Commoner gallery windows, but in summer Arthur would spend many hours of the night alone in the garden with his telescope and transit instrument, making his own observations. Good judges of astronomy told his father that Arthur's knowledge of the subject was in any case remarkable for a boy, and still more so when it was remembered that he was self-taught. His father used to ask him in the morning what he had seen, and every one took the deepest interest in what he could teach us."

From ARTHUR

" WALTON, *August* 1858.

". . . As I came from Highbridge to Glaston-
bury, the sky seemed to be clearing in a most
satisfactory manner ; but alas ! who can calculate
upon the events of futurity (as Julia Mannering
says, or something very like it). With the setting
of the sun came the rising of the clouds ; however,
Mr. Hickley says it promises well for a fine evening,
and the wind is N.E., so what more can I desire ?
Last night before going to bed we were looking at
the hopeless sky, when we were surprised by a
sudden serenade struck up in a field opposite—three
donkeys singing a canon. This morning, as I was
sitting reading, I was attracted by an odd sort of
humming. It was not like a bee, fly, or wasp. On
looking about, I saw that a humming-bird moth
had got into the room. It soon whisked out of
window. I followed it about the garden for some
time, watching how gingerly it dipped its long
trunk into each flower without resting upon it. I
have seen several about the garden to-day ; one
came in just now and sucked close under me, and
even under my shadow, so that it would have been
easy to catch it ; but even had I cared to do so, I
could not abuse such confidence. It seemed to
reject all other flowers but verbenas, phloxes, and
petunias ; I suppose because those have such con-
venient holes in them for the trunks of the insects.—
Since I wrote the last sentence I have been watching
a moth for a quarter of an hour : when it would
get tired of the verbenas I could not think ; it
seemed to take the red ones first and then the
white and purple ones. At last I got tired of
watching, and so came in to finish my letter. I
saw the sun this morning ; it had a very large spot ;
also Venus I saw. Mr. Hickley says that the sky

is in a very favourable state.   Such a fine beautiful blue."

KITTY'S STORY

" Mary's wedding took place on July 20, 1858, a brilliant summer's day.   In the morning we found that the servants had made a gorgeous wreath solid with white roses over the entrance to the front staircase.   She was married by Warden Barter (who had baptised her) in the little old church of St. Swithun, which had been placed over the King's Gate for the workmen when they were building the Cathedral.   Decorations in church were almost unknown then, but friends had decked the church as a surprise to us, and the font was filled with water-lilies and passion-flowers.   The bride was surrounded by her seven white-robed sisters wearing forget-me-nots.   After the honeymoon, spent on the Wye and in Scotland, the Riddings paid us a short visit at Winchester before settling in Oxford, in the same little house (25, New Inn Hall Street) in which our parents had spent their first year of married life before coming to Winchester.[1]   Dora and I drove with them to say good-bye to the Kebles.   It was a still grey autumn day.   We left the carriage at the lych-gate and walked up the churchyard under the limes, which were turning yellow.

" That autumn was memorable for the great comet.[2]   Every evening it appeared in the west, with its tall graceful feather of a tail, nearly upright, stretching half-way up the sky.   The moment when it looked most beautiful was when Arcturus passed through its tail, and was seen through it as a golden mist.   The autumn was

[1] Now St. Michael's Street.   No. 25 was the house next beyond the buildings of the Oxford Union Society.
[2] Donati's Comet.

singularly unhealthy, warm and damp, and on
St. Simon and St. Jude's Day, which was wet and
muggy, Edith and Arthur spent the afternoon in
the porch of the Chapel sketching the memorial
to the Wykehamist officers who fell in the Crimea.
In the central niche was a dedicatory inscription
ending with the words :

"Think upon them, thou who art passing by to-day,
　Child of the same family, bought by the same Lord.
　Keep thy foot when thou goest into this house of God,
　There watch thine armour, and make thyself ready by
　　　　prayer
　　　　　　　To fight and to die
　　　　　The faithful soldier and servant
　　　　　　　　Of Christ
　　　　　　And of thy Country.
He is not the God of the dead, but of the living, for all
　　　　live unto Him.

"Arthur, who was now eighteen and a senior
College prefect,[1] and had gained two silver medals,
was working for the Goddard Scholarship. He
caught a heavy, feverish cold, and went continent.
He did not shake it off, and came home to be
nursed. There was low fever about in the town,
but Arthur did not seem very ill, only very weak,
with a constant quick pulse and absolutely no
appetite. He used to come, slowly and languidly,
into the drawing-room, with a drooping head and
a little cough. Sometimes he pulled a chair to the
piano and played and sang 'Deh vieni,' or something of the kind. That November Emily and
I were confirmed with the boys in the College
Chapel, and on Advent Sunday Arthur was so
anxious to go to the midday Communion that
leave was given him to go in after the sermon.
His great friend (William Awdry, a College

---

[1] The senior College prefects at this time were : W. A. Fearon,
Prefect of Library ; A. Moberly, Prefect of School ; C. Martin, Prefect
of Hall ; E. H. Harrison and F. G. Eyre, Prefects of Chapel.

prefect)[1] fetched him from Seventh Chamber, where he had waited, and brought him in with his feeble step. A day or two afterwards he became much worse. It was a time of great depression. The boys both at Eton and Winchester had to be dispersed on account of illness and deaths. The Warden's butler died ; so did our butler, and one of the housemaids, and our housekeeper had an alarming illness, but recovered. The state of the atmosphere was so peculiar that on coming back from the service on the Sunday before Christmas, when it was just dark, the little midges and gnats were flying about in crowds in the warm, damp air."

From MR. KEBLE

"HURSLEY, *Dec.* 6, 1858.

" Indeed you will have the best of our prayers ; poor enough some of them are, but some, I trust, not unlikely, for His sake, to avail somewhat. I feared from J. P. Young's note that you were in much trouble, but I did not know that it was more than we had heard of in your own house. May God grant that this alarm may soon pass away, and may His heavy hand be speedily withdrawn and your fatherly heart be comforted in every way. The best of a father's comfort, dear friend, you most assuredly have (if one may say so without presumption) in abundant measure. May He increase and multiply it to you a thousandfold, and to your dear wife, who will know how much and how tenderly she is thought of by mine.".

From MRS. KEBLE

" One word I must say to tell you how thankful we are for the better account which has come to

[1] Fourteenth in the School.

us through Otterbourne.   I am sure you and yours
must have the help of many prayers from loving
hearts, who on their part have the greatest comfort
in thinking and feeling Who it is that 'tarrieth
about you.'"

From Mr. Keble

" It is a day or two since we heard of Arthur.
I trust the relief continues.   It was *such* a comfort
to us : what must it have been to you !   With
Christmas love (more and more of it every year),
                     " Ever yours,
                          " John Keble."

From Mary Anne Moberly

" My dear Brother,
          " Your letter was the first that came to me
in my deep sorrow, and very precious and comforting it was to me.   Yes, at first grief will have its
way, and the parting with a darling child, never to
see his face again on earth, makes one's flesh quail
and quiver with anguish ; and in this case the loss
to me is peculiarly severe, for Arthur was *my* boy,
my companion.   His gentle, earnest love for his
parents was most touching, and came out strongly
at the very last, and his gentle, refined tastes were
the brightness of my life during the last years.
I always looked forward to the summer holidays
for the pleasure of being in the country with
Arthur ; there he took a keen interest in everything around us, from the glorious stars to the
wild flowers and insects, and the poetical turn of
his mind made the information which he could
always give upon these subjects very pleasant to
us.   Yes, it has all been very merciful, and *he* was
the right one to go.   Unfitted for the roughnesses

of the world by his clinging to home and gentle quietness, we bless God that we have been allowed to lay our gentle boy to sleep ourselves and to tend him lovingly to the end.

"During the many long days and nights of delirium, in which he talked incessantly and his mind roamed without rudder or compass, never did a word escape him which we could have wished unsaid. ' Now let us sing the evening hymn,' he would say ; and in the midst of his wildest imaginations the voice of prayer would *instantly* stop him. While the Commendatory Prayer was being read, he even tried to still the heavy laboured breathing which told too surely of approaching death ; and never shall I forget the earnest deep gaze of love at his father and me after it, a loving farewell of intense affection ; or his solemn voice as he repeated the end of the Blessing—' now and for ever, now and for ever, now and for ever.' While I live, that 'now and for ever' will ring in my heart. And oh ! the expression of heavenly joy upon the pale face, so as to make it like that of an angel. It was a great trial to part with that pale dear form, but the trial was lessened by having him laid in the solemn, beautiful Cloister.

"The last leave out day he walked with Edith in the Cloisters, admiring their quiet beauty and telling her how lovely they are by moonlight. And there his body rests to wait the coming of his Lord ! He is our firstfruits in Paradise. It seems already to hallow and sanctify everything, so that we cannot be careless or neglectful ; and our Christmas has been such a happy and holy one ! I made a holly cross to lay on his dear breast, and the children put up a holly text in my room, full of hidden meaning to us, ' Unto us a Child is born.' We had the great comfort of the Holy Communion in Chapel quietly on Christmas Day."

From MR. KEBLE

" What can I say to you, dear friend, to thank you as I ought for your most comfortable letter? I knew it would be full of comfort, but this is somehow beyond my expectation. It looks to me like a fresh world opened for you, both of Sorrow and of Consolation. Well do I know what thoughts I ought to have of it, so far as I am myself concerned ; but for you all one's heart can rest on nothing but leaving you, as it were, to Him Whom you can all but see taking your child up in His arms and giving him His final blessing. I hope not to forget what you speak of in my prayers, such as they are. I shall ask for that for which I hope as confidently as I well can for any special mercy—that this merciful trial may be fully blessed to all the purposes for which it is sent ; for correction, where need may be ; for high and heavenly improvement to you all. May you have many a more joyful Christmas. I do not think you will ever have a much *happier* one in this world. Forgive me if I say what I ought not. . . . This evening brings a much worse account than before of Keenie.[1] So His people seem to be fast entering into their rest, or rather, His rest."

From MARY RIDDING

"25, NEW INN HALL ST., *March* 1859.

" MY DEAREST MAMMA,

" George has been obliged to go to College, and has commissioned me to write and thank you for your birthday letter to him. I begin to find that I was rash in allowing him to go out every evening for *only* an hour, for I might have known that it would be *always* an hour and a half, and

---

[1] Mrs. Thomas Keble, junior.

sometimes more. However, it is a good lesson for having grumbled so much ; and now that I leave my music to be practised then, I can amuse myself very well. I sometimes try having the cat for a companion, but if she can't sit in my lap all the time, she grows restless and won't stay upstairs like a reasonable cat. We have breakfast punctually at 8.30, and stay downstairs working till 10, when George goes to College. Then I order dinner, and water my flowers, and read Pascal till 11. I am reading ' Un Discours sur l'Amour,' which is very funny in some parts. Then I paint and work and amuse myself with home letters till luncheon. I read Prescott at odd times, and have almost finished ' Quentin Durward.' On Wednesdays and Fridays at 4.30 I go to St. Peter's-in-the-East. Last night we went to hear the Dean of Westminster preach in St. Mary's. I was very anxious to see him, and was not disappointed in his appearance at all, though I was in his sermon. But then, I am sorry to say, I went into a most comfortable doze during the first of his three practical observations at the end. George has given me a most beautiful stand of flowers, with two beautiful geraniums, a heliotrope (so very sweet), and a deep purple cineraria. There is just room for my rose too, and I like keeping the window open to see them enjoying the fresh air. My azalea is in full beauty, and I have also got some bunches of violets which smell so very sweet. I am looking forward to the Vacation very soon now. This Term has flown away so very quickly that I can hardly believe it."

ANOTHER

" I have been so happy with all my letters and parcels this morning. I don't think I have ever really had such a happy birthday, and being twenty-one is much better than I ever expected. There is such a difference between this and my last birthday, when I was *beginning* to grow a little older, but when everything was new and I was only feeling my way, as it were ; and when (I may say it to you) now I look back, I really did not know what loving was. Every month that we have been married, I have been growing happier and happier, knowing my dear husband better, and therefore loving him and reverencing him more and more. And he teaches me and helps me to be good in such a kind, gentle way ; and you, who knew me so well before, must be able to think how I must have tried him sometimes. . . . Your dear letter of this morning was almost too much for me, it was so very nice ; and though I have read it twice, I have not half learnt it yet. Your workbag is the prettiest thing I ever saw ; I shall always keep my dear little works in it."

From MARY ANNE MOBERLY

" FIELDHOUSE.

" DEAREST HUSBAND,

" It has been a most delicious evening, and we have had a charming walk all together, even Selwyn, though he has been on his feet nearly all day. We went through the Grotto wood and as far as the turning to Halsted, and the sunset light was beautiful ; but my heart is so very full constantly that I hardly know how to bear it, and everything makes it yearn so for the *one* who is so mixed up with it all and is gone from us. Every dear beautiful thing is full of aching pain, though there is real peace and thankfulness at the bottom of my heart for *him*. I hope it will be better by and by, for it is very hard to be cheerful. I do so long for you. If you were here, I know I

10

should not venture to speak about it, but I could take your arm and that would do me good. This is the first day I have been in Hursley church.

" Selwyn is as happy as a prince ; he has been to all his favourite walks to-day, and driven the cows down to Potkiln this evening. He says, ' Oh, what a *jolly* place the farm is ! ' "

GEORGE MOBERLY'S JOURNAL

" *Domi, June* 24 (1859).—Hoc ipso die, anno proximo, cum Arturo carissimo rus ibamus. Inter redeundum uxor mea sæpius dixit se vidisse duos homines duas sandapilas ferentes ex casâ Potkiln exire—quod mirum in modum cum doloribus postea evenientibus consentire putavimus. Redit idem dies, eodem modo festus. Redeunt signa doloris et metûs. O Deus Optime, Maxime ; nè graviorem in nostram domum immittas manum ! aut saltem nos, quodcunque venturum sit, sanctos, submissos, gratos, acceptos in Christo facias ! " [1]

Alice, Edith, and Dora stayed in Oxford for a

[1] Potkiln Green stretched from the farm to the wooded lane by which we reached the high road from Southampton to Winchester. Potkiln house stood alone on the green, and was divided into several tenements where our farm servants lived with their families. Every one within it was well known to my mother, who knew that no illness or death had taken place there. My mother, who, after the first shock, accepted the appearance as kindly preparation for all that followed, was driving back alone to Winchester on St. John Baptist Day, after a merry hay-making party in which many boys in the School had taken part.

" I believe that my father told me after Arthur's death of my mother's. first vision, for I certainly heard of it as being connected with him and Dacre, our butler, who, it was hoped, was the second indicated ; but the second vision was never told to any of us, and it was a great shock to know of it after my father's death from the entry in his diary. During the eight following summers spent at the farm the visions never returned, and my mother never had a like experience before or after those two years."—ALICE ARBUTHNOT MOBERLY.

bright and happy Commemoration, the special
interest of which was the engagement of Mr. James
Du Boulay to Miss Alice Cornish. Mr. Du Boulay
was an old Wykehamist, Fellow of Exeter College,
and a great friend of George Ridding's. Mrs.
George Cornish was the widow of Mr. Keble's
early friend at Corpus. She was present at Oxford
with her daughters, the youngest of whom was the
beautiful Alice Cornish. This was the beginning
of another set of friendships for us. After Commemoration the sisters returned to the farm and
the Riddings took up their abode in College Street,
intending to remain there till August, when Mary's
confinement was expected.

July 18 was a delicious summer's day, and the
Riddings drove out to the farm and had tea with
us on the lawn. Mary enjoyed it so much, that
she promised to come and spend the anniversary of
her wedding day in the same manner. Hearing
the next day that Mary was tired and unwell, my
mother went instantly to College Street without a
moment's delay. The first we knew of that terrible
evening and night was from a letter which reached
us early on the 20th, to say that Mary had died that
morning. In the afternoon my father and George
Ridding came out to the farm and took Edith and
Dora back with them. Each day, until we all
went into Winchester to lay Mary in the College
Cloisters beside Arthur, George Ridding and Edith
drove out to us, in order that he might have the
relief of wandering alone in the woods.

From MARY ANNE MOBERLY

" MY DEAR BROTHER,

" I thought that no word of comfort could be of any avail from any earthly friend in such crushing sorrow. But you wrote in the words of Holy Scripture, and they seemed a cordial, coming from such a dear and loving brother; much, very much were they needed, and your prayers too, for our support. For in the first days the anguish was overpowering—we seemed bowed to the earth, and as if no relief could lift us up; but it *has* come. We have had the strength and comfort which so many kind friends have asked for us, and we can now say from our hearts, ' It is well,' ' the Lord hath given and the Lord hath taken away; blessed be the name of the Lord.' It seemed such a mysterious dispensation, and often during that terrible night I asked that it might be *my* life for the *young life* ; but He Who is all wisdom, as well as all mercy, judged it right to be otherwise ; we must surely have needed the chastisement to turn us more entirely to God and to heavenly things. For *her* indeed we ought to rejoice, even though she was taken in the midst of such great earthly happiness and with the brightest hopes of new joys soon. We know that these could be but disappointing and unsatisfying compared with her present joy and peace in the presence of her Lord. Yes, she is at rest. She and dear Arthur *together*, we trust, and now we feel as if this life had altogether changed its aspect for us, as if we were but waiting God's pleasure to lay others to rest in. His own good time.

" We had been in some degree weaned from dearest Mary's constant companionship during the last year, but still we met often, and when we did so, we were more and more struck with the wonderful growth and *blossoming* of her love for us, which seemed overflowing with the most tender filial duty and affection, and now the memory of it is very precious.   She seemed to feel that it would not be for long, and indeed we find that ever since Christmas she has said that she should never recover, and told her husband on leaving Oxford, that she should never be there again.   So her religious feelings ripened and deepened, and she was preparing for her great change, while we were only pleased to see how her character had opened out and strengthened in her married life.   Poor little dear!   This baby was much desired and so lovingly worked for, and we thankfully trust that her unconsciousness lasted all that time, and so spared her the disappointment of its loss.   My dear Charles, what a night was that after it!   There was a slight thunderstorm at 7 o'clock a.m., and then her strength began to sink and her consciousness to return.   Her father said prayers for her aloud.   It was almost a comfort to hear the terrible breathing relax, and after a few quivering sighs to know that her poor body was at rest and her spirit with her Saviour. . . . George thinks for every one, and is so tender to the children, especially Maggie.   I sometimes feel as if it were all a dream.   Everything is so much as usual, and then some trifle wakes one up to all the reality of grief—her songs, her drawings, her handiwork everywhere. . . ."

An epidemic of sore throats among us that summer caused us all to be taken to Weymouth for a month of general refreshing.   George Ridding went with us.   Here, with the help of sea bathing, the ships in the harbour, the long walks to the Chesil Beach for moss agates and to see the big waves, and the expeditions to Portland, cheerfulness was resumed and a fresh turn given to our thoughts.

The Farm

It used to be a place of mere delight,
For there our children gambolled in our sight
    From morn till night,
    From morn till dewy night.

Whether in April's early budding bowers,
Laden with baskets full of primrose flowers,
    A few stol'n hours
    From work—a few stol'n hours.

Or in the brightness of a summer day
A troop of girls and boys in untired play,
    Scattering the hay,
    Scattering the cocks of hay.

Or housed awhile in our dear verdant nest
The little party that we loved the best,
    Taking our rest,
    Taking our six weeks' rest.

Our eldest boy, of grave and serious look,
Girt round with girls, deep buried in a book,
    In the dear Nook,
    In the dear shady Nook.

Or when the sundown fired the western sky,
We led our merry populous company,
    Mamma and I,
    Gentle Mamma and I.

So year by year our happy children grew
Amid our simple pleasures, sweet though few,
    Loving and true,
    Most loving and most true.

It used to be a place of mere delight;
But holier memories haunt the green to-night,
    Sweet, calm and bright,
    Sweet, calm and very bright.

One earnest boy of gentle words and ways,
Who taught our eyes to thread the starry maze,
  Who loved to gaze,
  Upward on heaven to gaze.

One loving girl, fresh from her Parents' side,
A husband's tenderest love too shortly tried,
  A twelvemonth's Bride,
  A twelvemonth's happy Bride.

Do they not haunt with us this well-loved scene?
Do they not walk with us the accustomed green?
  Near, tho' unseen—
  Near always, tho' unseen?

Yes! trackless as those wandering airs of even,
To come and go, those souls to whom is given
  The Birth of Heaven,
  The Spirit-Birth of Heaven!

Now every sound that floats upon the breeze,
The sunshine and the gloom, the birds, the bees,
  All speak of Peace,
  All speak of Heavenly Peace.

Peace! not the mirthful wildness of unrest,
Peace! in the silence of the faithful breast:
  God's last and best,
  God's latest gift and best.

G. M., 1859.

CHAPTER V

" The Child's heart was full of joy even to the brim.   He sat himself down and almost thought he should like to take root there . . . for he felt a deep delight in the still, secluded, twilight existence of the mosses and small herbs, which felt not the storm, nor the frost, nor the scorching sunbeam ; but dwelt quietly among their many friends and neighbours, feasting in peace and good fellowship on the dew and the cool shadows which the mighty trees shed upon them.

" To them it was a high festival when a sunbeam chanced to visit their lowly home ; whilst the tops of the lofty trees could find joy and beauty only in the purple rays of morning and evening."

The Story without an End.

Annie's Story

" One of my father's chief characteristics was his sparkling brightness in conversation : as Dean Church said, ' alarming sometimes, even in its bright kindness, from his flashes of repartee, and the terrors of his quick and unexpected wit.' It was complete enjoyment to us to hear his keen argumentative talk when he was addressing his friends and equals ; but some of us younger ones were shy when he spoke to us, knowing how quickly he saw anything humorous in what we might have said, and slightly dreading his incisive speech. From boyhood he had had the clearest and most delicate articulation, whilst his love and knowledge of music enabled him to modulate his voice with ease. His singing of Italian songs was

unique; no one could sing the high running
passages so exquisitely as he, and nothing was more
charming to us than either his spirited singing of
Jacobite songs to his own accompaniment, or his
dreamy extemporising on the piano, weaving in
passages of his favourites, Mozart and Handel.   He
had drawn well as a young man, and encouraged us
all to sketch.   Of ancient and modern poets Pindar
and Coleridge were oftenest on his lips ; and nothing
pleased him more than to give one of his animated
accounts of Napoleon's wars, or of more ancient
battlefields, describing in detail the positions and
strategies of the armies.   When Uncle Richard
Church stayed with us, we used to observe laughingly
that the first half-hour was generally spent in a
discussion between him and my father as to the
relative greatness of Napoleon's generals, and in
going over some details of the Peninsular war, in
which they both took the greatest interest.

   " In tone of mind and in general politics my
father was a Liberal ; but he generally voted with
the Conservatives at elections on account of the
Church questions involved.   He used to call himself
'an inconsistent Liberal,' his immediate friends being
all strong Conservatives.   He wanted reforms too
at Winchester, which it was not in his power to
carry out fully.   Dear personal friend as Warden
Barter was, on some subjects there was a reserve
between them.   The Headmaster often felt himself
thwarted by the Warden and Fellows, as an official
body, especially in the matter of the appointments
of under masters ; sometimes he said that he thought
they resented his Balliol origin, his Liberal views,
and his friendship with Mr. Keble.   In that direction
also, he was not completely at ease, and often
realised that he was disappointing his Hursley
friends, and those at Otterbourne as well, by his
inability to agree with them on all points.   Perhaps

all these difficulties helped to give him occasionally a stiffness of address which looked like coldness, whereas he greatly desired sympathy and was easily wounded.   When this slight reserve was overcome by affection and intimacy, nothing could exceed his warmth and fullness of love.   One of his soldier friends having found this out, said to us, ' He has such a rich heart.'   Edith writes, ' He was always *the* loving, caressing father, almost playfellow ; his fun was so satisfying, so entirely amusing and amused, and the repartees between him and us were unfailing.'

" We received most of our religious teaching from the tone of our elders.   In those days we were almost the only women to go to the College Chapel services, where we constantly heard the deep-hearted words spoken by Warden Barter and the Headmaster, who shared all the sermons between them.   During the Indian Mutiny one of them in a sermon told the story of a young soldier taken prisoner by the Sepoys, who, when his fellow prisoner was offered life on the condition of renouncing the Faith, said, ' We must not deny the Lord Jesus,' and was instantly shot dead.   My father added, in a deeply thrilled voice, ' I cannot desire a nobler lot for one of my own sons.'   It was the enthusiasm of these men for all that was Christian and lofty which taught us so much.

" How we loved those bright saints' days when, with a crowd of boys, he walked with us over the downs !   I remember one walk shortly after the Crimean war, when some of our military friends from the barracks had joined us, we all played at taking the Russian forts up and down the grassy ' humps,' the boys fighting with sticks and umbrellas, and every one taking part on one side or the other, and all getting very hot and excited.   Fun of all sorts my father delighted in, and he was the life and centre of all paper games when stories and verses had to be written. His own productions were always the best and the merriest, and how he would laugh over the attempts of the children and the jokes of the schoolboys! In the holidays, Walter, as a small schoolboy, always sat, if possible, next to him at meals, when (in spite of all our usual rules of decorum) they chaffed one another until it generally ended in a hand-to-hand fight, and Walter was deposited under the table.

" My mother's face was finely formed, with straight brows and dark hair and eyelashes over blue-grey eyes; these, with the long, delicately shaped aquiline nose, were lovely. Her long white throat and graceful bearing made her look taller than she really was. She possessed a most characteristic love of beautiful things. She looked upon it as a duty to make herself and everything round her as perfect as possible. Her dress, for instance, was always of the best materials, and she insisted on having it sewn with silk on both sides; when we asked her, irreverently, what difference it could make whether they were sewn with silk or cotton, she would reply, ' I should know that it was cotton, and I should not like that.' She made all her own close caps of Honiton lace, with lappets to her shoulders, because the fashionable shapes were neither tasteful nor simple enough. She loved to be surrounded with flowers, but they were all carefully chosen for their sweetness and colouring (she disliked yellow flowers); ordinary garden flowers gave her no especial pleasure, and even as little children we only offered her roses out of our gardens, or bunches of scented geranium leaves, lemon verbena, or mignonette. She kept a little bottle of attar of roses in her workbox, and her rooms had an indefinable fragrance of lavender and violets about them, for which she carefully cut the

lavender every summer, and collected rose leaves
for potpourri. Bottled scents were far too coarse
for her, and if she suspected musk to be in them
they were sent away at once. Her wrath at being
subjected to such smells as gas, coal-smoke, or
lamp-oil, etc., was strong and despairing ; and no
member of her large household ventured to strike
a match, or blow out a candle, in any room into
which she was likely to come within half an hour
after the rash act. If possible, she would never
touch a penny, and if it could not be avoided,
hurried to wash her hands ; she always washed the
silver or gold coins with soap and water before
giving them in the offertory. Amused as we
often were at these and other dainty fancies, yet
we recognised that they imparted an air of exceed-
ing refinement, such as we never perceived in the
same degree elsewhere.

"My mother's knowledge of the best Italian
society showed itself in her parties and large
assemblies ; so much trouble was taken that they
were generally well done ; but entertainments were
an effort, and fatigued her. As children we were
rather puzzled by her pretty manners, for we
sometimes knew that she was bored and teased
by guests, and then straightway we observed her
hearty greeting, half curtsying, and heard her
gracious words. But we gradually perceived that
the unwillingness was chiefly shyness, and that the
feeling of annoyance had hidden for the moment
her truer self, which long training in good manners
enabled her to recover without effort. No change
of sky was lost upon her, and it was always at
her instance that the whole family turned out on
summer evenings to Halsted common to see the
gorgeous sunsets. She always knew which planet
was due, and in what stage the moon was ; and
how she enjoyed a thunderstorm ! My father used

to call her ' a connoisseur in thunderstorms.'   Her
enthusiasm for these things infected all the household ; we considered it necessary to know the
history of the past storms, and to tell the story for
years after.

"But along with all this great joy in outward
beauty was another characteristic as deep and
strong—a strain of austerity towards herself—and
in the combination of the two lay the uniqueness
of her character.   Nothing that she called self-
indulgence did she allow herself, and even when
quite old she would allow neither daughter nor
maid to save her trouble, lest she should get into
bad habits.   My father used to tell us that within
a year of their marriage he was much shocked by
my mother appearing in a close cap tied under her
chin ; all her pretty hair, which had been done up
in horns at the top of her shapely head, was laid
flat.   This was done from the idea that it was
proper for married women to wear caps.   No
expostulations had any effect, and though she was
only just twenty-three years old, from that time
caps were the rule during the day ; she still dressed
her hair elaborately for the evenings.

"My mother was extremely shy and reserved.
During the first year of her married life she
managed not to call her husband anything, and as
soon as Alice could speak adopted the child's name
for him, addressing him as 'Papa' from that time
forward.   I remember perfectly, when they had
been married more than twenty years, hearing him
coax her to call him by his name ; he refused to
give up a charming cloak he had bought for her
until it was said.   After a long time, and with
the greatest difficulty, she whispered, 'Thank you,
George'; but it was never said again.

"She was not naturally sociable ; her stately
grace had something too grave and awe-inspiring

in it for her to be well known by a great variety
of people; yet even the Winchester schoolboys,
with whom she had but little in common, felt the
influence of her character. A Wykehamist wrote
thirty years later: 'I have been looking back to
my boyhood and young manhood, as she came
across it, and all along I see how elevating she
was, and I know now how her mind, combined
with her high ideal and personal beauty, has impressed me; yet with a certain awe, which also
in its way had a charm.' Anything in religious
people which bordered on mere enthusiasm, without corresponding effort and deepening reverence,
was distrusted and discouraged by her; but the
high spirituality of the Kebles and Yonges, which
allowed of no self-indulgence or sentimentality, but
called upon all their powers of culture, spiritual
insight, and balanced common sense, suited her
entirely.

" Her rule over her many sons and daughters
was quiet, equal, and very firm, but she was not
demonstrative. She loved to be alone, and spent
many hours reading in her room; but even then
she never lost touch with us, and we felt her all-
pervading eye. On hot summer mornings at the
farm the little children could not run across the
garden without their hats, but they heard her
warning voice from the bowery upstairs window,
' Come out of the sun, come out of the sun ' (a
reminiscence, probably, of Italian dangers). She
never minded being interrupted by us, and was
always ready to answer the many extraordinary
petitions that we brought to her door. During
the nine months of the year in Winchester the
family reading of Psalms and Lessons took place
in her sitting-room immediately after breakfast,
followed by recitations of verse and spelling by the
little children, who had often tried the gravity of

MARY ANNE MOBERLY.
By George Richmond.

p. 158]

the elders by reading 'statutes' as 'statues' and 'idols' as 'dolls,' and by taking still wilder shots at difficult verses of the Psalms. Then my mother retired for an hour's quiet reading, coming back to the older children for two hours of regular lessons. From 4 p.m. until 6 she superintended the reading aloud of all stages of history and the learning by heart for the next day. This went on for years and years without any irregularity, in spite of social duties and bad headaches. In the evenings she and my father gave themselves up to the family for at least an hour, and though she might be writing letters, my mother would become enthusiastic with us over the play of Shakespeare or Waverley novel which was being read aloud.

" Those who were admitted to her friendship delighted in her quiet spiritual strength. Her sons were greatly influenced by her unquestioning faith, and when George Ridding, from the time of his great sorrow, took an intimate place in the family, it was clearly a pleasure to him to sit by her and feel her restfulness in spiritual matters. She made him completely at home amongst us, and in all plans for the holidays calculated on his being with us as much as her own sons. Wherever we might be, he called our house 'home,' and treated it as home ; and a great acquisition he was to our party. Coming as a second 'George,' he had to submit to being called by his full name or having it shortened into ' G. R.,' which soon became ' Jara.'

" Our own George was still at Oxford. He had gained a First Class in Moderations when he was barely nineteen and a half years old, and three University prizes, viz., the Stanhope, the Ellerton, and the Arnold, and was now Fellow of Corpus Christi College. In 1860 he was ordained by Bishop S. Wilberforce, and became curate to Mr. Capel Cure at St. Peter's-in-the-East in Oxford.

A permanent cripple and very delicate, he was a constant source of anxiety to our parents on account of his many illnesses; yet he had passed through his school and college careers with credit, and was now fairly launched on his clerical course.

" The society at Winchester at that time was very delightful and well centralised. Dean Garnier entertained largely, and Warden Barter had kept open house, especially to Wykehamists. The Headmaster also gave large dinner-parties during the half-year, so that the various circles of the Cathedral, the College, the Barracks, and the Town met often and most pleasantly. It became a grief to the Headmaster to find that, as expenses grew, he could ask Wykehamists less and less to his house, and that family necessities required the early meal unsuitable to chance guests. My mother had, gradually, to give up going out in the evenings; so to evening entertainments her daughters had to go by themselves, and some other chaperon was found to conduct them to balls. She was wonderfully trustful of us all, but we missed the training that otherwise we might have had. Of course some members of the large party of girls had their occasional difficulties and excitements, and her perfect confidence was a great help to us.

" Edith was the heroine and centre of the house. She was the lively sister who caused things to happen, and suggested all sorts of comings and goings, and had the spirit to carry them through. A great favourite with the outside world, she went away more often than any of us, and it was chiefly through her that the younger ones gained some notion of the gay world that lay beyond us. She was so sparkling and brilliantly merry that her sayings and doings formed the staple of the family jokes. In spite of great fits of wrath, considered by herself to be merely 'righteous indignation,' which

upset the house from time to time, Edith had the
rare gift of a charm which was undefinable.   From
the old, old days when, as children, she and George
found a mysterious dragon-fly pond in the farm
woods, which could never be found again, a halo
of romance hung round her in our eyes.   Her
freshness and quaint speeches were the delight of
our friends.   We quite recognised that, though
there was not the smallest real likeness between
Edith and any of the characters in Miss Yonge's
books, Miss Yonge's instinct was often to make
the third sister of her many large imaginary
families the interesting and entertaining one.   The
birthdays of these phantom people, in the early
books, were apt to coincide with ours, and Edith
asked that her birthday might be given to ' Harry
May.'   It was to Edith that the first copy of ' The
Daisy Chain ' was sent.   It was Alice's vocation
to take charge of our mother and help to teach the
children, whilst Edith made the house attractive to
visitors, friends, and boys.   Every one knew Edith
and her love of all sociable ways and outdoor
amusements.   She sketched and sang well, and
she and Kitty constantly rode out to the meets
with Captain Forrest and his daughters.   It was
Edith who gardened vigorously in summer and
promoted skating parties in winter, at a time when
ladies' skating was only beginning to be possible ;
and all was done with a heartiness of enjoyment
and an ease which caused us of inferior degree to
worship her."

From Mary Anne Moberly

" Fieldhouse, 1860.

" . . . This has been the softest of S.W. days,
with delicious smells of hay and roses wafted
into the window, but raining most of the day till
the sun came out brightly before tea, and at eight

11

o'clock such a thick mist began to rise that in half
an hour it was perfectly white and we could see
nothing beyond the railings. The Yonges came
to tea ; they must have been drenched in mist
before they got home. They say that Coleridge
Patteson is to be the Bishop of Melanesia. His
father has written to tell Charlotte of it. Miss
Keble has rallied and is better. . . ."

ANOTHER

" We went to church in the morning, and in
the afternoon papa drove the little ones to church
in the pony carriage. Miss Keble is still living,
but Mrs. Keble says that it is very distressing
now—she cannot sleep, and wanders from weakness.
Mr. and Mrs. Thomas Keble are come, and that is
a great comfort to them all. . . ."

From MR. KEBLE

"HURSLEY, *Aug.* 10, 1860.

" MY DEAR MOBERLY,

" . . . If you are not engaged, or if it is
not for any reason undesirable for you, to-morrow
evening, would you take my place, as an old
friend, by assisting at the Funeral service for my
sister ? (*i.e.*, the weather not being bad). Perhaps
we ought not to ask it, but it has come across
us both as a comfort at the time, and as a thing
comfortable to remember by and by ; your being
so near having put it into our heads. It is to be at
5 p.m., so we cannot have Holy Communion, as we
wished ; but seven the next morning will, we trust,
be near enough for us. *If you do not really prefer
Pitt,*[1] there are some reasons why I could wish you
to preach in this church on Sunday. I am a little

---

[1] A hamlet of Hursley.

afraid of the curates, lest in their kindness they should think it necessary to be more *express* than some of us could so well bear on what has happened. I think you will understand me ; but perhaps it is fancy. Anyhow, I must *put you on your honour* to do as is most comfortable to you. . . ."

From MR. KEBLE

"HURSLEY, *Sept.* 23, 1860.

" MY DEAR MOBERLY,
    " I am looking over Mr. Mansel's book : is it not a treasure ? Have you seen ' Essays and Reviews,' by Temple, etc. ? *Do* write some Bampton Lectures. It would be the right man in the right place. I am writing in less than owl light."

ANOTHER

"*Oct.* 16, 1860.

" . . . Could you kindly lend me for a little while the sermon which you preached here the Sunday after my dear sister went away, on ' Rejoice in the Lord ' ? I think I know of a person to whom it might be very useful. . . ."

From MISS YONGE

" *Dec.* 1860.

" MY DEAR ALICE,
    " I trow you are not expecting me to-night, and a great pity it is, but it will be mitigated if Dr. Moberly will only be so kind as to lend us the lecture to read at home, in which case the Institution shall honestly have the price of our tickets. If you will tell the cart to call we will send in Froude, vol. v., and ' Cornwallis.' I am afraid you are not in the way of the glory of the snow. It was like a succession of fairy palaces all the way to church this morning, and we have

just come in from revelling in it by the lovely little crescent moon, with the sunset light far away. Even waggons have not stained it yet, and the hill is one great twelfth cake: and the cabbages are divided into Esquimaux huts and lawyers' wigs. I am afraid Mrs. Moberly feels the cold, and still more afraid that Mrs. Keble does. . . ."

From MR. KEBLE

"HURSLEY, *Feb.* 1, 1861.

" MY DEAR MOBERLY,

" May Henry Williams and Heygate come out to us to-morrow? I am sadly disappointed at not hearing so good a report of our dear friend. But much rejoiced at the Bamptonward hint in your note the other day. Your iron, I think, is hot, and I hope you will have time to strike while it is so. . . ."

ANOTHER

". . . We were saddened by the account of dear Barter. We pray for him constantly in church. Would they like his name mentioned? I almost feel unkind not to have told you about P. Y.,[1] but I was in *such* a hurry. Is not hurry an essentially cruel thing? If so, I am like a wolf just now, but always very lovingly yours,

"J. KEBLE."

ANOTHER

" *Feb.* 16, 1861.

". . . God bless you, dear friend, and all around you, and your College, now dearer than ever, since you are more left alone with it.

" Your very loving

"JOHN KEBLE."

[1] Rev. Peter Young.

From George Moberly to George

" *Feb.* 8.—The Warden is alive, but reasonable hope is well-nigh gone. I stood by his bedside for a few minutes this morning, but he was asleep. Yesterday evening, when he had a glass of port wine, he said, cheerily, ' I shall be up to breakfast to-morrow at 10 o'clock.' . . . I am bent on writing to Scott to decline being put in nomination for the Bamptons for the present. My time is so occupied, and my spirits so little up to great undertakings, and the plan I had sketched so vast, that I fear I should break down.

" *Feb.* 9.—Our dear friend is gone from us. . . . About an hour before the end he chanted the Magnificat and Nunc Dimittis, and having omitted in the Gloria ' and to the Son,' repeated it again, putting in the words. How characteristic ! O that my last end may be like that of my dear old friend !

" *Feb.* 15.—We have laid our dear, kind, noble-hearted friend by his mother's side in the Cloister. There were very many present. The Bishop of Winchester read the service, looking very old and agitated. The Dean and Chapter, Dean Hook, half a dozen New College men, and a vast number of friends, clergy, tradespeople, and neighbours. The College boys in surplices stood at the east end of the Chapel : the commoners in the ante-Chapel. The dear old Dean Garnier is very unhappy. He sat with us half an hour yesterday full of grief. The Bishop of Salisbury has let me off my sermon to-night ; it would have been very grievous to have left Winchester instantly after the service."

From Mr. Keble

" . . . There is nobody, I feel sure, nobody on earth, who can exactly take the part which he did, with his sweet and noble and, as I always thought, *royal* ways : not giving up an inch of principle, yet known to be the friend of every one and making all friends to one another.   But now he is gone to be made perfect with Him from Whom he learned all this and more.   God help us to remember him as we ought, and forgive us for not having made more of his good example while he was here.   It is hard even here to realise that one is not to see his countenance and hear his voice any more on earth."

GEORGE MOBERLY'S JOURNAL

" Walford has a Cambridge assistant, a Mr. Hawkins, for whom I have fitted up a room in Commoners with desks, and I hope this will be a useful move.   The young tutors are lively, and we begin work in a fresh lively way.

" Robert is better.   I hope that the pony and cod liver oil together have done good.   But now he is grown so tall I am constantly reminded of my dear Arthur, and tremble for his strength.   He is only fifteen and a half years old, and by sixteen he will be the second senior (if not senior) College boy and as tall as a man.   Yesterday the first Flag of the girls' manufacture arrived, and was unpacked with great interest and expectation ; it is the blue one with the College arms." [1]

From GEORGE MOBERLY
" *Oct.* 1861.

" MY DEAR ALICE,
    " I am overwhelmed by an immense packet of questions from the Public Schools Commission,

---

[1] The College Rifle Corps was started in 1860, and the following year colours were presented to it.   Robert Pound was the first captain. Herbert Stewart (afterwards killed at Abu Klea as a young General) was present as one of the crowd of boy spectators, but being then second captain both of cricket and football, was not a Volunteer.

which will take a vast amount of time and labour to answer, and will additionally operate to sit down upon my letters. I go to Eton after seeing Adrian Porter, who is very ill indeed. . . . Johnnie has invested some of his fortune in a fiddle, on which the six juniors play by turns. Selwyn flatters himself that he plays ' God Save the Queen '; but, God save the Queen if she is only to be saved by such a wonderful ditty ! Jack and Edward, however, make out a little tune. The little ones are hearty, but Selwyn has a head like a mop gone mad."

From Mr. Keble

" My dear Moberly,

" I am ashamed to trouble you : but will you lend me the precious volume of ' Essays and Reviews ' once more ? I have a ' call ' to look at Dr. William's—and I cannot make up my mind either to buy, hire, or steal the book. Have you any strong opinion on the desirableness of the Bishop of Sarum's move ? or on the best way of conducting it ? "

From Mrs. Keble

" *Dec.* 1861.

" My dear Alice,

" Will you kindly tell me by which train your brothers come from Guildford ? Edward Young is to come with them, and I must send to meet him. One can hardly think much of anything but the Queen in her affliction, which seems to bring her so much nearer to us all. And will you tell me if the Du Boulays have found a house in Winchester to suit them ? Mrs. Cornish tells me that they had not up to the time of her leaving them."

From GEORGE MOBERLY

"*June* 1862.

" DEAREST ALICE,

"The vexatious rain selects Remedies, so on Thursday and Tuesday we grumbled at home. We wonder with all our small (but united) faculties whether you got to the Royal School yesterday, and, if so, whether you draggled in the long wet grass at Surly Hall. . . . Commoner Speaking was a glorious anniversary. Through the rain went various representatives of the fair sex, and the boys covered themselves with no end of glory. The Fives Courts grow up nearly as fast as the Tower grows down. A ghastly chasm opens in the wall of Hall and Chapel.[1] The breakfast bell has rung, but no girls appear. Oh! here is a step and a whiffling of petticoats on the stairs. . . ."

ANNIE'S STORY

"For some years the Headmaster had become happier about school, and high classes were being gained at the Universities. This seemed to be the result of the introduction of competition into Senior Part Fifth in 1854; also by the change from the old plan of nominations to that of open elections into College, in 1855, and the enlargement of the staff of masters. 'Commoners,' too, was flourishing, but Dr. Moberly had, for some time, been uneasy about the healthiness of the buildings, and in 1859 he had initiated the opening of tutors' houses. When, in 1862, Grass Court and College Meads were thrown into one, he longed to see ' Meads ' enlarged ; but the difficulty of the

[1] Owing to the deaths of the Wardens of Winchester and New College, in 1861 and 1862, there were no celebrations of Domum for two years. At this time the College tower was being rebuilt as a memorial of the two Wardens.

canals (which came close to the wall) seemed at the time insuperable.

" In the late autumn of 1862 George Ridding was appointed Second master, and in January 1863 he took possession of his father's old home in College. For some years he had shared the Headmaster's anxieties and aspirations for the school, and from the moment of his arrival my father felt him to be the greatest possible support, and the school gained enormously. To the home circle George Ridding's arrival was delightful; and in return for many good things, such as drives into the country and expeditions to London for concerts and picture-galleries, he threw himself with zest into all the freedom and fun of family life. For four years he had been a welcome guest in every room in the house—in the study, as well as in the drawing-room with the elder girls, and in the schoolroom. Sometimes he would refresh himself with horse-races in the nursery (the horses represented by turned-down chairs), much to the detriment of the chairs and of the ceilings below. Then he would dive into my mother's sitting-room, apparently to sympathise with her on the terrible racket going on overhead, without confessing where he had come from, or how far he was responsible for the pandemonium upstairs. To his sisters-in-law this most brotherly of brothers came with all the freshness of the Oxford tutor, who subjected every topic to debate, and required us to argue over everything we most cared about, even when we all knew that he and we were all of one mind. The merry indignation excited by his assumed attitude of criticism towards family traditions was reflected in Maggie's overheard ' aside' to Selwyn, that ' a Radical is the short for a rascal.' No doubt it was excellent education to have to fight for what we were certain (and his later writings provéd) he prized as much as we did ; and he evidently enjoyed a company of sisters with whom he sometimes posed as the breaker-down of prejudices and sometimes as the most old-fashioned of the party ; for in many a long talk he tried to impress upon us that he was the true Conservative, whilst the Headmaster was the Radical at heart. A word gravely spoken, three years later, to one of the sisters, about the difference between the Oxford tutor's theorising attitude with which he had come to Winchester, and the actual experience gained by his first years of residence, and the value he attached to that experience, was very interesting to us, in however many ways it might be interpreted."

About this time Bishop Coleridge Patteson wrote from New Zealand asking my father to correspond with him.   Bishop Patteson was personally unacquainted with my parents, but his name as the first Bishop of Melanesia was a household word. He was a cousin of the Yonges, and his sister Fanny constantly stayed at Hursley ; he had been a friend of George Ridding's at Oxford. The series of letters which now began was a great pleasure to all concerned.   Some portions referring to my father, Hursley, and Otterbourne are extracted from them.

From BISHOP PATTESON

"ST. ANDREW'S COLLEGE, KOHIMARAMA.
Aug. 29, 1863.

"MY DEAR DR. MOBERLY,
    "Thank you for a very kind and most interesting letter written in May.   If you knew the value to us of such letters as you have written,

containing your impressions and opinions of things in general, men, books, etc., you would be well rewarded for your trouble, I assure you. To myself, I must say to you in all sincerity, such letters are invaluable; they are a real help to me, not only in that they supply information from a very good authority on many questions which I much desire to understand, but even more because I rise up or kneel down after reading them, and think to myself, 'How little such men who so think of me really know me; how different I ought to be'; and then it is another help to me to try and become, by God's grace, less unlike what you take me to be. Indeed you must forgive me for writing thus freely. I live very much alone. . . . I see but little even of my dear Primate. We are by land four or five miles apart, and meet perhaps once or twice a month to transact necessary business. . . . Were I in England, I know scarcely any place to which I should go sooner than Winchester, Hursley, and Otterbourne; and then I should doubtless talk, as I now write, freely. All that you say of the state of mind generally in England on religious questions is most deeply interesting. What a matter of thankfulness that you can say, 'With all the sins and shortcomings that there are among us, there is an unmistakable spreading of devotion and the wish to serve God rightly on the part of many.' I could not help feeling sorry at first as I read that you had declined the Bishopric of Gibraltar. . . ."

On March 10, 1863, the Prince of Wales was married to Princess Alexandra of Denmark, and for two days nothing was thought about but feasts, illuminations, and processions of pageants through the streets. On the day itself we went to the

railway bank and saw the Prince and Princess pass
on their way to Osborne; for at each station their
train slackened sufficiently to let the crowds see
them. Mrs. Alfred Gatty [1] and her daughter,
"Aunt Judy," [2] were staying with us at the time,
on account of her son Stephen's illness in College.
This was the beginning of a correspondence with
my mother. They left us to stay with the Tenny-
sons at Farringford, in the Isle of Wight.

From MRS. GATTY

"I.W., *March* 1863.

"MY DEAR MRS. MOBERLY,

". . . I forgot to tell your daughters a
small joke we had in store for them—viz., that
Mrs. Ferris, [3] on talking over the torchlight procession, told us that *Britannia was tired*, and
therefore did not go round by College Street! It
struck me that perhaps the four Quarters of the
World were fatigued also, and that was the reason
of your not making them out satisfactorily. We
heard the ' Welcome ' read aloud in Mr. Tennyson's
sonorous way of reading and grand voice; it has a
very fine effect, and would almost have converted
Miss Yonge. You must know how pleasant it is
to me to know that ' Aunt Judy ' has won her way
into the regard of the children of the house and
that of the parents also. Moreover, I do not forget
that the original Aunt Judy has already had the
pleasure of being under your roof. . . . I am quite .
tickled by your anecdote of Selwyn; his objections.
to his first school were the most original I ever

---

[1] Author of " Parables from Nature," " Aunt Judy's Tales," et .
[2] Afterwards Mrs. Ewing, author of " Jackanapes : The Story of a
Short Life," etc.
[3] Matron of College Sick House.

heard.   It would have done well in an Aunt Judy tale."

ANOTHER

"You were so very kind as to send me your daughter's cards, and sincerely do we congratulate you and yours on the happy event.   I heard from Miss Yonge the pleasantest possible account, and I do feel with you in the joy you must experience. May I ask if you have read 'The Water Babies'? I ask everyone, for it has enchanted me to such an extent that I dip into it again and again as a sort of refreshment.   It is also very interesting to try and make out the allegory.   If you and your party have read it, let me hear the general opinion. Whether the stream into which Tom fell is Baptism; whether Mrs. Be-done-by-as-you-did is Nature, and Mrs. Do-as-you-would-be-done-by Grace, or whether these two are the Law and the Gospel. Whether the back-stairs are Art or Fashion, and whether the thirty-nine things the book teaches are the Thirty-nine Articles?   He has, as I think, made a great mistake in making the Dragon-fly come out of the grub under the water, but I speak from old accounts, and from the particular case we watched in a foot-pan here ; and here the grub walked up the Iris leaves first and then cracked, so that the Dragon-fly came out.   We found the empty case on the leaf, all the six legs in the usual attitude, just as if the tenant occupied it still. Mr. Kingsley's nature descriptions are, however, for the most part inimitable.   In short, both book and illustrations appear to me delicious."

ANOTHER

"As to 'The Water Babies,' I make it my request that you will read the book and judge for yourself.   I cannot persuade myself that it is not a spiritual allegory, though I own I doubted if it hung together as a whole from end to end. I have never discussed it with Miss Yonge, and perhaps I am more carried away than I am able to make allowance for, by the exquisite breezy and watery naturalness and brilliancy of the whole thing. . . . Truly I think mothers are just the people to enjoy 'The Water Babies' to the very depths of their being, so I shall set Dr. Moberly and Miss Yonge on one side—as no judges at all.

" Your kind and gratifying letter gave me much pleasure, and moreover I followed all your trains of thought in speaking of your daughter with deep interest. But I am quite satisfied that Providence never intends us to read the riddle of the future in the past, unless the riddle be one of *moral* teaching. Princess Charlotte dies, Princess Victoria lives to see nine children born and her husband buried! Our hopes and fears are all defied by such events. Good children from bad parents, bad ones from good ones. Even education defied now and then, that we may feel everything to be ruled above and beyond us. But of course you have gone through all these thoughts too.

" I do hear such confirmation of your accounts of the Barter race, that I trust your ' Katie's ' marriage will be a cause of lifelong happiness to you.[1] Aunt Judy was perfectly well till, by over-fatigue, she caught cold and a sore throat. It has passed over, but one cannot make even the dearest young people wise. . . ."

[1] Elspeth Catherine Moberly married Rev. Henry Barter, 1863, nephew of Warden Barter, son of Rev. Charles Barter, of Sarsden, Oxon.

H. Barter was born 1835 : Tomline Prize at Eton, 1852 ; Math. Post Mastership, Merton College, Oxford, 1853 ; Prox. access. Jun. Math. Prize, 1853 ; 2nd Class in Classical Mods., 1855 ; Math. Greats, 1857 ; ordained deacon, curate of Bradford-on-Avon, Wilts, 1858; priest, 1860; curate of Old Windsor, 1860 ; Vicar of Lamborne, Berks, 1862 ; of Shipton-under-Wychwood, 1868 ; of Sonning, Berks, 1899 ; Proctor in Convocation for the Oxford Diocese, 1899. Died May 24, 1901.

From A Friend to Mrs. Moberly

"*May* 1864.

" Your very kind note has been like dew on the grass to me : not that my remembrance of, or my true love and honour of you were withered or faded ; but that you should still so care for me, brought with it comfort and refreshment which I cannot express. My times spent under your roof recall thoughts not of this world, and your dear image often rises before me amid the sun and dust of this world's work, reminding me that daily duties, fuller and heavier than even mine, *may* be done by the measure of Eternity, and affording me a true help and encouragement. I think of George, especially on Sundays at St. Peter's-in-the-East, at Oxford : the modulations of his clear sweet voice still seem to ring in my ears. . . ."

From Miss Yonge

" My dear Alice,
        " I was thinking of sending ' The Mice at Play ' to Maggie, but somehow I felt that the note must be to one who could remember the old days, when the three bright faces it brings to mind were with us. If you had been people who shrank from such recollections instead of cherishing them, I would of course never have disinterred this old affair, but I know you will like the recurrence to those merry old days and bright remembrances. . . ."

From Mr. Keble

" My dear Moberly,
        " Will you kindly lend me again the ' Essays and Reviews ' for a day or so (if you can bear to be without so precious a Manual so long), as I want

to verify a quotation. I will not keep it, as before, for months. How I do wish that you had leisure to give us all your views on making the most of the opportunities, and dealing with the risks, of the present 1864. Both seem to be coming on in immense amount. As far as I could judge, I was rather comforted than alarmed by what I was able to pick up at Cuddesdon and Oxford. Is there any chance of your being at Fieldhouse to-morrow, and if you are, may I come up and steal half an hour from you ?

    " Ever your loving and grateful
                          " JOHN KEBLE."

ANOTHER

" HURSLEY, October 1864.

" MY DEAR MOBERLY,

    " I was sorry to miss you when you called the other day. It looks as if the Hursley ' season' were fast drawing to a close. Of course you know of the Park moving to Rome, and to-day the N.E. wind warns <i>us</i> that we must not stay too long. φεῦ φεῦ.

    " Your most loving and ever grateful
                          " JOHN KEBLE.

" I do so much thank you and Mrs. Moberly for sparing us your children ; they and their music were to me a complete charm in the house."

The Kebles had for some time been in a very delicate condition of health. On account of Mrs. Keble's difficulty of breathing, they had spent several winters at Penzance, Torquay, and Bournemouth. In the autumn of 1864 Mr. Keble had a paralytic seizure. He partially recovered, and we saw him during the summer of 1865, but looking sadly changed. My father saw him for

the last time at a luncheon party given with difficulty at Hursley vicarage. Mrs. Keble was ill
upstairs, Mr. Keble was sad and tired, so Mrs.
Thomas Keble did the honours. The other guests
were the Queen of the Sandwich Islands and
Archdeacon Utterton (afterwards Bishop of Guildford).

Their nephew, James Peter Young,[1] a former
College boy, went with them to Bournemouth ;
he took such care of them that they used to call
him both son and daughter. And by him we
were kept informed of their condition ; so that
Mr. Keble's death, on Thursday in Holy Week,
1866, did not come as a surprise.

From J. P. YOUNG

"BOURNEMOUTH, *March* 24, 1866.

"DEAR SIR,
    "It is all over. The doctors told us last
night at 7 that he was dying. From that time
till the end came, at one o'clock, he lay quietly
sinking ; no sign of animation except the regular,
quick breathing. Aunty bears up wonderfully.
I was with her a good deal last night. She was
very resigned. I read to her. She seems so like
a mother. Tom Keble, who has been here for the
last two days, is gone to Hursley for a few hours.
The funeral is fixed for Thursday, at Hursley."

From MRS. YONGE

"OTTERBOURNE, *Easter Eve*, 1866.

"It is quite a comfort, my dear Mrs. Moberly,
.to have your letter, and to answer it immediately.

---

[1] Afterwards Vicar of Grimsby, son of Rev. Peter Young.

And it is better to write than to see you; our hearts would be too full for speech. Charlotte and I can only trust ourselves to talk at times. It comes at the best possible time for us all; these services are so especially full of Mr. Keble. At the same time we are quite alive to the special mercy of his not having been left to linger a few sad, feeble years without her to comfort him, and I suspect that she feels that strongly herself. She has surprised us so often, she may yet rally; and she has learnt her lesson of submission and patient waiting so thoroughly that any way it must be well for her. The person I pity is Sir William Heathcote; fancy having to appoint a successor! Lady Heathcote says he was quite knocked down by it. Of Dr. Moberly's two invitations, to the house of mourning and the house of feasting, it is not difficult to guess which he will accept. Bitter as the sorrow is, I think it would have been worse but for the warning of last year; he had written so cheerfully of late, we had almost forgotten his precarious condition.

"It will always be a pleasure to Charlotte to think how welcome her Saturday's letters have always been to them. I do not know how to leave off writing; it seems the only thing I have spirits to do. . . ."

From M. A. MOBERLY

"WINCHESTER, *Easter Week*, 1866.

"MY DEAR ALICE,

"Uncle Richard Church arrived on Wednesday, Sir Frederick and Lady Rogers as well, and they all dined and slept here. They were so bright and full of talk that it greatly refreshed papa. Yesterday morning they all went together to Hursley, for the early Celebration at 8 o'clock, at which there were about 70 people present. The

coffin had been laid before the Altar the evening
before.   Afterwards our four drove up to the
farm and breakfasted (Hursley and the inn were
crowded), coming down again for the morning service.   It was sad that you were all at Sea View;
but George and Annie, the only two here, went
over.   The day was brilliant, the sky cloudless
and warm, if not *hot*.   They seem to have been
struck with the festive look of everything : the
villagers in their best clothes and the flowers for
Easter.   The Altar-cloth was white worked with
gold, the pall purple silk with a deep red border
and a gold cross on the top ; the reredos was hung
with black and white silk.   Mr. Keble's seat in the
chancel was guarded by cords of black and white
silk, and a lovely wreath of white camellias laid on
the cushion.

"The church seemed glowing with sunlight
streaming through the stained windows, and there
was much singing ; the first butterfly danced about
over the heads of the congregation, and seemed to
be dropping gold dust from its wings.   The pall-
bearers, all former curates, wore white surplices.
Papa was one of the eight personal friends to follow
the mourners, with Sir William Heathcote, the
Bishop of Salisbury,[1] Dr. Pusey, Mr. Spranger, the
Bishop of Brechin,[2] and Mr. Liddon.   The church
was crowded, many Oxford and London clergymen
being there, and many having to stand.   The
23rd Psalm was sung, as it was sung the first day
of the Kebles' arrival at Hursley : it was sung at
the grave, which is close to Miss Keble's, under
the vicarage wall—a large double grave.   On the
coffin was a large gilt cross with trefoil ends, reaching the whole length of it.   Immediately after the
service the bells rang a peal : not muffled, but
joyful.

[1] Bishop Walter Kerr Hamilton.
[2] Bishop Forbes.

" The dear old Dean [1] was there.   I was so glad that the Cathedral bell tolled for an hour.   Warden Lee changed the day for his wedding ; and to-day we have the Cathedral and College bells ringing continuously for it.

" Mrs. Peter Young came in just now.   She says that Mrs. Keble is quite calm, and no worse ; but she cannot last long, as further symptoms have set in and she is suffering greatly.   She *longs* to go. . . ."

From G. MOBERLY *to* BISHOP PATTESON

" WINCHESTER, *April* 17, 1866.

" . . . And now our minds are all full of the loss we have recently sustained by the death of dear Mr. Keble. . . . Mrs. Keble, for many weeks, has seemed to be at the point of death.   He was reading prayers by her bedside when he grew faint. . . . From that time his strength gradually failed, and in a week he quietly sank.   His wandering words were of course wild and inconsecutive ; but ' the upper room ' and ' full of lilies ' were the most intelligible expressions of his last hours.   His wife was unable to be with him, but she discovered his death when a print of the Crucifixion which had always been in his room was brought in and put at the bottom of her bed.   She said at once, ' I knew it, and I thanked God, and I *do* thank God, that He has taken him, and that he is with his Saviour now.' . . . We cannot mourn.   He was full of years.   He had done his work.   And most surely no man has lived in the Church of England for many generations who has left a deeper or more sacred mark upon his own age, or left behind him a more enduring legacy for the good and edification of future generations, than our

---

[1] Dean Garnier.

dear friend. It would be selfish to think amid all this of one's own grief; but to me it is the loss of my dearest friend, and one who for the greater part of 30 years had honoured me with an intimacy and confidence to which I had no sort of claim, but which I most dearly prized."

From J. P. YOUNG

"BROOKSIDE, BOURNEMOUTH.

"DEAR SIR,
    "Thank you very much for your letter. Aunty has been too ill to see it to-day. I feel very proud that I can be in any way the channel through which such letters come to her. She was in great pain last night, and got little, or no, sleep. The anodynes she took have made her sleepy to-day. I don't think she has been in much pain. I heard from Mr. Liddon the other day some particulars about the College scheme. The people here are going to put up a memorial window in the church above the place where uncle used to sit when he came in, as he always did, in the middle of the Communion service.

ANOTHER

"BOURNEMOUTH, *May* 1866.

"DEAR SIR,
    "You have perhaps heard from Hursley of Aunty's death. She died this morning about 12 o'clock. It must have been very sudden at the last, though she was so ill this morning that the doctor was sent for at 6 a.m. When I saw her at 11 she seemed comfortable and said something about my lifting her. I was away at the time. They say it was very quiet. I saw her almost directly afterwards, before the colour had quite gone. I had thought the end could not be far off. Mrs. Thomas Keble is very much overcome

at present, but I hope she will get a good night's
rest and be refreshed. . . ."

ANNIE'S STORY

" A few days later, at Hursley, the same
wonderful scene as we had witnessed just a month
earlier was repeated. The same cloudless sky, the
brilliant rhododendrons in full bloom, and the
glowing sunlight cheered us again. The same Psalm
was sung, and the triumphant peal of bells rang
out again at the end of the service ; but a smaller
company had gathered together. Mrs. Keble had
arranged every detail of both services, and had
selected me, as representing her godchildren, to be
one of her pall-bearers.

" The Kebles had for years thrown themselves
unreservedly into the concerns of the merry multitude in College Street. They had delighted in
George's literary tastes and Oxford successes : had
been interested in the astronomical excitements :
they had watched Robert's self-controlled ways
and shared our pleasure when he gained one of the
Winchester scholarships at New College. Being
one of their godchildren, I had always been included
in any invitation to us to stay at the vicarage ; but
my recollections of those visits chiefly concern
tiny points interesting to a child and to a growing
girl. The sight of Dr. Newman's miniature bust
on Mr. Keble's study table with a white veil always
placed over it was very mysterious to us children.
Mr. and Mrs. Keble were very stern at anything
which seemed to them foolish, and their tone of
marked disapproval on hearing of a delicate girl
insisting on going to an early Celebration against
advice made a great impression, and the grave voice
in which they said, ' it is not even common sense.'
A certain great lady they spoke of as ' a very pious
goose.' I shall never forget the tone of his voice

when he told us that a murderer (of whom every one was speaking at the time) was caught and would be hanged. The kindling of his eye set me wondering whether the Psalms of denunciation were not the utterances of advanced spirituality rather than its opposite. I still seem to see Mr. Keble at family prayers with his hand shading his eyes as he repeated Bishop Wilson's prayers by heart.

" No doubt some of us saw more of the Kebles in their own house than the others, but until many of the party were grown up, we all alike knew Mr. Keble in church. Robert, for instance, was twenty years old when Mr. Keble died, and for fifteen or sixteen years can hardly have passed a summer Sunday without hearing him preach, catechise, and read the Lessons in his deeply reverent manner. That strong, intellectual, spiritual Churchmanship greatly influenced us. The home lessons were burnt into us at Hursley, as we heard the earnest teaching that the outward ceremonials depended for their reality on the inward spiritual gifts ; but those spiritual gifts being present (as covenanted to Christians), the sacred whole of inward and outward together could not be too deeply reverenced.

" One of the last summers, my father sent for a photographer to take some family groups at Fieldhouse. Afterwards they went to Hursley and, to my father's satisfaction, found Miss Yonge drinking tea with Mr. and Mrs. Keble on the vicarage lawn. Very shyly they all allowed themselves to be photographed, but only on condition that the Headmaster formed one of the group. My father wrote to Bishop Patteson, on sending the picture to him, ' The group is not successful, though the pose of Mr. Keble himself is characteristic ; but the great tranquillity of the scene, the foliage of the trees, and the church are as good as can be.'

" In the same year in which Mr. and Mrs. Keble died, the great white and red rose trees covering the south side of the vicarage up to the chimneys also died. This has quite altered the look of the house. Strange to say, immediately after Warden Barter's death a grand wistaria tree, trained to reach over seventy feet of wall in his garden in College, died suddenly."

From MISS YONGE

"WANTAGE, *May* 1866.

" MY DEAR MRS. MOBERLY,
        " Only think of Mr. Butler's [1] being so kind as to take me to Fairford yesterday—18 miles, with his brisk black pony. And there with the beautiful sunshine we saw everything to the greatest advantage. The colouring of the memorable windows is much what the east window of the Cathedral was before it was cleaned and spoilt ; the same rich dusky blue and red. But these grand colours were as charily used as the bright tints on a bird's wing ; and the drawing was all in a sort of brown or grey with a ruddy tint, the hair golden with a great richness and depth. The church was built *to* the windows, a great solemn deep-chancelled church with three aisles going very far east, and the general arrangement of the glass is certainly that of Hursley. Restoration has murdered two small bits, and all England should lift up its voice to save the rest.
        " We had an old clerk to take us about, who had been in the Keble service as a boy and used to draw Miss Keble about the garden. They tolled the bell for three hours on the day of the funeral. Then we made him show us the house, which is now lived in by the doctor. It is of that grey or brown stone so common here. The garden door

---

[1] Afterwards Dean of Lincoln.

HURSLEY VICARAGE, 1861.

p. 184]

opened on to a little bit of lawn with a cedar tree and a seat under it. Just beyond is a narrow, long field with a path round it like ours, only smaller— and grand elms with rooks' nests in them ; snowdrops, periwinkles, and stars of Bethlehem growing in the grass.

" We are enjoying our outing greatly, and are both much the more brilliant for it. On Tuesday we go to the Miss Pattesons.

" I am sure no one could see church or house at Fairford without seeing how the calm and mystery must have influenced the whole nature.

" We had a shake of the hand of Robert in Oxford, in boating costume, and looking ready for a pantomime. . ."

One result of the Public Schools Commission in 1861 was the appointment of a Governing Body intended gradually to take the place of the Warden and Fellows ; consequently Mr. Quicke's Fellowship, which fell in in 1864, was not filled up. We knew that our father meant to stand for the next. It was a great change to us already, not to be the only womankind to attend the College Chapel, and the cricket and football matches, and to feel boundless enthusiasm for the school and all its traditions, good and bad. The companionship of others was pleasant enough, but the thought that we should before long have to leave Winchester made us restless and unhappy.

HOME LETTERS

" FIELDHOUSE, *July* 27, 1866.

" . . . We are having cooler grey weather ; the hillside is so clear and dark and looks so near, that we seem to be able to see quite into the woods. Alice and Edith have been alternately at Otterbourne, and Bob writes to Johnnie to invite him to a walking tour either in Wales or at the Lakes. G. R. and Edith have just driven over from Winchester, and the others have gone down to Hursley to sketch in the vicarage garden.

"When it is dark we walk about the garden in twos and threes, having an enthralling subject of conversation, for Mr. Charles Williams has died, and we can see on to our actually leaving Winchester at Easter."

"WINCHESTER, *Sept.* 28, 1866.

". . . Yesterday all the Fellows were in Chapel before their meeting at 2 p.m. To our surprise mamma arranged to drive to the farm, taking Edith with her, saying that the news could wait. They had hardly gone when Johnnie ran in with the announcement of the election. This was soon confirmed by the Cathedral and College bells striking up, whilst congratulations began to pour in ; but our feelings were dreadfully mixed about it. After a time my father came upstairs and said quietly, 'George Ridding is Headmaster.' As soon as my father had joined the Fellows in the Warden's gallery, he found it was already settled, and they had asked him to go and offer the vacant post to G. R., who had accepted it. More congratulations followed and more complication of feelings. It was a relief when the driving party returned, and my mother was with us to take the lead. She heard G. Ridding's step on the stairs, and went out to meet him and gave him a kiss. The immediate consequence of this was that he ran downstairs again and was seen no more by us that evening. The evening was one of illuminations and bonfires, cheering and singing in the school ;

and the noise in Hall that night was tremendous. . ."

GEORGE MOBERLY'S JOURNAL

"*July* 8, 1866.—Again in the vernacular. How much has happened since I closed the Latin volume !—namely, the illness and death of my dear friends Mr. and Mrs. Keble, whose loss alters Hursley and its aspect to us so grievously . . . and the Continental war ; how suddenly the fire has blazed up, and how suddenly it seems likely to die out ! The Archimage of the Tuileries will sweep all the table into his own pocket, I suppose. . . . Then the change of Ministry . . . and my poor boy Fraser, who, after two days' very imminent condition of danger, seems this morning as if he might recover. Lastly, the birth of a little grandson at Lamborne.[1] But I must not forget eight First Classes in this year, all the Chancellor's prizes of the year, the Gaisford verse, the Hebrew Scholarship, the Queen's Fellowship, the Magdalen demyship—altogether an entirely unprecedented success for a school, specially for a small one. We are looking forward to the restoration of the reredos in Chapel, and to the Public Schools Bill. Of course my tenure must be near its end, and I suppose that a vacant Fellowship would terminate it—somewhat abruptly.

"*July* 27.—Mr. Charles Williams has died, making a vacant Fellowship. It is my wisdom to offer for it, partly because I have been here long enough, and the school will be the better for a change ; partly because I have been ill every spring and most autumns of late ; partly because after this vacancy two more must fall before another is filled up.

"*Sept.*—The school has met again. We have

---

[1] Charles Barter.

had two wild nights of theatricals in Commoner
Hall: pretty and successful. The half-year begins
vigorously. My classes all in bright earnest. . . .
The future looks grim, and I seem to have reached
the beginning of the end. . . . I feel my heart
cling twenty times more closely and warmly to
my boys for thinking that I am probably about to
leave them.

"*Sept.* 28.—Yesterday I was elected a Fellow of
the College: just forty years after my election to
be a Fellow of Balliol! Very different indeed the
two occasions. That was the promising Prologue,
this is the somewhat depressing Epilogue of a long
and varied Drama—over now.

"*Oct.*—Kind letters from near friends and from
surprisingly distant ones. I have only a certain
number more lessons to give and words to say
before I drop the cæstus and relinquish the art.
I must find a house and face the future with a
good heart. My sons will suffer, for they will not
be able to go to the University. Even Johnnie, I
fear, will have to leave Oxford. I only hope
I shall see cheerful looks and hear unrepining
words. . . .

"*Nov.* 12.—The days run away, and five more
weeks will see the final end of my teaching. How
I shall miss it! Yet my Pindar will be for a time
an occupation, and I have an idea of putting my
Confirmation lectures into shape.

"*Nov.* 18.—We have had an astonishing exhibition of shooting-stars, predicted by the astronomers,
and wonderfully brilliant. I saw none; but some
of the girls were up, and the rest of mankind have
been all alive about it. I am going to give the
boys a great supper. My boys for Confirmation
please me.

"*Dec.* 1.—Confirmation over. Advent Communion to-morrow. I have lectured in Chapel

this evening, and expect fully 170 boys. I have been speaking for the Curates' Augmentation Fund, and have undertaken a lecture for the working men on 'A Thousand Years Ago.'

"*Dec.*—Thursday last I received from the Bishop of Winchester the offer of the living of Brighstone. Everything is in favour of taking it, except the prospect of not being able to get into the house. I had not contemplated parochial work, and the climate is probably soft and moist. The church is said to be beautiful. . . . We have elected Hornby as Second master—a gentleman, a scholar, an Etonian.[1] . . . Only one broken week more; and then, the cable once cut, I shall not be sorry to find a home away from Winchester. I consider the Bishop's offer, coupled with his most handsome letter, exceedingly gratifying.

"*Dec.* 10.—I have accepted Brighstone. May the blessing of God rest upon it and me and mine, for Christ's sake.

"*Dec.* 25.—A letter from George tells us that, being unwell at Mentone, he sent for the doctor, who told him that there is no hope of his life. He is in God's hands; but the hearts at home shake sadly. And now that good G. Ridding goes off to-morrow to Mentone to see him, and takes Alice as well.

"*Jan.* 1867.—A whole sad week has passed, and behold! the doctor having sentenced George to death and left him under the weight ten days, now wholly shifts his ground. . . .

"I purpose reading in next Sunday, and am beginning to dismantle the study in order to hand it over to George Ridding at the beginning of next half."

[1] Later Headmaster and Provost of Eton.

From BISHOP PATTESON

"KOHIMARAMA, N.Z., *Jan.* 2, 1867.

"MY DEAR DR. MOBERLY,

". . . I have seen in the paper that you have resigned the Headmastership and taken a Fellowship, and that Ridding succeeds you. This is news indeed. I cannot help hoping that you may soon have a wider sphere of usefulness opened to you, though indeed a Winchester Fellowship is a retreat that sounds delicious. Under the shadow of that glorious Cathedral, helping to rule your grand old College, with your son-in-law in your place, I rejoice to think of you. If you are left there (which I much doubt) you will write us books and sermons, etc. I should like to be with you and ask you questions about many things, and see Hursley and Otterbourne, places which I never saw. And yet I know full well that I should be uneasy if I were absent from Melanesia, and of course I never dream of such a thing. Miss Rennell, whom no doubt you knew, and whom I used to call my aunt, has passed away from this world, I hear. How well I remember as a little boy stopping in the Deanery! I remember the old Dean and the Cathedral, and how, playing close to the buttresses of the old grey Choir, I stopped in my play with awe and wonder to hear the solemn chant within, and felt as if I were under His shadow. I know no such associations as those of Winchester Cathedral, but I saw it but once, and for a minute only, in after years. . . . My very kind regards and congratulations to Ridding. If you must retire, I could not wish the School a better man. Dear fellow! I never think of him without a pang. But God, Who took from him his young wife, is, I doubt not, all to him."

Home Letters.

" Jan. 1867.

". . . Our great news is that Emily is engaged to be married to William Awdry.[1] . . . We are expecting Alice and G. R. to-night, from Mentone ; they have been snowed up at Avignon and so delayed. Their train had to be dug out of the snow. . . ."

" Feb. 1867.

". . . Many changes have been taking place here. The glee club now comes into chapel in surplices ; it produces a splendid body of sound, and the hymns are grand. My father chanted this evening, and as it was the first time his voice had been heard anywhere this half-year, all the boys looked up with interest. Another change is that, instead of calling names at the end of the service, the prefects go down the rows marking off those boys who are absent. It only takes two minutes, and is much more orderly, but being a change, we think it proper to resent it ! Mr. Hornby, the new Second master, is an old friend of G. R.'s (they were proctors together at Oxford), and they are now living together in College. The boys have had ' bounds ' extended, so that Hursley has become a favourite walk. The late Head-master is very merry, and tells G. R. and Mr. Hornby that he wishes the boys would make a great riot to show that they have not suddenly become so very good. We are really afraid that

[1] See page 139. Balliol College, : 1st Class. B.A. 1865 ; Ellerton Prize, 1867 ; Fellow of Queen's College, 1866 ; Second Master of Winchester College, 1868-72 ; Headmaster, Hurstpierpoint, 1872 ; Canon Residentiary of Chichester and Principal of Theol. College, 1879 ; Vicar of Amport, Hants, 1886-96 ; Suffragan Bishop of Southampton, 1895 ; Bishop in Osaka, Japan, 1896 : in South Tokyo, Japan, 1898. Died at Winchester, Jan. 4, 1910.

we shall soon like the ' improvements ' very much !
This evening the choir sang ' O taste and see ' very
well, and it was a pleasure to us in this trying
time.   The moon shone like gold through the
Jesse window, making some of the panes perfectly
brilliant.

"We are delighted to find out that exactly
two hundred years ago Bishop Ken was made
in the same year Fellow of Winchester College
and Rector of Brighstone, so that we feel quite
Wykehamically comfortable."

" FIELDHOUSE, *May* 1867.

" . . . We have made the first move to the
farm for the last time. Emily, Maggie, Walter,
Selwyn, and I are here now, and Kitty and her
two children come on Friday.   Maggie and I
wandered about College the last days, and sat in
chapel for a long time, hearing all the clocks
strike at intervals.   The last sound we carried
away with us from Winchester was, ' He watching
over Israel,' sung softly in the distance by the
glee club, whilst we leant out of G. R.'s window
in College, watching the tower and the gurgoyles
against the gentle blue sky.   It has been difficult
to feel in the least good about leaving, and hopeless
not to seem sad these last days.   Now I am looking
out of my mother's lattice window, with the
banksia roses round it in full blossom ; the scythe
is being sharpened in the garden below, and the
nightingales are singing all round in the copses.
The great meadow is studded with cowslips, and
shadows are passing quickly over the sea of woods
which, slightly veiled in green, stretch away into
the blue distance.   The great quietness and the
country scents and sounds are so delightful that
we cannot help thoroughly enjoying them though
we believe ourselves to be miserable."

"FIELDHOUSE, *June* 1867.

" Maggie and I spent four days at Brighstone learning the place and the people. How delicious home was when we came back ! We found Edith, Dora, and Kitty here. Some of us spent the evening in Greenclose, sitting on a faggot stack in bright moonlight ; every now and then a belated pheasant coughed, whilst the nightjars were purring all round, and there was a perfect chorus of nightingales. The next day was gloriously fine. Emily and Willy Awdry and the three youngest brothers came from Winchester early, and later Alice and G. R. and brakes full of boys arrived. We spent the very hot afternoon lying in the shade in the garden and meadow, until it was cool enough for a grand strawberry picking. After tea four of the sisters and dozens of schoolboys started for a walk in the woods. We lingered behind in case the parents were coming as well, and finding that they thought it too hot, Alice, G. R., and I ran off into the woods, but could not find the others. We sat down on a log in the fir-wood behind the Redan oak. It was getting late, and the firs were very black on one side of us, whilst floods of deep crimson sunset light poured in on the other. When we came back, we met Edith coming across the Greenclose fields to meet us and say that the boys had gone. Alice and G. R. followed them to Winchester, we thinking that we were parting for ever so long ; but—no such thing.

" The sisters were sleeping in the large room, which had once been the nursery, and the room inside it. We were getting up early to see Kitty off, when about 7 a.m. a carriage was heard coming up the lane, and a minute or two later G. Ridding's head was thrust into our room and he shouted out, ' Bob has got the Newdigate.' Alice was there too. They had found the telegram when they reached

13

Winchester the night before, and had started off at
the top of the morning to bring us the news.   We
looked into 'The Daisy Chain' to see what happened
when ' Norman May ' won the same Prize fifteen
years before, and finding the words ' the doctor was
greatly pleased,' a note was sent to Miss Yonge
with the words added between inverted commas.

" William Awdry has gained the Ellerton Prize,
and another Wykehamist the English Essay ; after
the wonderful successes of last year, this makes our
father very happy.   He suggests that the two
new carriage-horses shall be called ' Ellerton ' and
' Newdigate,' or ' Bill ' and ' Bob,' for short.

" We went, a most happy party, to Oxford, and
enjoyed glorious summer weather, and were entertained by numbers of Wykehamist brothers.

" Our centres were with George at Corpus and
with Robert and Johnnie at New College, but
William Awdry at Queen's and Leonard [1] at All
Souls' also considered themselves our hosts.   We
thoroughly enjoyed the scene in the theatre and
Robert's recitation of the ' Newdigate'; and
after the heat of the Masonic fête in St. John's
gardens were grateful for the cool and quiet of
New College chapel at 5 o'clock.   The next morning
we saw Robert take his B.A. degree, and spent
another hot day seeing colleges, and ending with
a row to Iffley in the evening.   We lingered over
Thursday in order to go round by Eton to see
the cricket match with Winchester ; but alas ! the
match did not last two days, so we made our way
back to Winchester, where G. R. was getting up
a regatta for those boys who were to have gone to
Eton as spectators.   Very strange it was to see our
old home being painted and ' done up ' and largely
altered inside.   We were all up for early chapel,

---

[1] A son of G. Moberly's brother, William Moberly.

asked leave to go to the Warden's garden for the last time, walked up ' Hills,' and drove out to the farm in the evening."

GEORGE MOBERLY'S JOURNAL

" *Brighstone, July* 1867.—I have been across the Solent 21 times during this long breaking up of my old home. Yesterday I left Fieldhouse finally as a home; and on Wednesday was at service at Hursley for the last time; but the place was beset with people and tourists promenading the church-yard after service, to my great vexation. Once here, we will make the best of it; but for eight months mind and body have been a-straddle across the Solent. I have to go back for the College meeting, election, and the training school.

"Six Firsts in Mods., the Craven, the Latin Essay, and the Ellerton and Newdigate Prizes. The Bell Scholarship. B.N.C. Fellowship. Very good so far in 1867."

CHAPTER VI

BRIGHSTONE

" Ecco chi crescerà li nostri amori."
Paradiso, Cant. 5.

From BISHOP SAMUEL WILBERFORCE

"WROXTON ABBEY, *Dec.* 15, 1866.

" MY DEAR DR. MOBERLY,

" I cannot hear of your acceptance of dear Brighstone without a throbbing heart. Would that it were something far more worthy of your great services to the Church. But if *such* a place was to be taken by you, I cannot but rejoice that it is Brighstone, Bishop Ken's home ; and the scene of my ten years of paradise life. You will sometimes let me come and see the grave I dug and the trees I planted there.

" I am ever most sincerely yours,

".S. OXON."

HOME LETTERS

"BRIGHSTONE, I.W., *July* 1867.

" . . . Though the day was wet, we have had a delightful Domum. Half the party were already in the Isle of Wight, the others followed from Winchester. It was a very stormy crossing, but a most beautiful rainbow spanning the Southampton Water showed itself as we landed at Cowes.

Brighstone is about a mile from the sea on the south-west coast, seven miles from Freshwater on one side, and about the same distance from St. Catherine's Point on the other; both downs are visible from the lanes above the village. The lower down behind Brighstone is called by the villagers 'Wilberforce Down,' after old Mr. Wilberforce, who lived with his son at the Rectory and used to walk there. It is covered with gorse and heather, and charming blackberry lanes lead up to it. From the top we look upon a stretch of ocean, and have satisfied ourselves that there is no land between Brighstone and the Azores. The great chalk down, which forms the backbone of the island, rises behind the lower ridge of green sandstone, and from this high down there are grand views of the Solent, Spithead, St. Catherine's, and the beacon at Freshwater. We go up it occasionally to see the 'mother country' and try to make out the Hursley woods and Ladwell hill. The coast is wild and lonely, and, the bay being dangerous, there are constant wrecks; owing to the complicated currents there are neither fishing nor pleasure boats, but there are three lifeboats within five miles of coast. Many are the stories of former wrecks; strange cargoes of umbrellas, wines, apples, and convicts, having been thrown on the shore. Nearly every man in the village seems to belong to the crew of the lifeboat, and the hymn for those at sea is a great reality here; it is sung on Sundays whenever the wind blows, with all ears attentive meanwhile to the possible sound of minute guns from the sea.

"The house is most uncommon and very pretty. The garden slopes down to the south, and ends in a 'wilderness' of roses. At the bottom there is a wall bordered with old yew-trees, where, we were told, Bishop Ken had composed his morning and evening hymns; but we had just come from

Winchester and knew the traditional site there, so we shook our heads and were not convinced. There is a fuchsia tree nine feet high in the garden, and myrtles climb to the top of the house ; we hear that our predecessors used to burn a myrtle log every Christmas. The sea is visible from the windows.

" It is all wonderfully new to us : the quiet village life, with its strong sea element ; the intense loneliness ; the daily vision of the Blackgang and Freshwater coach, suggestive of a great world somewhere else ; the sea-fogs ; the Isle of Wight luxuriance of flowers : everything is new. The brothers will soon be gone and we remain here, as far as we can see, for ever ; but we won't find it dull, if we can help it."

" BRIGHSTONE, *August* 1867.

" We happen to be all together again, and it is Sunday. Having to go to the school at 5 p.m., a new thing has been instituted—viz. tea at 4.45 in the anteroom. This is a delightful room between the drawing-room and dining-rooms, open to the staircase, and darkened with oak panelling, having an apse with small narrow lancet windows giving a green light on account of the ivy growing thickly outside.

" The church is old and dark, with an appropriate east window of our Lord in the boat and a great green wave. We have just come back from church, where the setting sunlight poured in from the west window at the beginning, but by the end of the service it was too dark to see. New lights in the church will be a necessity. A little wandering in the twilight garden, and then such a long supper table. As our predecessors were here for nearly fifty years and had no family, our crowd is a great excitement to the village. The new Rector's sermons from the first greatly attracted the people. They are full of Church teaching, but are expressed so well and carefully, and the argument on which the teaching rests is explained so clearly, that even in this stronghold of dissent, where almost every grown man is a preacher in the dissenting chapel, they draw and do not repel. The congregations are large and attentive ; and Russell, the old clerk, who remembers the Wilberforces here, has already told us confidentially that the village opinion is that ' the Doctor is one of the picked six and will soon be hoisted ! "

" Sept. 1867.

" Mrs. and Miss Yonge have been staying here, and during their visit Brighstone had its Harvest Thanksgiving Service. We spent the afternoon wreathing the church with scarlet geraniums and brilliant flowers, and Miss Yonge undertook to make the double triangle of grapes and corn for the east end ; our helpers were greatly interested to see her with her dress tucked up sweeping out the chancel with a long-handled broom. The church was thronged ; nearly every one in the place must have come to the service, and at the end the bells rang merrily. Before coming in we ran down the garden through the soaking grass to see the moon rise large and red.

"The next day we sketched on the cliff, and tried our hands upon a most gorgeous sunset over the sea. The colouring was magnificent, and a long golden glistering path of glory lay on the sea, with St. Alban's Head just visible in a bright mysterious haze. The pools in the rocks and the sands had turned crimson and purple.

" The Yonges have left us ; and Papa and Alice have gone to spend Sunday in Winchester. How our mouths watered ! Just at the time they were crossing we went up the ' high down ' and looked over a wonderful view of sea and sky. There was a fresh wind blowing, the sun was shining, and birds were starting up round us amongst the furze bushes. We had great fun in looking at our shadows, for we have left off our crinolines. It feels very funny and certainly looks so, but it is so comfortable without them that we wonder we never tried it before.

" There is a great deal of dissent here. Personally my father gets on very well with the people, who are ready to be very good friends. He proposed giving a weekly evening lecture on the Acts of the Apostles, and they are proving very successful and are exceedingly well attended. Young men, boys, coastguardsmen, women, servants, etc., come with their Bibles in the dark and through the rain. We make large maps which every one can see, and he tells the history of the times in his liveliest way, taking verse by verse, commenting on each. We end with the evening hymn, generally Bishop Ken's, in honour of Brighstone. Some of the people have asked to be taught to sing in parts, so a choral society has been started. We hope a Church choir may emerge from it, but the Rector refuses to hurry on anything which does not grow spontaneously out of the people's own wish and ambition. Uncle Richard Church, Helen, and young Helen[1] have been here; they greatly like the place.

" The singing class progresses admirably. My father must come a few more times to harangue about crotchets and quavers and then Edith has undertaken to conduct. We all enjoy it immensely. The schoolmaster leads the basses, and our coachman is the show tenor. There is such a muffling up these dark nights to go to the school. As we have wandered so often into the bushes, mamma has presented us with a lantern."

---

[1] Afterwards Mrs. Francis Paget.

" Dec. 1867.

" Robert has been elected to a senior student-ship at Christ Church, and we are all rejoicing over it. On Monday the Christmas holidays begin, and we are expecting the arrival of a party of twelve— viz., three sisters, five brothers, George Ridding, Kitty's two babies and their nurse. Mamma says, ' The house *must* learn to hold us all ; I will never tell any son or daughter when they offer to come home that there is no room for them.' Yesterday we saw the lifeboat practise in a great gale. It was a wonderful sight. We could hardly keep our footing on the cliff; the rain and spray drove into our faces, and on account of the thick atmosphere no horizon was to be seen. The boat entirely disappeared between the boiling waves and then rode up high on the top of them."

" Jan. 1868.

" Yesterday evening we had a regular Christmas rout with our pleasant opposite neighbours. We were just sitting down to an immensely long table, expecting Henry Barter, Robert, and Walter, who had been walking to Blackgang, and were making themselves clean and tidy, when—in rushed George Ridding ' very much the reverse,' as Edith exclaimed ; he had been back to Winchester for the day. The evening was brilliant with three most successful tableaux. Walter spent some time in front of my looking glass, as he said, ' making myself look vile,' and fully succeeded, for he made a frightful Shylock.

" The first penny reading ever held in Brighstone has taken place. Old Russell brought his Bible, thinking that it would consist in every one's reading aloud a verse by turns ; so he was somewhat dis-appointed. The trial scene in the *Merchant of Venice* was a great success, and G. R.'s spirited reading of ' Daniel O'Rourke ' will not soon be forgotten."

" *Feb.* 1868.

" Have you heard of the tremendous reforms George Ridding contemplates at Winchester and Mr. Hornby at Eton ? We have been composing a valentine to send them. The family has produced the poem and Edith has drawn a pen-and-ink likeness of G. R. gazing through his eyeglass into the sky, saying, ' Why, I can't find anything else to sweep, so I must sweep away the *boys* and the *buildings* ! ' "

George Moberly's Journal

" Hornby elected Headmaster of Eton. We have advertised for a Second master. . . .

" Dear Mrs. Yonge perceptibly fading. I fear she will hardly see the summer. Alice is at Otterbourne.

" In a few weeks my two first Bampton Lectures come off. Keble, the Epistles, and Pindar all hang fire. I have plenty of work for a long time ; and how much time for my work ? Threescore years do not promise much. Perhaps Richard Church may come here before long, and he will enliven me. . . . The girls interest themselves in parish affairs very nicely, particularly old Edith. Good news from George at Mentone. Edward is to stand for C. C. C., and writes to me for grammatical help, which is very pleasant to me.

" *March.*—My first two Bamptons are over. . . . Gladstone's resolutions portentous, and I feel some doubt of his success. This is politics. Hitherto I have felt him conscientious. . . . I do not know of more than five of my catechumens coming to Communion next Sunday, but I hope for ten. I have daily morning service, and on the last four days evening service with addresses."

HOME LETTERS

April 1868.

" Spring is here. The trees are getting green and the apple and pear blossoms are appearing, and the gorse is in full bloom on the cliff. We now have daily morning service, and in the evenings lately there has been a congregation of about thirty people. A Confirmation has lately been held here, and the Rector is working hard to get all the candidates to the Easter Communion. The dissenters are very busy just now. A few weeks ago an opposition sermon was advertised in the village, to be preached by Captain —— in a barn, on one of the lecture evenings. Captain ——was a schoolboy at Winchester not very long ago, so my father sent him a very polite message through the clerk, asking him to call at the Rectory, or to let my father know where he was lodging. Nothing more was heard of him ; he did not preach, but passed on quickly to the next village. We suppose that he did not know ' the Doctor ' was living here, or thought that he was being ' sent for.'

" I hear a great noise : two pigs are frantically cantering about the garden, with Bob, Walter, Maggie, and Selwyn armed with big sticks, and Bruin flying after them round the bushes. An army of ducks walked into the drawing-room an hour ago."

"LAMBORNE, *April* 1868.

" Edith and I are staying with Kitty and Henry Barter, and we all went yesterday to Oxford for the laying the first stone of Keble College. It was beautifully fine, and we met my father, Robert, and Johnnie in Oxford. We were just in time for the Litany at St. Mary's and Bishop Wilberforce's sermon. Immediately after we followed in the crowd to see the stone laid by the Archbishop of

Canterbury. The New College choir sang the
psalms and hymns. The number of old friends
we saw there was astonishing. All the Hursley
world, of course, and many from Winchester. We
succeeded in our great object, and shook hands
with Bishop Selwyn of New Zealand. Our morning drive over the Berkshire downs had made us so
hungry that we could not resist having luncheon,
and therefore we were too late to get seats in the
theatre; but we went in later, and heard Bishop
Selwyn's mention of Miss Yonge, and ' The Daisy
Chain,' and the ship for the Melanesian Mission,
and had the pleasure of seeing her quite unable to
keep in a broad smile of happiness. . . . Then to
Winchester."

" WINCHESTER, *April* 1868.

"All the sounds here are so delightful and home-
like : the rooks in the elm-tree in Commoners'
court ; the jackdaws round the College tower ;
and the click of the gate leading into cloisters.
The buttresses and gurgoyles, the quiet grey
corners, the Chapel—every part is full of association. It will always be more home than any other
place. My father says, ' Brighstone is a very good
place, but it doesn't wag its tail at me, as Winchester does.' "

" BRIGHSTONE, *Aug.* 1868.

" We are all assembled for Emily's wedding—
six brothers, seven sisters, George Ridding, and
Henry Barter. We were in the middle of decorations and attempts to make more room, when,
at 5 p.m., the flood-gates opened and thirteen
Awdrys poured in. We were thirty-two at
dinner, and, except Sir John and Lady Awdry
and our parents, all the rest claimed to be brothers
and sisters. The gentlemen are sleeping in the
village ; and last night, instead of going back at

once to their lodgings, they all went, by moonlight, for a long night walk along the shore, and enjoyed it immensely. The next day was fine, and the wedding took place duly. Emily wore a wreath of real myrtle. In the middle of rather a tumultuous tea-party on the lawn, added to by Emily's class of girls and Edith's boys, Bishop Wilberforce arrived. He was only passing through, but could not do so without looking in.

" In the evening, leaving the four parents alone, we all went to the school, carrying flat candlesticks to light us and the claret-cup over from the break-fast to refresh us ; and there, in the dusty, dark school, we danced for two hours to the sound of a buzzing harmonium, played with great spirit by each sister in turn. The old men and women, who had a dinner the next day, expressed a wish for a wedding once a month ; and Barnes (our old butler, now butler at New College), who came for the occasion to wait, says that he could come for another wedding before the end of the vacation, and adds that there are a great many nice young gentlemen at New College ! "

From MARY ANNE MOBERLY

" BRIGHSTONE, *Aug.* 1868.

" The Bishop of Oxford seemed rather to enjoy coming in upon a wedding-party. He had a cup of tea in the verandah, looked into his own arbour which he made himself, went to the church with Russell, and then walked to the shore. He called upon several people, and pleased them by telling them that Henry Barter was one of his clergy, and that he had ordained William Awdry. The old men and women thoroughly enjoyed their feast. Russell said, ' Ah, we be under the palms now,' and made an oration. Papa has gone to Calbourne to meet the Bishop of Winchester and the little son of

King Theodore of Abyssinia. Alice has gone to Otterbourne for a long visit : she finds Mrs. Yonge extremely feeble, but able to be talked to and to hear about the wedding."

ANOTHER

"*Sept.* 1868.

" MY VERY DEAR CHILDREN EMSIE AND WILLY,

" I cannot let the post go without a few words to thank you both for your most welcome and loving birthday letters. If anything can make an old woman's birthday bright, it is the loving remembrance of her children, which is not lessened by the little fretfulnesses of passing years. As you may suppose, Michaelmas Day was made very sorrowful by the tidings of dear Mrs. Yonge's death. It came as a shock at last, and we feel that it leaves a dreary blank in our small remaining circle of friends, though we are thankful for her that she has won her rest. . . .

" We hear this morning that our dear good Walter is senior by a hundred marks in the holiday task examination ; he quite deserves it for his industry. The brothers are very happy to be allowed to go and see you in College now we are gone. It will make all the difference to them. . . ."

From MISS YONGE

"OTTERBOURNE, *Sept.* 30, 1868.

" MY DEAR MRS. MOBERLY,

" Thank you for your kind, sweet, cheering note. It does seem to me truly that it is the burden of the flesh she is freed from, so entirely labour and weariness had the mere act of living been to her for months past ; but with what sweet smiles ! I am glad your dear Alice so thoroughly shared the peacefulness of the earlier watch, as well as that last trying day, which I trust will have done her no harm. I hope she and the Goddaughter[1] may be with us on Friday. She, with George Yonge and (perhaps) Duke and Anne, are the only ones to be with us here now who were with us before. The others have 'all passed into the world of light,'—the dear Kebles, Lord Seaton, Warden Barter, my cousins James and John. All Alice's life I think she was the most loved and cheering young thing, out of the family, to both my father and mother; and how she helped us in 1854! . . . I have been really alone for some time, so the loneliness does not press so much as no doubt it will."

ANOTHER

"OTTERBOURNE, *Oct.* 1868.

" . . . Anne[2] and I were pleased to have a sight of Emily; there is more change in the latter than in the former in the fourteen years since they met. I hope you will not have to part with the Chester division of the family much before Christmas. Perhaps if you do not join them there very soon after they go, you would let me come to you for a little while. . . . I am not afraid of solitary days; after all, it is all well. . . ."

ANOTHER

" PUSLINCH.

" Many many thanks for your most kind letter, and for telling me of the happy prospect before Dora. . . . I have asked Mrs. Wilson to send on to you a letter of Bishop Patteson's, which I think you will feel refreshed by reading; please send it.

[1] Frances Emily Awdry.
[2] Miss Anne Yonge of Puslinch.

on to Miss Anne Mackenzie.[1] You are so very kind, and it would be very delightful to make one in the migration ; but I have only seen Miss Dyson for a day since *her* sorrow, and not at all since *mine*, and the meeting at Testwood has become such an institution that I could not fail in it, so I must wait until you are at Brighstone again, and I have always had a wish to see that in spring. I have just returned from Lady Seaton's. It is a house of shadows and memories to me."

G. Moberly's Journal

" *Oct.* 2, 1868.—Jacobson offers me the Canonry of Chester, and I suppose I shall accept it. It is bewildering to think of. Three months in Chester ! What of my parish ? My schoolboys ? What will become of my daily services ? . . . To-day is Mrs. Yonge's funeral. Ernest Hawkins is said to be dying. How our friends are passing into the next world !

" *Nov.* 7.—Wilbraham is here. It is pleasant to have a man to talk to. The first sheet of Keble's poems is revised ; the preface finished. On Monday I hope to be able to begin the ' Short Commentary.'

" *Nov.* 20.—Tait is Archbishop ; Lincoln, London ; Wordsworth, Lincoln.

" *Dec.* 2.—. . . I was installed Canon of Chester last Wednesday. Took part in a long Chapter meeting, and returned to Winton for Selwyn's confirmation. On Sunday 200 boys at Communion, including Walter and Selwyn.

" *Dec.* 13.—My last Sunday at home before the Chester campaign. It will be very expensive. Very funny paragraphs in the Chester papers. My singing the Litany ' excited surprise and admira-

[1] Sister of Bishop Charles Mackenzie, first Bishop of the Universities' Mission to Central Africa.

tion.' My 'venerable appearance showed well by the side of my less-favoured brethren.' If my 'ministrations should prove as acceptable as my presence is portly and characteristic, I shall be no unfit successor to Dr. MacNeill.'"

HOME LETTERS

"CHESTER, *January* 1869.

"After all, we are all here. The second detachment consisted of fifteen people and thirty-six packages. Edith, George Ridding, and the dogs arrived at midnight on Christmas Eve. This is a large house—a great boon to us : it is comfortable, but the furniture is very old, much of it of the last century. The Canons share one house, so they can seldom meet—or rather, their families cannot. Each one has a cupboard in which the goods of the different Canons are kept, and the choosing of a new carpet should require a Chapter meeting. The town is most interesting, but the streets at this moment are very dirty. This, it was explained to us, is owing to the Gulf Stream ! The Cathedral music is excellent. There is a crowded nave service on Sunday evenings, with a volunteer choir of a hundred voices. One of the Canons asked a bargee what he thought of the suggestion of discontinuing this service in summer, and the answer was, ' If we keep on coming, you have no right to leave it off.' The Miss Wilbrahams, who live here, have worked for years in the large Irish quarter of the town. The Deanery is next door, and Dean Howson, on looking in the first evening, must have been horrified at our numbers.

"It is snowing fast, and the Welsh hills from the old walls look like a range of Alps. We feel very gay after the deep silence of Brighstone, for there is much going out in the evenings, and we have been to several dances at the Castle. My

14

father and Alice dined and slept at Hawarden, and came upon the new Lord-Lieutenant just starting for Ireland ; the luggage was standing in the front hall. An Irish Archdeacon was there, helping to arrange matters relating to the Irish Church ; he was very unhappy, and talked a great deal to the new Canon. My father finds preaching in the Cathedral most interesting ; he constantly receives notes afterwards from strangers, asking questions, or making criticisms, but always showing interest in what was said. He declares that it is worth while preaching to such wide-awake people, after the sleepy south.

" The brothers have left for Oxford and Winchester, but Selwyn is to remain at home for a year, and my father will teach him. It is a great experiment. Selwyn is very quick at comprehending people, and is more like an equal in his love and understanding of his father than his little youngest son. He is a favourite with everyone.

" We have been repeatedly assured that it is commonly said that 'the Daisy Chain is in residence.' We have real difficulty in explaining that our only likeness to it, at the time it was written, was in our being a large family. All the striking coincidences have happened since its publication, and were of the nature of prophecy—viz., the pretty second daughter marrying ' George Rivers ' (which used to distress Mary), which happened when Mary was fourteen years old, long before Miss Yonge had ever heard George Ridding's name. Then the mixture of our two brothers-in-law, William Awdry and Charles Martin,[1] reminds people of ' Norman's '

[1] See page 139. Scholar of New College, Oxford, 1859 ; Stanhope Prize, 1862 ; First Class and B.A., 1863 ; Senior Student of Christ Church, 1864 ; Assistant Master at Harrow, 1869 ; Warden of St. Peter's College, Radley, 1871 ; Rector of Woodnorton, Norfolk, 1879 ; Poulshot, Wiltshire, 1883 ; Dartington, Devonshire, 1891 ; Rural Dean of Totnes ; died 1910.

old schoolfellow, 'Charles Cheviot,' settling down as master in the old school at Stoneborough. But W. Awdry became Second master at Winchester last year, and Dora and Charles Martin were only engaged to be married last month, whilst the book was published in 1856! Robert got the Newdigate thirteen years later, having been ten years old when 'Norman May' was invented, and when even George had not yet gone to Oxford, or gained any of his future University prizes. The quasi-engagement between 'Blanche' and 'Hector Ernescliffe' has a very dim likeness to Kitty and Henry Barter's fancy for each other from girl and boy days, but Miss Yonge could never have heard of it until their engagement in 1863. Yesterday Selwyn was asked whether he was 'Tom,' and had the pleasure of answering, ' "The Daisy Chain" was written before I was born.' We can hardly call it a connection with the book that, when Miss Yonge began writing sequels to her stories, my father made her promise that she would never allow 'Ethel May' to be married, nor 'Dr. May' to die." [1]

From GEORGE MOBERLY

"BRIGHSTONE, *April* 1869.

"I have agreed to edit the Keble correspondence with some misgiving, for I am not at all satisfied with my performance in the Poems, and I fear they regard me as more entirely in agreement with Mr. Keble's views than I am. Kind words from Sir John Coleridge about my work in the Poems. Macmillan declines the Pindar on the ground of 'too much in hand.' I have finished six chapters of the Romans. Now that I have the Keble correspondence before me, I should like to get that

---

[1] This last promise became a difficulty; for before Miss Yonge had done writing, "Dr. May" had become so old that it was obvious that he ought to die; but she always laughingly recalled her promise.

work off my hands ; and with good daily industry
I might perhaps do so by the end of May."

HOME LETTERS

"BRIGHSTONE, *July* 1869.

" The choral society has given a most successful
concert.   The villagers came in crowds, labourers
hurrying from the hayfields to be in good time.
We have had three engaged couples here—George
and Esther de Castro, Dora and Charles Martin,
and Johnnie and Caroline Hunter.   It is really
serious for us in a small house.   Fortunately we
have had glorious weather the last fortnight, and
the garden is looking perfect with all the white
lilies in bloom.   Yesterday we walked to Brooke
along the cliff, with Johnnie and Carrie.   The sea
was the deepest purple and green against the red
cliffs, and the seagulls floated upwards in flocks,
crying and yapping as we passed.   Ships are shy of
our dangerous bay, and we do not see any beyond
an occasional ocean steamer on the extreme horizon.
The great loneliness adds a grandeur to our sea.
Nothing disturbs the gulls and cormorants.   From
the downs there is a sort of opalescent colouring
over sea and sky, owing to our being on an island.

" We are getting quite at home on our island,
though at first we fancied it would be so small that
there might be some danger of walking over the
edge, and felt surprised to see houses and men of
the usual size.   But we do not yet call it ' *the* island,'
as is done in the village, or talk of the inhabitants
of England as ' overreigners.' "

"BRIGHSTONE, *Aug.* 1869.

" A great change is in front of us.   Bishop
Hamilton of Salisbury has been very ill for some
time, and not long ago my father received a sound-
ing letter as to whether he would be likely to

accept the bishopric. Quite accidentally the post failed us for some days, and we first heard of the Bishop's death from Mr. Robert Wilson, of Rownhams, who came to stay here. On Thursday morning the post arrived duly, and in the course of half a second every individual recognised the signature on the outside of one of the letters, though all read it upside down and some were in the anteroom. Edith said in a low voice, ' I am done for.' She has been so especially happy here ; and by their kindliness and unfeigned sympathy she and my father were bringing every one round them—dissenters and all.

" Now the first shock is over, my father is certainly rejoicing in the prospect of ' being at work again ' ; and besides, owing to the relaxing air, he is never quite well here. My mother is very quiet about leaving, though she has thoroughly enjoyed the country and her many friends amongst the villagers. The household and village are much excited ; the housemaids cried, as they made the beds, between joy at ' the Doctor ' being made a Bishop and grief at leaving Brighstone, the choral society, and all their friends here. Russell, the old clerk, is triumphant : he considers that he has *brought up* and *sent out* two Bishops ! "

GEORGE MOBERLY'S JOURNAL

"*Aug.* 5, 1869.—A mighty change ! I have accepted the Bishopric of Salisbury. . . . God guide and sanctify me, and make me less unfit to follow in the holy steps of my two predecessors, and bless me in this high, responsible, and sacred office. What a prospect of work, trouble, and absence of peace of mind it opens before me and Mary ! I shall, of course, relinquish the Keble papers.

"*Aug.* 8.—Letters from Liddon, Hook, Lear, and Wilson. There is cordial kindness towards me : thank God for it ! How shall I succeed to so great a man and so great a work ?

"*Aug.* 15.—I am overwhelmed with letters—202 in three days. I have answered at the rate of 40 a day.

"*Aug.* 21.—I was at Sarum on Tuesday, and saw Mrs. Hamilton. Went over the Palace and gardens, dined and slept at Bishopstone." [1]

HOME LETTERS

"BRIGHSTONE, 1869.

" Maggie is now seventeen years old, and has ' come out ' at a Regatta ball at Yarmouth. She went in white with myrtle in her hair, and must have looked charming, for Mrs. Cameron took a fancy to her and made her three sons dance with her. Mrs. Cameron put her arm round Maggie's waist and begged her to bring her father to Freshwater to be photographed, and added, ' And then, my dear, you had better come with him and be photographed too.' She came back from Westover to-day loaded with magnolias, begonias, and ice-plants. Edward and Walter, who have just returned from a tour in the Lakes with Robert, are greatly impressed with Maggie's turning into a grown-up young lady, whilst Selwyn is quite pathetic and says sadly, ' Oh, Maggie, you *are* a swell ! '

" BRIGHSTONE, *Sept.* 1869.

" Dora's wedding took place yesterday. Though Charles's family is of more moderate dimensions than the Awdrys, we had to make great preparations. There has been a great gale blowing all the

---

[1] Dr. Liddon and I received him in the library, and showed him over everything. When he was gone, we walked up and down talking it over, and I have now a withered flower H. P. L. picked under the library window, saying, " Sic transit."—H. L. S. L. (Mrs. Sidney Lear).

week, and though it was not quite so terrific on Tuesday, yet it was a bad day, everything being enveloped in a fog which constantly fell in a thick drizzle. Fortunately, it held up as we went to church. Uncle Richard Church read the Service and Mr. Fearon was the best man.[1] The harvest decorations were still up, and the music was very grand, for the choral society offered its assistance. When the bride and bridegroom drove off, they would not tell us where they were going to, but assured us that nothing would induce them to leave the island as long as the wind blows great guns.

"As soon as they were gone, we put on our oldest clothes to face the weather and look at the sea. It was wonderfully grand ; the great waves rolling and roaring on to the shore, whilst gleams of pale sunshine sometimes lighted up the crests of the waves and turned the yellow foam in the pools into peacock bubbles. We could not hear ourselves speak, and got thoroughly drenched with the spray and foam, which flew about wildly. With streaming hair and battered clothes we fought our way home to find an elegant tea laid out in the anteroom, reminding us that we were still going on with the wedding day. We were glad to have the lights brought in and to shut out the storm.

"There has been no tidal wave, and Brighstone has not been swept away, though the papers did their best to frighten us. The chief wave has been that of new Bishops : Mr. Mackarness is going to Oxford and Bishop Wilberforce to Winchester."

"BRIGHSTONE, *Oct.* 1869.

"The entire party, excepting our mother and Annie, went to Westminster Abbey for the Con-

[1] Page 139. Afterwards Headmaster of Winchester College and Archdeacon and Canon of Winchester.

secration. We could hardly find places, though the doors had only been opened five minutes ; and during the service we were constantly discovering well-known faces. Amongst others there were Miss Yonge, Mr. Wilson, Mr. Peter Young, and numbers of Wykehamists. Bishops Wilberforce and Jacobson were the presenting Bishops. It was a glorious service ; whilst the rochet was being put on the choir sang ' How lovely are the messengers,' and later the treble solo of Atwood's ' Come, Holy Ghost' seemed to float up to the roof. There were four hundred communicants.

" A home party of eighteen lunched together, after which Willy Awdry took Selwyn for a walk to show him London in the shortest possible space of time. At Waterloo Miss Yonge joined the party, and we had an extremely merry journey to Winchester. Papa walked down to College with Selwyn, who, to his intense amusement, gently chaffed him all the way, though really immensely proud of *his* Bishop. The Cathedral and College bells were ringing merrily. This morning George Ridding and Selwyn went to the station to see every one off."

HOME LETTERS

" Nov. 1869.

" The enthronement will be to-morrow, and the first Confirmation tour will begin on Monday morning. My father went to do homage at Windsor yesterday. The Queen was going to hold a Council, so he travelled in a special train with a large party of gentlemen, and six royal carriages were waiting at the station to take them to the Castle. The Castle was looking most beautiful in the rich autumn sunlight. They all waited together in the corridor, where he had some talk with Mr. Gladstone, and congratulated the Mayor of Chester, who was waiting with others to be knighted. We begged for a description of the Queen, but our Bishop said he did not know how she looked, except that she was very much amused when he tried to get to the door backwards and took a wrong shot at it."

"Alice and Edith, who were the last to leave Brighstone, say that they received enough affection and good wishes from every one to last them all their lives. One very poor woman had made them three most ingenious horsehair rings with beads.

"Of tangible results of our stay here there are few indeed. The church is now fully lighted for evening service, largely through the concerts given by the village choral society. There is a choir of men and boys, but unsurpliced and sitting round the organ at the west end of the church; at present singing in parts is a great incentive to attending choir practices; we hope that the further steps of putting on surplices and sitting at the east end will follow by their own wish, as so much else has done. The third addition is a gift from Miss Yonge of the two oak chairs within the altar rails. For us there are friendships which we value greatly, making the circle of those we love very much larger."

GEORGE MOBERLY'S JOURNAL

"*Brighstone, Sept.* 1869.—George has accepted the temporary charge of the chaplaincy at Mentone. Robert is to be tutor at Christ Church at once. Selwyn darling has begun bravely and successfully at Winchester. Diocesan cares come like drops of an approaching thunderstorm. I am on the point of sending the Keble MSS. to Wilson.

"*October.*—Mr. Heygate, of Southend, succeeds me here; a good man, a Churchman. I have had a very pleasant talk with old J——, which confirms me in the thought that the people here have drawn much nearer to the Church and Church teaching than they were. It is cheering to find how affectionate they are.

" On Thursday I was consecrated Bishop of Salisbury by Tait. It was inexpressibly solemn. An immense congregation ; multitudes of my own friends ; sixty or seventy clergy in gowns. Richard Church preached excellently. Surely I ought to be better and holier after all that has happened and all those good, friendly, dear prayers. God be with us all, for Christ's sake. Amen."

CHAPTER VII

FIRST YEARS AT SALISBURY

Where'er I roam in this fair English land,
The vision of a temple meets my eyes :
Modest without ; within, all glorious rise
Its love-enclustered columns, and expand
Their slender arms.   Like olive plants they stand,
Each answering each, in home's soft sympathies,
Sisters and brothers.   At the Altar sighs
Parental fondness, and with anxious hand
Tenders its offering of young vows and prayers.
The same and not the same, go where I will,
The vision beams ! ten thousand shrines, all one.

Lyra Apostolica.

From BISHOP PATTESON

"NORFOLK ISLAND, *Nov.* 1869.

" MY DEAR DR. MOBERLY,
"Since my return from the islands a rumour
has reached us that the Bishop of Winchester has
resigned his See, and that *you* are his successor.
It is almost too good to be true.   But if it be true,
and I do earnestly trust and pray that it may be
so, indeed it will give hope and courage and fresh
life to many and many a fainting soul.   If I may
presume to say so, it is (as Mrs. Selwyn said to me
when *he* was appointed to Lichfield) ' a solemn and
anxious thing to undertake a great charge on the
top of such great expectations.' . . . Your letters
have always been a very great help to me.   I felt

that I accepted your remarks on the questions of the day ; indeed, since my dear father's death, and Judge Coleridge's inability to write so frequently as of yore, your letters, with those of Edwin Palmer, Miss Yonge, and occasionally one from G. Ridding or some one of the few, very few, like-minded friends—are the only ones on which I can rely for sound useful criticism of things and persons. Your last present to me was your Bampton Lectures, of which I need not say how both the subject and the mode of treating it make them specially valuable just now. And there is a strong personal feeling about the work and writings of one, when the public man is also the private friend, which gives a special zest to the enjoyment of reading a work of this kind. Certainly it is one of the many blessings of my life that I should somehow have been allowed to grow into this degree of intimacy with you, whom I have always known by name though I don't remember ever to have seen you. I think I first as a child became familiar with your name through good Miss Rennell, the old Dean's daughter. What a joy this would have been to dear Mr. and Mrs. Keble ! What a joy it is to C. Yonge, and there may be others close to Winchester whose lives have been closely bound up with yours.

" *Nov.* 27.—I leave this as I wrote it, though now I hear that you are Bishop of *Salisbury*, not of Winchester. I hardly stop to think whether it is Winchester or Salisbury, so great is my thankfulness and joy at the report being substantially true. Indeed, when one thinks of the peculiar difficulties of the two dioceses, it is difficult to have a choice. Salisbury must be in a very peculiar condition. . . . Hence, though it did seem that Winchester was a natural sphere for you, I can't help feeling that at Salisbury you can do (D.V.) what perhaps scarcely

SALISBURY CATHEDRAL

any one else could do. And now I rejoice that you had the opportunity of speaking with no uncertain sound in your Bampton lectures. Any one can tell what the Bishop of Salisbury holds on the great questions of Church doctrine and Church government. The diocese knows already its Bishop, not only by many former books but by his latest book. Surely you will have the confidence of all Churchmen, and be blessed to do a great work for the glory of God and the edification of the Church.

" And now, my dear Bishop of Salisbury, you will excuse my writing on so freely—too freely, I fear. I do like to think of you in that most perfect of cathedrals; send me some day a photograph of your beautiful cathedral.

" Yours very faithfully,
" J. C. PATTESON."

GEORGE MOBERLY'S JOURNAL

" *Salisbury*, 1869.—When last I wrote I was at Brighstone. I left it a few days after, to my very great regret, for I dearly loved it, and the people were full of affectionate sorrow at parting with us. I was enthroned with much ceremony on Nov. 13th, and on the 14th was carried off to confirm, and in the next three weeks had confirmed about 2,400 people. The Confirmations were delightfully interesting to me. Got on pretty well with my addresses, though they get to be very like one another. At Portland I preached to the convicts and confirmed 41. At Weymouth confirmed 175 sailor boys, presided at two S.P.G. meetings, and came home with a very bad cold. . . ."

HOME LETTERS

" WINCHESTER, *Nov.* 1869.

" Edith and I are still with George Ridding in Winchester. We have been greatly amused at the boys' wrath and protests against 'G. R.'s utter profanity' last Sunday in setting 200 lines each to 50 boys whose offence was *shirking Chapel.* Selwyn has just been up arguing hotly and declaring that their sense of duty and conscience refused to let them do anything so wrong, and going into difficult questions as to where obedience should end in such cases. One boy by way of protest wrote out the fourth commandment many times !

"We went over to Salisbury last leave out day. The drawing-room is a delicious room, 60 feet long, but not a bit too big. There are three large Queen Anne windows, at the two ends and on one side. At the north end there is a beautiful view of the Cathedral standing on the green shaven lawn with large cedar trees in front, and above them the spire rises in great peace and dignity into the blue sky. The south window is em-bowered in magnolia and pomegranate trees, and looks out upon a formal garden, bright with geraniums ; and a broad gravel walk, upon which pigeons were promenading, follows the whole length of the house. A low stone balustrade divides this garden from the field in which our three cows are tethered. In the field is a big pond surrounded with trees, and in the middle of it is a small wooded island. The house is large, with long passages, and at one end is an old oak double stair-case having two open landings. Before the floors were put in, it formed one side of the original entrance hall.

"The Dean (Hamilton) is an invalid, so his preaching-turns in the Cathedral, at Christmas, Easter, and Whitsuntide, generally fall to the Bishop. The four Canons are Archdeacon Hony, Canon Fisher, Canon Gordon, and Canon Lear. Canon Lear is an old Wykehamist, the son of a former Dean of Salisbury, and brother of Mrs. Walter Hamilton, the late Bishop's widow."

"At the confirmation at Portland, the Bishop preached to 1500 prisoners. The same afternoon he confirmed the boys on the *Boscawen* training-ship. The contrast between the downcast look and the cropped heads of the prisoners with the fresh, manly sailor lads, having *such* heads of hair, was most striking."[1]

"The first ordination Sunday was bright and fine. Mr. Robert Wilson, of Rownhams, preached: he and Uncle Richard Church are two of the examining chaplains. Mr. Wilson has accepted a prebendal stall here, and as he and Bishop Hamilton were dear friends, it is a pleasure to all concerned. Mr. Yeatman, an old Wykehamist,[2] was ordained, and his mother and sister[3] joined us in

[1] Later on, Bishop Moberly instituted the plan of sitting to confirm, and only one at a time, unless the numbers were over one hundred, in which case two were confirmed together.

"I have recently adopted a practice borrowed from that of Bishop Selwyn, of Lichfield.' It is, to ask the separate answer of each candidate to the great question asked in the Service. For this purpose I shall be greatly obliged to the clergyman at whose church the Confirmation takes place to furnish me with a list of the Christian and surnames of all the candidates, and to take care that they are seated in church exactly in the same order in which their names appear on the list. When, then, I have asked the question *once* only, I shall call upon the boy or girl nearest to me by their Christian name, to answer 'I do,' and having answered it, to kneel down and pray for the grace of God to enable them to keep their vow; for which purpose it is very desirable that they should be furnished with an appropriate prayer. I adopted this practice last year in Wiltshire, and found it useful and impressive. I think that the clergy also, where it was tried, shared my impression, as did also the congregations present."—*Charge,* 1879.

[2] Afterwards chaplain to Bishop Moberly; second clerical Secretary to the Salisbury Synod, 1875; Vicar of Netherbury, Dorsetshire; St. Bartholomew's, Sydenham; Suffragan Bishop of Southwark, Coadjutor to the Bishop of Rochester; Bishop of Worcester.

[3] Afterwards the first Head of the College of Grey Ladies, at Blackheath.

the evening, when we had a party of forty, including the students of the Theological College. It is a great pleasure to the Bishop to find another old Wykehamist (Rev. John Daubeny) here as Principal of the Theological College."

"We are to be all together this Christmas, an event which has not happened for years, as George has been so much at Mentone during the winters. He has just become English chaplain at Bonn, and is to be married in February.

"At Chester last winter we sisters dressed ourselves alike, and found that it had puzzled those people who had desired to know one sister from another. Remembering this, and feeling mischievous, we propose to do the same again."

"We have made acquaintance with Ethel Hamilton, the late Bishop's eldest daughter, about twenty years old. She came bravely to call on us, though greatly tried, and a few days later walked round the garden with Edith. She has been sitting with me in their old schoolroom, and asked me eagerly where was the eighth sister who had been with us in Cathedral the Sunday we were all together. I inquired laughingly whether seven sisters were not enough, and on her persisting that there had been eight, asked for a description of the person she had seen. She gave me one very carefully, and I said, 'You have described my sister Mary, who died ten years ago.' The subject dropped immediately, and we have not referred to it since." [1]

[1] Many years later, when we were living at The Hall, New Street, Salisbury, I told my mother of this conversation. Hearing that I had never shown Ethel any picture of Mary, she begged me to do so. That evening I went to the Close to say good-bye to the Hamiltons before returning to Oxford. Ethel said, "What have you got there?" Putting an old coloured daguerreotype of Mary into her hands, I answered, "It is the likeness of some one you have never seen." As she looked at it her face flushed up to her hair, and she said, "It is the sister who

"The canvas screen is being put up across the nave to divide it from the choir, which is to be restored as a memorial to Bishop Hamilton. It is a pleasure to see the screen shutting off the Lady Chapel removed at last. It must be lighter and airier in the nave, where we shall now be for many years. We have had to sit in boxes round the choir behind the stalls, and to enter them from staircases in the aisles. The box is small and stuffy, the ceiling very low, and the old red baize smells fusty to a degree. There are no lights in the Cathedral, so on winter Sunday afternoons there can be no sermons, and the Dean and the minor canon in course have each a little flickering candle. Every one else is in pitch darkness, unless private candles are brought. We never expect to see into

was with you all in Cathedral the first Christmas you were here. I recognise her perfectly." Ethel then told me that when we first arrived at Salisbury, she had been staying at Highnam Court, in Gloucestershire, with her uncle and aunt, Mr. and Mrs. Gambier Parry; that on Christmas Eve she had, for the first time, returned to their new abode in the Close, and that the thought of us at the Palace had been a great trial to her. On one of the Sundays immediately after Christmas she went to the Celebration at the Cathedral, and, being well out of sight herself in one of the boxes behind the stalls, became aware that we were opposite to her in the stalls. She thought, "I *will* accept them : I *will* look at them, and try to like them." She lifted her head and gave us a steady look, and, more than once, counted *eight sisters in bonnets just alike*. Her eye fell especially on this sister, and she said to herself, "That is a pretty face, with a sweet upward look. I will make a friend of her." She saw this sister again, standing with us in a group at the Altar rail, and noticed her with pleasure. Afterwards, when Ethel was introduced to one and another, she looked in vain for this sister, and at last asked about her. Of course I wanted to hear more, and asked many questions; and Ethel exclaimed, "How I wish you had questioned me about it before, when it was all fresh and I could have told you so much ; now it is so long ago."

Ethel Hamilton was our dear friend through our whole time at Salisbury. If anything, she was lacking in imagination ; her honesty, downrightness, and accuracy of mind and word were so great, that we used to tell her that her efforts to avoid the smallest exaggeration made her letters quite prosy. She died in 1895.

15

our books in the afternoon. No evening service can be held in the Cathedral, and the Lent sermons have to be in the parish churches."

" Yesterday a diocesan conference on the Education Bill was held in the drawing-room ; about 120 gentlemen came—clergy, landlords, tradesmen, church-people, and dissenters. People were pleased at all shades of opinion having been called together, and at the good chairmanship. The Bishop has gone this morning to the Revision committee of the New Testament at Westminster, and next Sunday he will be confirming and preaching at Westbury. There is no doubt that he is in his element, and thoroughly enjoying having to do with people again."

G. Moberly's Journal

" *Salisbury, April* 1870.—. . . Preached on Sunday on the Temptation at St. James', Chapel Royal ; walked home with the Gladstones. At 7 p.m. preached at St. Paul's to a mighty congregation on the Transfiguration. I was also caught for a confirmation at King's College School. It was pleasant to renew an old acquaintance with Dr. Barry, and very interesting to confirm schoolboys for the first time. To-morrow to Beaminster ; next day Sherborne, school and Abbey ; next day St. Thomas' sermon. Sunday sermon at Harnham and confirmation at St. Martin's. I have a vast amount to do ; and, but for occasional infirmity of body, enjoy it.

" *May.*—Much in Town : this time for Convocation. On the 19th will be the second reading of the Wife's Sister Bill. I take a part in the debates, and his Lordship of —— seems to think it his particular duty and power to sit down upon me. The Keble College opening will be on June 23rd, the day after Lord Salisbury's Installation as Chancellor."

HOME LETTERS

"SALISBURY, *May* 1870.

" We find out now what a lovely garden this is. Trees close it in, and we have discovered where the delicious deep shadows are, filling the pond with green reflections. The horse-chestnuts are in full bloom, and the crimson and white thorns are coming out in the meadow and in the shrubberies. The weather is hot and beautiful, and we sit out all day on the lawn under the Cathedral. The Miss Paynes from Chester are staying with us, and are punting with Maggie on the pond. Yesterday we took them to Winchester. After lunch we sat in the new cricket-field lately made by George Ridding (who has turned the canals) and watched the M.C.C. match. The meadows were looking lovely, the river blue and sparkling, and a blue haze over the downs. We went to hear G. R. call names on school steps. Many old friends were in the cricket-field as well as Mr. and Mrs. William Lyttelton, who are staying with the Awdrys in College. Maggie and Selwyn were delighted to meet and take a walk together ; he is senior in Classicus Paper, and in a great state of happiness."

" WINCHESTER, *June* 1870.

" What a glorious victory Winchester has won ! When it came to eleven to win the excitement was intense. At two to win the Eton field standing near us tore up the grass ; it was he who let the ball slip and gave us the winning run. The scene then was peculiar : every one ran about shaking hands with every one else, with their hats stuck on the back of their heads, shouting, not to say screaming. The boys were never tired of carrying

Herbert Awdry and Guinness about : Guinness battered and his arms nearly shaken off. There were good speeches afterwards in Hall, showing the kindly feeling between Eton and Winchester.

" Have you had an account of the Keble College opening ? The day before was spent in decorating the temporary chapel. Kitty, Maggie, Robert, and Johnnie, with the Miss Wilbrahams, helped the Keble people from early morning till 12.30 at night. Kitty and Maggie found it impossible to go back to Shipton, so lay down for a few hours in a lodging at Oxford and went on with the work early next morning. Charlotte Yonge joined them, and after the great services went back with them to Shipton-under-Wychwood. Though dreadfully tired, they managed to get in a good deal of talk."

GEORGE MOBERLY'S JOURNAL

" *June* 1870.—I cannot go to Oxford because of the Revision committee. . . . The Charge looms before me. I am bitterly assaulted for the West-minster Abbey Communion. . . . Richard and Helen Church, with their three girls, are with us. To-day to Winchester for the Election and opening of the Moberly Library.[1]

" *July.*—I have been to Winton with Mary and half a dozen children—a dinner-party and concert. Tuesday the Library ; very cordial, very interest-ing, very fatiguing. Sir William Erle most affec-tionate. Dinner in Hall, speeches, and Domum. Home next day ; Bishops Harris and Macdougall

---

[1] "George Ridding rushed up to Emily in the Second master's house and said, ' Have you a Vulgate here ? I want an inscription for the Library archway, and it must begin and end with words of two letters.' She turned over a leaf or two of the Vulgate, and pointed to 'Si hæc scitis, beati eritis si feceritis ea.' ' The very thing ! ' he exclaimed, and with the open book in his hands ran down to the architect, who was waiting below ; and the words were placed at once on the lintel."

and Dean Hook to dinner. Thursday a largely-attended Communion, and 120 people to lunch ; followed by an evening meeting for S.P.G.

"*Aug.*—Sir William Heathcote is a Privy Councillor ; and I have had the pleasure of writing to congratulate him. I regret that I could not take part in the Education debate ; it was prevented by the engagements in Winton and Salisbury, made long ago. Public affairs very momentous. The French defeated at Wissembourg ; routed at Wörth by the Crown Prince ; driven from Saarbrücke by General von Steinmetz : must now encounter a general pitched battle against three armies full of victory. Anything less than complete success is ruin to the Emperor and submission to terms.

" *Aug.* 16.—The first day of Visitation is over. I put in three pages about the Westminster Communion, which I hope may have quieted uneasiness. I have been very busy about a conference on the state of diocesan education in view of the working of the Education Bill.

" *Bournemouth, Sept.* 1870. — My sermon and paper for the Congress are looming thunder-like before me. Paris is in the agony of a coming siege. Alas for the loss of H.M.S. *Captain !* I preach this morning at St. Peter's, but do not celebrate, my usage and that of the clergy at St. Peter's not being uniform.

" *Salisbury, October.*—I came here yesterday for a conference on the Education Bill, which has been continued to-day ; not, I think, without fair promise of good effect. We had Lords Shaftesbury, Ailesbury, Nelson, and Heytesbury, and many clergy and laity : much union of feeling.

" *Oct.* 28.—The anniversary of my consecration. God pardon me for all the shortcomings, for all sins of commission and omission, that have marked the first year of my episcopate.

"*Nov.* 23.—Preach to-night in the Theological College, on Sunday in the nave ; next week at St. Paul's, for the consecration of the Bishops of Sierra Leone and Mauritius. I am beginning to break ground about a Diocesan Synod. I think of asking six wise men to come here and talk, a cleric and a layman from each archdeaconry, and then a sort of convocation of Notables to frame a constitution with duties—Lord Nelson, Sanctuary, Farrer, and others. I have written to Hony. . . .

"*Nov.* 27.—I have been preaching to a very large congregation in the nave, lighted for the first time with gas. The contrast with last year was remarkable. Then, on Advent Sunday afternoon, a few ladies in the boxes, ill-lighted by candles, attended prayers without a sermon.

"*Jan.* 31, 1871.—I have had a meeting at my house to shape plans for a Conference or Synod. We met Hony,[1] Sanctuary,[2] Huxtable,[3] Raikes,[4] Farrer,[5] Lear,[6] and Lord Heytesbury. It was highly satisfactory, and so were the letters I received from others. We propose the Conference in the Chapter House on August 9th.

"*Feb.*—I think I must give up my Fellowship at Winchester : simply and solely for —— sake ! I cannot ensure his election, but I must give him the chance. Paris fallen ! and the terms of peace proposed gigantically hard. " Dame Europa " has been attributed to the Dean of Salisbury, to Archdeacon Hony, to Lear, to Armfield, to me, to Stanley, and no doubt to many others.[7]

[1] W E. Hony, Archdeacon of Sarum 1846-75.
[2] Thomas Sanctuary, Archdeacon of Dorset 1862-89.
[3] Anthony Huxtable, Archdeacon of Dorset 1836-62.
[4] Charles Raikes, Esq., C.S.I.
[5] Oliver W. Farrer, Esq., of Binnegar Hall, Wareham.
[6] Francis Lear, Archdeacon of Sarum, 1875.
[7] A political skit called " Dame Europa's School," by Mr. Pullen, Minor Canon of Salisbury.

" *Feb.* 14.—To-day a long debate on the Revision Question ; what the result will be I cannot foresee. It looks like an overthrow of the whole Revision. I spoke—too eagerly, and trod on the toes of at least two bishops, and exposed myself to a telling reply from Temple.

" *Feb.* 17.—Stormy debates in Convocation. We have been gloriously inconsistent, first laying out the broadest basis of critical scholarship, then turning a man out for Socinianism, and then letting ourselves be overruled by the Lower House. But I stand to it all. The theological difficulty was imported by Stanley, and we, having condemned the evil that came of it, gladly got back to the breadth of the original resolution. . . .

" *Feb.* 27.—Though it is Ember week and I am wanted at home, I have come to be at the Jerusalem Chamber. I had resolved to appear on general grounds, but a letter from ——, announcing his non-appearance, because of Vance Smith's declared intention to come, enforces my original purpose. I shall have to take the chair ; and we must expect a storm, if on nothing else, on the position of the co-opted members of the company. . . . Scott and Bickersteth strongly urge my presence.

" *March.*—Dear George is the father of a little son, now four weeks old. He is also presented to the living of Duntesbourne Rous, in Gloucestershire. Bob is gone over to Bonn, with a nurse, to superintend the passage home of little George the Third." [1]

From MISS YONGE
" OTTERBOURNE.

" MY DEAR EMILY,
        " An odd question, but can you tell me what Edward first taught himself on the violin ? I want

[1] George Keble Moberly.

Lance Underwood to do it, and must mention some tune. . . ."

From Selwyn

"Winchester, *March* 19, 1871.

"Dear Edward,

"I hope you managed to make enough personal and other remarks in your letter. All the same, it was a pleasant surprise to see a letter in that bad handwriting of yours. Well! I should be ashamed of being afraid of the scarlet fever; why, I (hardy boy) rub my hands at the bare idea of our having eighteen cases, and two of them awfully bad. The athletics are on Thursday, and the heats on Tuesday. A mill with the cads (N.B.—Edward loq. : What??) is expected, since only those who have tickets are going to be allowed to enter.

"I know what it will be when you get this. The gong will have sounded a long time, and nine will have struck by the Cathedral and stable clocks, when you wake and get up, and opening the door, will find Walter asleep, or perhaps wide awake thinking. Laddie will come under the window and wonder when you are coming down; and at last, frowning, you will go into the dining-room with a resigned face and a sarcastic remark about Walter (to screen yourself). Edith or Maggie will be making the coffee, and the other one of them will be on the other side of you. On your way into the dining-room, you will have seen Rachel dusting the piano, and Henry doing something to the lamps, whilst Edwin is making up the fire.

"Finally, at the extreme end of breakfast, a cheerful step will be heard, and Walter will come in, and, kissing mamma very loud, will chuck Maggie under the chin and sit down to begin. Mamma will make some remark in a low voice about the boys coming down late, which Walter will affect not to hear, whilst Alice answers it from the top of the table. It will probably be, ' Come, Walter, you are very late.' Edith will say, ' Walter, did you hear me call you this morning ? ' I can't go any further, but could fill a book with the sayings and doings of the family. Oh! what jokes you are !

" Your affectionate brother,

" SELWYN.

" I intend to come on the 25th."

From MARY ANNE MOBERLY

"SALISBURY, *April 5,* 1871

" DEAREST ALICE,

" This is a sad disappointment about dear Selwyn, the very day he was to have come home ; I only hope the disappointment will not make him more ill. You must not over-exert yourself or take less food, not even on Good Friday. I hardly think you should stay in College after being much with him ; perhaps you might sleep at G. Ridding's."

" Here mamma tells me to go on : my love and blessing are rich in Kingsgate Street with my dear eldest and youngest. I do not wish you to be guided by anything but the doctor's advice, and to that I hope you will adhere exactly. . . . My dear child, I don't like your being away ; but I rejoice at my boy having your company. If I were not too full of business with all these sermons I should come over. Give my darling boy my kindest love.

" Your most affectionate father,

" GEORGE SARUM."

HOME LETTERS

" On St. Matthias' day Selwyn came to Salisbury for leave out, and we had a particularly happy day.

We were all very much struck by his increased height and broad shoulders, along with a greater manliness of bearing which had come since we had last seen him.   He had always been the most charming of schoolboys, and now, within two months of being seventeen years old, he seemed suddenly to have become a man.   Something of this must have made his father shake hands with him on his leaving, instead of giving him the usual kiss.   We remarked on this, and objected, and the Bishop said, ' He is too old to kiss,' and then, taking Selwyn's face in his two hands, said most lovingly, ' but he shall not be too old this time.' "

" The holidays were to begin on Wednesday in Holy Week, and the night before Selwyn felt unwell. The boys who were packing in his room suggested that he should send his luggage on with one of them and follow when he could ; but Selwyn answered, with his usual gentle considerateness, 'I could not do that, for if my luggage were to arrive alone, my father would be anxious until I appeared.' The next morning he ' went continent,' and, scarlet fever having declared itself, he was sent into lodgings in Kingsgate Street with a nurse. The next day, Thursday in Holy Week, our father received a telegram from George Ridding : 'Decidedly worse and bad.   Alice comes to me.   Mrs. Ferris to him.   Your room ready.'   Mamma's face suddenly flushed, but without a word she went to get ready.   Papa and Robert caught the next train, and mamma with Beard[1] (who had nursed Selwyn from his birth) followed as soon as possible.   The next telegram, ' More comfortable,' was a great relief, and so was Robert's return.   On Good

[1] Mrs. Ann Beard came to us as nurse when there were seven children in the nursery, and three more followed. In a few weeks she gave notice to leave, but was persuaded to try to go on ; and remained forty-six years.

Friday morning our father returned greatly comforted ; he had to preach that evening in the
Cathedral, which he did to a large congregation,
ignorant, of course, of his great anxiety. On the
morning of Easter eve papa and Robert went
back to Winchester : they were only just in time,
for Selwyn died that morning."

"We have had a long letter from Alice this
morning, saying that mamma is fairly well, but full
of headache. She and my father spend their time
in the schoolroom in College Street, and keep
entirely away from every one for fear of infection ;
but they had a Celebration on Easter Day. Beard
came back for a few hours to-day. She said that
when she first went into Selwyn's room on Thursday he was so charmed to see her and said, ' You
dear Beardie to come and see me ! ' She said, ' Miss
Edith sent me ' (for it had been Edith's arrangement), and he exclaimed, ' *Dear* old Edie ! ' He
told Mrs. Ferris all about Salisbury and Laddie,
and that he had had such a nice leave out to
Emily. In his delirium on Friday night, he said,
' Papa has so many, he can spare the youngest.'
Beard asked if his head ached. ' No,' he answered,
' I have no pain anywhere. I feel as though I
should like a good walk.' He lay not only smiling
but laughing to himself ; he read inscriptions on
the ceiling, and grew quite angry because they could
not see them. He said, ' Now I see a bright eye
looking at me,' and then assured them that some
one had come in and was standing by his bed, and
that he must get up and go with him. Mamma
asked him whether he sent his love to Maggie.
' Oh, yes, and to Edward and Walter—to every one
of them all.' He constantly mentioned Walter.
On hearing that it was Good Friday, he remarked
that it would be ' beautiful when we get to Easter

eve.' He had talked a great deal about going home to Salisbury until the last morning, when mamma told him that he was going home—to his *real* home. He quite understood, and from that time said no more about Salisbury.

"When his father came into the room he saw that there was no hope left. Selwyn greeted him with smiles, and could not bear to lose sight of him for a moment, and made him and mamma each hold a hand : he repeated the Lord's Prayer after them with difficulty, but smiled brightly and constantly, to show that he understood all that was said and knew them all. George Ridding was there. His father's and mother's arms were round Selwyn when he died, quite peacefully and smiling to the last. Beard was much overcome. Mamma quiet and composed.

"Robert, meanwhile, was waiting in College Street with Alice and Emily, and after the sad party came back to the old home he returned to us at Salisbury. We were all sitting on the garden steps outside the schoolroom door, making Easter wreaths for the Chapel, when Edith appeared, with Robert behind her. We knew more from her face than from her words how it was. No one spoke, and Maggie soon disappeared. After a time Edith brought her out into the garden, and we all walked up and down the meadow with arms linked together. It was a soft, grey evening, and the thrushes were singing loudly. Not long after, Mrs. Walter Hamilton called, and, for the first time since she left the Palace, came up into the drawing-room. She shook hands with the brothers and made herself known to them, and took Maggie into her arms and cried with her, saying how dearly they all loved Selwyn, with his bright, gracious, lovable ways ; how often he had gone with Clement (Hamilton), to have tea with them, though we had hardly known it ; and how people in Salisbury who scarcely knew him spoke of him as ' that nice boy ' and had a remembrance of something bright and winning.

"Emily and Willy Awdry arrived that evening, making nine of us to go to early Communion on Easter morning. The joyful music and the great Easter hymns have been such a pleasure. Arthur died just before Christmas and Selwyn just before Easter, so we shall have the two associations. Arthur was Selwyn's godfather, and they died about the same age at school."

From REV. E. SERGEANT

"CULVERLEA, WINCHESTER, *Easter Sunday*

"MY DEAR LORD,

". . . I know that you gave me a pure Christian boy to take charge of, and I was proud to have him, and felt grateful for your confidence. I hoped all good things of him. I never heard him say one wrong or unkind word ; he was gentle, very sensitive, very obedient. I am sure he was respected in the school ; he was generally liked, and a great favourite with a few. His natural reserve a little prevented me from becoming very intimate with him, but I always hoped some day to know him more intimately. I am now full of regret that I did not strive to know him better, for I quite feel that I have lost no common treasure from my house, but one of its very best inmates. He seemed to me to be the most natural and modest of boys. He once—in one of the few long conversations I had with him—spoke of the praise I had bestowed on him with a half joy and half regret, the pleasure arising evidently from the feeling of satisfaction it had given you, and the regret from the modest desire of disclaiming any merit. He seemed almost too much afraid of being overpraised. His last conversation with me was on the subject of our house comforts ; and he had good-naturedly promised to explain to you some points about them, which, he admitted, he might, in his zeal, have rendered too prominent. May God bless you, my dear Lord, always, and, when the first sharp pain has passed away, draw you towards us who are still working on at your own old Winchester. Your letter read like a farewell, but you did not say it— nor will I."

From MISS F. WILBRAHAM

" What can I say, my dear and sisterly friend, but that your tidings just received have filled my heart to overflowing with grief, and yet with heavenly thoughts and fears ? Tears come faster than words at the thought of the darling boy, so bright and angel-like even in death, now with the angels and with the spirits of just men made perfect, and with the dear holy friend who took him from my arms and signed the sign of the Cross on his forehead. And he is in that Holy Presence too, the crown of all our longings. . . . Thank you more than ever for making him mine. Annie's letter made my heart thrill with its details, especially of his having an ' À Kempis ' by him and reading it nightly—dear, gentle, good boy !"

HOME LETTER

"SALISBURY, *April* 1871.

" We all went to Winchester yesterday. It was an exquisite day, perfectly warm and sunny. The rain the day before had made everything green, and such primroses and anemones ; and the clouds, soft and fleecy, made passing shadows on the fields and woods. Mamma had made a large white azalea cross, Clement Hamilton one of red and

white azaleas, Edith one of primroses, and Edwin
(the footman) a wreath of daisies and yew. Every
one carried flowers. There were many people in
the cemetery chapel, amongst others Sir William
Heathcote (Selwyn's godfather), General Wilbraham from Netley, many of the Winchester masters
and clergy from the town. Warden Lee had asked
to read the Service. The grave is on the breezy
hillside at the edge of the slope—St. Catherine's
Hill in the bright afternoon light, St. Cross basking
below, and the distance towards the Isle of Wight
blue and soft. . . .

" George Ridding has felt it dreadfully. Alice
says tears have been constantly in his eyes, at
which he was as much surprised as she. Finding
him so easily overcome, we insisted on his coming
back to Salisbury with us. When Alice said good-
bye to old Mr. Ridding (who lives with George)
she kissed his hand, and he said, ' Bless you all for
taking such care of my boy !' When we reached
home, mamma, who was tired and full of headache, went straight to bed, but we had evening
chapel and sang ' Jesus lives.' The feeling of the
smiling death has brought the happiest comfort.
My father says, ' I feel sure that that bright smile
will greet us again some day, if we do not miss
our inheritance.' At noon to-day G. Ridding went
off to Cambridge, and he is thinking of either taking
Edith to Sidmouth or of going somewhere with
Mr. Du Boulay. He owns that he needs a change."

From EDWARD

"C. C. C., OXFORD, 1871.

". . . I am in the Schools in about a fortnight
to pass in Science, so I am reading hard ; then
will come the refreshing week at Winchester.
We intend to take long walks to the farm and
woods by different routes, finding out old places

where we caught rare butterflies and where Selwyn used to spend such a long time. We also wish to sketch from the cemetery, from Hills, from Ladwell hill, etc. Walter is reading away at history, and walks over to Radley very often. Papa and Maggie have been at Shipton and Radley, and we are going over there to-day for Maggie's birthday. To-morrow Robert has asked us all to lunch in Christ Church common room, with many other Wykehamists to meet papa. We then adjourn to some garden until time for Magdalen chapel, where Dr. Stainer is going to play a special voluntary."

GEORGE MOBERLY'S JOURNAL

" *April.*—I have shrunk from writing these days, and I shrink still. But I must record in tenderest grief and love and comfort the sudden illness and death of my dearest, dearest Selwyn. I hardly know how to write it, or to bear it. Yet, with all the pain and distress, it has been full of true comfort, and the loving words of his friends and the common testimony of his masters and school-fellows to his goodness are unspeakably soothing. How gladly, but for the sake of the others, would we have gone through the gentle gate that opened so unexpectedly for my darling boy!

" *July* 6, 1871.—I see I have taken a book containing *purposes unfulfilled*—

"' For who the lessons cons
  Of task-taught virtue, he is naught,
  Tottering from wish to wish, much purposed,
    little wrought!'

" To-day I have consecrated Hindon Church, having been staying the night at Lady West-minster's. To-day Lord Pembroke is of age. His father was 21 when we went to France. Strange, that Thornton's metrical version of our tour comes to me to-day from Benjamin Harrison.   To-morrow institutions and Wilton.   Saturday, Lambeth and Athanasian Creed.

" *July.*—Lambeth   yesterday—very   fatiguing. We talked for 2½ hours : several for relegating the Creed to the end of the Book along with the Articles. . . . I spoke for the omission of this Clause as against the whole character of Christian teaching, which in the matter of election, baptism, etc., promises strongly on the affirmative side, and declines the *negative*, which might seem logically wanting to complete the doctrine.   We resolved to take measures for retranslating : a Conference with the Cambridge professors of Divinity.

" *Aug.* 1.—Dean Mansel has died suddenly.   I cannot think who will go to St. Paul's.

" *Aug.* 11.—It is a great thing indeed to have held the Diocesan Conference, and to have held it with such complete and most gratifying success.   We had about 450 people, but Lord Shaftesbury threw me overboard at the last moment.   The feeling was perfect, and I felt that my plan was safe.   The first Resolution was passed before luncheon.[1]   The second excited opposition on both sides, but the amendments were all overruled by large majorities and the thing carried :[2] so too the third.[3]   Lord

---

[1] *First Resolution.*—"That this Conference is of opinion that it is desirable to institute a permanent Synod in the Diocese of Salisbury."

[2] *Second   Resolution.*—"That the Synod consist of the following official members : the Lords Lieutenant and the High Sheriffs of the two Counties (being communicants), the Dean of the Cathedral, the three Archdeacons, and the Chancellor of the Diocese ; and of clergymen elected by the clergy, and laymen (being communicants) elected by the lay Churchmen of the parishes, to serve for each division of the Rural Deaneries of the Diocese, in the proportion of 4 clergymen and 6 laymen for each Sub-Deanery, undertaking to serve for three years."

[3] *Third   Resolution.*—"That the duty of the Synod be twofold : first, with the consent of the societies now engaged in those duties, to take charge of the chief operations conducted by voluntary associations within the Diocese, such as those of Church Education, the supply of

16

Bath, Lord Eldon, Sir Alexander Malet all spoke. It was over by 5 p.m.   Nothing could have been more cordial.

" Yesterday the Crown Prince and Princess of Germany were here in the Cathedral and garden.

" *Aug.* 22.—The Deanery of St. Paul's is still in the clouds.   It was in the *Guardian* before Richard had heard of it ; and in the *Times* after he had written to refuse it.

" *Aug.*—Richard telegraphs that he accepts the Deanery ; will he still be my chaplain ?   If he resigns, I wish I could find one among my pupils. . . . I busy myself with Revision papers. I hope Richard will succeed me here.

" *Sept.* 11.—The Synodical elections are going on.   I cannot doubt that I shall have the sympathy of the Diocese in the beginning of the Synod. Then comes the question of its doings, and its debatings, the question of its practical value and success.

" *Sept.* 19.—Mr. —— and his people decline to have anything to do with the Synod.   This is the second instance.   There will be others, say 30 or 40, in all.   A letter against it in the *Times*—all for the Norwich model, which is simply a five-centred Conference. . . .

" *Nov.* 19.—The first session of the Synod of Salisbury is over : [1] with, I may venture to say,

Clergy and of Churches, and Church Missions ; second, to be of conference and counsel with the Bishop in regard to ecclesiastical affairs of importance to the Diocese."

[1] There were three special points of difference between the Salisbury Synod and such Diocesan Conferences as had been already started in England.

1. *The Name.*   The Bishop knew that the gathering was not according to mediæval precedent, but believed it to be according to primitive spirit.   He did not undervalue the true and necessary proportions which the different elements of the Church bore to one another, but he believed that the part taken by the laity in the welfare of the Church in the early times was much more considerable than in later ages, when

amazing success. Of the total number of 345, not less than 320 were present. The proceedings were altogether amicable, and devoid of anything like party division or unkind feeling. If I should criticise, I should say we were too unanimous. Difficult questions were delegated to committees, of which we have many ; some of them with tremendously hard tasks assigned to them. We are to meet again (D.V.), on April 9th, in order to be in time for the Parliamentary measures of next year affecting the Church. I verily believe that in no other diocese in England such a success was possible. It is owing to the 34 years of orderly and churchlike government of Bishops Denison and Hamilton. I am now reaping the benefit of the respectful love and confidence of those two Episcopates. Literally we have only three or four opponents.

HOME LETTERS

*"*Salisbury*, Nov. 1871.*

" The Synod has got under weigh at last, and should prove to be of very great importance and the people were merely to receive what they heard authoritatively declared by clergy and bishops. He strongly objected to the name *Conference,* as he wanted it to be a representative body to work, not to waste itself in idle talk.

2. *In the number of ex-officio members.* If they began with a body of 70 persons nominated by the Bishop (rural deans and prebendaries of the Cathedral), it would alter the essential character of the body it was proposed to establish. He thought representation should be the real basis and the real strength of the Synod ; and that members (even the clergy) would feel themselves in a stronger position as elected to represent others, than they would as nominated by the Bishop or his predecessors.

3. *The members of Synod should bring forward their own subjects for discussion,* the organizing Committee being satisfied that it was a proper subject for discussion and accorded with the constitution of the Synod. This, the Bishop thought, would secure liveliness and continuous interest, especially as it was a rule that every subject was to have some practical outcome.

interest ; partly because very few dioceses have, at present, anything of the kind, and because it is on a pattern of its own, according to which the Bishop neither appoints the subjects for discussion nor the speakers. More than one Bishop spoke to the Bishop of the superiority of this plan over theirs ; but they placed the possibility of the success of his venture in his excellent chairmanship, which enabled him to avert all ill feeling, however burning the question under discussion might be. He hails the discussion of a 'burning question,' believing it to be far the best thing to have it fairly debated and both sides fairly stated. He does not wish the elected members to be all of one sort, but to represent, as far as possible, every honest difference of opinion amongst churchmen.

"Sitting silently by, as we did, we could not doubt that his chairmanship helped greatly. His brilliance of speech and flashes of wit told both ways; but the judgment of his opinions, at more than one critical moment, carried the assembly with him.

"The Synod will take place each year in the second week after Easter, and will last for two days. Many of the residents in the Close and town offer hospitality, and the large evening party at the Palace on the first day will give us the pleasure of making acquaintance with my father's diocesan friends.

"The last proposition for stopping the echo in the Chapter House is that each speaker should put up his umbrella to act as his own sounding-board. Miss Yonge writes that Mr. —— told her that when he first read the notice for elections in church, one of the old men said that they were 'to elect two lame men and a sinner! . . .'"

"*November* 1871.

"Uncle Richard and Helen are making their move from Whatley to St. Paul's, so the girls are with us ; they rout up Maggie and make her dance in the evenings, and she brightens under it. . . . The rumour of Bishop Patteson's murder reached us in the evening, and at Chapel the Bishop nearly broke down and spoke to the assembled household about Bishop Patteson and the work going on in Melanesia."

From Miss Yonge

" Otterbourne, *Nov.* 1871.

" . . . I have little hope of a contradiction ; it is the same island where they martyred the two boys before, and no one ever set his face more as a flint to meet whatever might come than he did. Once before it nearly happened. How one must pray that this blood may be the seed of the Church ! The last I had heard was of a grand, crowning success of ninety-seven baptised at once at Mota. . . . So he has brought his sheaves with him ! When I know more you shall hear, but his sisters are abroad ; I do not think they ever looked to see his face here. . . ."

Another

" Innocents' Day.

" . . . I tremble to say that I am to write his life, and I am probably going to Lichfield to talk it over with the Selwyns and Abrahams. It is very awful, for it is embalming the Saint for the Church. I hope the Bishop will let me have copies of the letters to him. . . ."

Another

" *Jan.* 1, 1872.

" . . . There is a full detail of all that is known in a letter from Mr. Brooke in the new number of *Mission Life* . . . both bring out more of the pain and grief than the first, which rests on one like a vision of the crystal sea and the palm.   But the sweet smile bears one on through it all.   I go to Lichfield on Monday ; Mrs. Selwyn says that her Bishop is overflowing with recollections of the early days of the mission. . . . Some islands have been quite depopulated by those wretches.   I believe Satan always does stir up something dreadful when his kingdom is being taken from him, but when he can only make martyrs it is well. . . .”

GEORGE MOBERLY'S JOURNAL

" *Dec.* 6.—I am startled by the arrival of a formal reply to my sermon and appendix[1] by Dr. Pusey. He misses my point and actually writes as though I said that doctrine was not necessary ! in despite of many most express passages to the contrary. . . . The Bishop of Oxford seems to follow my synodical lead. . . .

" *Dec.* 24.—Edward is in the second class, but I hear from Dr. —— that he and another man were put aside as candidates for the first.   But *aliter visum est.*

" *Jan.* 4, 1873.—Excellent reports from my *colonies.*   Edward is beginning to act as my private secretary.   I shall gradually make great use of him.

" *May.*—I preached this forenoon, rather contro- versially I fear ; but it seems to be needed.   I cannot go in for the modern Romanising doctrines.

" *July.*—The Archbishop has sent me the draft of a Report on Confession, drawn up at a meeting at which I could not be present on account of confirmations, which is to be resolved upon at a meeting when I shall be in Visitation.   I do not like the draft, and have freely criticised it.   I doubt whether I can sign it as it stands, though its sentiments are not entirely different from my own.

[1] Concerning the Athanasian Creed.

"*July* 19.—I have received an amended draft of the Bishops' declaration about Confession. I do not like it, and am greatly distressed at the short notice of the meetings of the committee, rendering it impossible for me to be present ; and if this form be adopted, I shall be unable to accept it. . . .

"*July* 21.—Shocked by the sudden death of Bishop Wilberforce. We stood together for the first Ireland, when neither won. We stood together for Balliol in 1826, when I won. I argued with him endlessly when he was Canon and Archdeacon of Winchester. I followed him to Brighstone. A great man has fallen in our Israel. . . .

"*Sept.* 20.—Johnnie and Carrie have a little son, to be called Arthur Norman : so now we count eleven grandchildren.

"*Nov.*—Richard Church brings his two girls to be confirmed here. Plenty of work—so many applications for sermons.

"*Feb.* 1874.—Dora's little boy is to be another Selwyn.[1] How often I think to meet my Selwyn about the house.

"*April.*—The Synod is over, harmoniously and prosperously. Next day I went to Town to a Bishops' meeting about the Archbishop's Bill for the Regulation of Public Worship, where I am supposed to have compromised myself by taking part in amendments. I dislike the Bill wholly ; but it seems to be thought that I cannot in honour oppose it. . . .

"*April, St. Paul's Deanery.*—Convocation. The Archbishop's Bill is put off till May 11th, and is, I think, doomed, at which I heartily rejoice. Something is really needed ; but this is a terrible measure.

"*May.*—The Bill was read the second time

[1] Charles Selwyn Martin.

without division. I did not speak, though at one time I rose to do so, but —— took the wind out of my sails. I do not see how to mend the Bill into a passable shape. . . . .

"*June* 30.—The Archbishop's Bill carried me to Town. I divided, alone of all the Bishops, against going into Committee, and have got more notice therefrom than I liked.[1] I spoke somewhat strongly on the 8th Clause, but the papers did not report me.

"*Aug.* 11.—The Bill is passed, shorn of the appeal from the Bishops to the Archbishop's discretion. His Grace rides on the crest of the wave of lay frenzy, and the Bishops are at a sad discount. . . ."

[1] The isolated action of the Bishop of Salisbury brought upon him at the time a good deal of attention from churchmen, and was the cause of a representative of the Church of England Working Men's Society being sent eleven years later to the service at Salisbury Cathedral, July 10, 1885.

First Reading, April 20, 1874.

Second Reading, May 11. Passed after long debate.

Proposed, June 4, that their Lordships should go into Committee on the Bill.

Amendment moved by the Duke of Marlborough : "That this House, while recognising the importance of a revision of the law for the restraint of ecclesiastical offences, considers it inexpedient to proceed with the said Bill at present."

The Bishop of Lincoln appealed for a reference to the Convocations first.

Amendment rejected by 137 to 29, the Bishop of Salisbury, alone of the Bishops, voting in the minority.

In Committee, various divisions on different points of detail ; one was on Lord Shaftesbury's clause constituting the office held later by Lord Penzance, which was adopted by 112 to 13.

Two Bishops (Carlisle and Oxford) voted in the minority.

Third Reading, June 25. Passed after debate and with many amendments of detail.

Aug. 4.—The House of Lords (by 44 to 32) refused to accept an amendment from the Commons giving a right of appeal from the discretion of the Bishops to the discretion of the Archbishop.

The Commons' amendment was supported by the Archbishops.

   ,,   ,,   ,, resisted by eight Bishops.

HOME LETTERS

" Our Bishop has been anxious for some time to combine the various C.M.S. meetings of the diocese with the great S.P.G. diocesan Festival which takes place every summer in Salisbury. The idea is a new one, but has been carried out, and the first combined Mission Festival of the new pattern has been most successful. Bishop Claughton, of Rochester, preached, and from 1,000 to 1,500 people were present at the garden meetings in the afternoon and evening. An equal number of missionaries from the two Societies were invited, and they spoke alternately. They seemed pleased to meet on the same platform. The rule that none but actual missionaries were to speak proved eminently successful. They were asked to ' soar above Societies,' and, as far as possible, not to mention any. All money collected was divided equally between the two Societies, excepting such as was given to any special object. The proceedings began the afternoon before with a children's mission service in the Cathedral, which advertised the next day's great united diocesan service and meetings. Whenever the weather allows, it is proposed to hold the meetings in a tent in the Palace grounds.

" The next day my father went to Templecombe, and finding the Prince of Wales waiting at the Salisbury railway station, had a long chat with him."

" You have heard our news, that Maggie is engaged to be married to Charles Awdry — a younger brother of William Awdry's ? Charlie is in W. H. Smith & Son's business. Writing to Miss Yonge, we could not refrain from asking her how it was that ' Gertrude May ' of ' The Daisy Chain ' married the person responsible for newspapers, and that 'Stella Underwood,' the youngest girl in 'The Pillars of the House,' married 'Charles Audley.' Miss Yonge answered that 'there are some things too strange to be explained.' Certainly her prophecies in the matter of names have been most comically complete ; but prophecies they were."

GEORGE MOBERLY'S JOURNAL

"*Dec.* 14. — An unusually large Ordination coming.[1] My Walter, now my youngest boy, hopes to be ordained on Sunday. He goes to Mr. Lowndes at Sturminster Newton.

"*March* 5, 1875.—All the Bishops signed the 'Address to the Clergy and Laity' except me for one reason, and the Bishop of Durham for the opposite reason. I have prepared a letter to the Archdeacons explaining the cause of my isolation. I was two days at the Jerusalem Chamber, with small satisfaction.

"*March* 22.—A fortnight of confirmations in bitter N.E. wind. My letter has excited notice ; not much blame, even warm praise, and abundance of thanks from my clergy for speaking kindly of them. . . ."

Extract from THE ARCHBISHOP'S PASTORAL

"While, however, we thankfully recognise these abundant mercies and blessings, we cannot but acknowledge with sorrow that serious evils disturb the peace of the Church and hinder its work. One of these evils is the interruption of the sympathy and mutual confidence which ought to exist between the clergy and laity. Changes in the mode

[1] In 1875 the examination of candidates for Ordination in the Salisbury diocese was separated by some weeks from the week before the Ordination, which was devoted to quiet services and addresses.

of performing divine service, in themselves sometimes of small importance, introduced without
authority, and often without due regard to the
feelings of parishioners, have excited apprehensions
that greater changes are to follow ; distrust has
been engendered, and the edification which ought
to result from united worship has been impeded.
The suspicions thus aroused, often no doubt un-
reasonable, have in some cases produced serious
alienation.   The refusal to obey legitimate authority
is another evil in the Church at the present time. . . .”

Extract from BISHOP MOBERLY'S LETTER TO HIS
ARCHDEACONS

“. . . The design of issuing a Pastoral letter from
the whole Episcopate to the clergy and laity under
the present circumstances of the Church was by
no one of our body more ardently desired or more
earnestly pressed than by me. . . . There seemed
to me to be an opportunity, if it were firmly,
tenderly, and discreetly used, of helping to restore
peace (where peace is much needed) among those
who are in their hearts as true as ourselves to the
Church of England and its great and recognised
teachers.   But nothing, I thought, was more to be
deprecated than any unnecessary revival of complaints already sufficiently urged, and any enumera-
tion of acts of disobedience and the like, already
amply provided for by the Act of Parliament which
is to come into operation on the 1st of July.   With
these feelings I took part in trying to amend the
draft address which was laid before the Bishops, but
was unable to carry the points on which I was most
anxious. . . . On the one hand, I cordially agreed
in deprecating the creeping innovations in divine
service of which the address spoke, and utterly
disapproved of the ‘ dissemination of doctrines and

encouragement of practices,' and especially of the 'multiplication' and 'circulation' of such manuals of doctrine and private devotion as it referred to. As to the 'interruption of sympathy and mutual confidence between clergy and laity,' amounting in some cases to serious 'alienation,' and the disobedience of clergy to Episcopal and other authority, I feared there might be some ground for these complaints, though I am thankful to say that I know of none in my own diocese.

"But, on the other hand, . . . I thought the address unlikely to do good, and not unlikely to do harm, and I wished that it should not be issued, and . . . recommended that it should be withheld. . . . It seemed to me that it would be unfair to my diocese to appear to include it without distinction under the general statements of the address, cowardly in myself to shrink from declaring my real mind in a case of so great importance, and injurious to the Church to run the risk of irritating rather than soothing the agitation which exists. . . ."

From BISHOP HORATIO POTTER, OF NEW YORK

"March 23, 1875.

"MY DEAR LORD BISHOP,
        "Pardon me for intruding upon you at this solemn time.   Late last night, on my return from a Visitation far up the Hudson River, my daughter brought me the daily English paper, in which, to my surprise, I saw the Pastoral of the Archbishops and Bishops: I knew at once what it probably contained.   I felt deep regret that a step should have been taken which I feared would increase agitation within the Church, and which would *help* those *outside* who wanted such help, to keep up a cry of 'great agitation and peril in the Church!'

" The very fact of such a movement by the entire Bench would be accepted as evidence of great and imminent peril. I did not read it; 1 knew of no *dissenting Bishop!* This morning I went to my nephew's church to confirm, and he informed me, to my great joy, that you had declined to sign. On coming home, I found my copy of the *Guardian* just arrived, containing the Pastoral and your Lordship's admirable letter. Excuse me for presuming to express an opinion of anything your Lordship writes and does. But you stand alone, and I have felt that the judgment of a calm observer three thousand miles away might interest you. I go along with every word you say.

" I know you have in England more of excess than we have, but after all it is comparatively small. Why could not the Bishops state the thing at its real magnitude, instead of conveying an exaggerated idea of it? If the Chief Pastors are in a panic and hurried into exceptional action, the Flock will be frightened, *maddened* more than is meet. Why speak so much of alienation between the clergy and the laity? It is the way to teach the lesson. With us, and I believe with you, it is the laity, or some of them, who love extremes as much as some of the clergy. . . . God save the Church of England! Again I give your Lordship my thanks for your firm and calm letter, and I again beg you to excuse my intrusion.

" Most truly and affectionately yours,
" H. POTTER, *Bishop of New York.*"

CHAPTER VIII

SALISBURY

For like a bee among the flowers,
Flutters from theme to theme this wandering strain of ours.
PINDAR, Pyth. x.

From REV. JOHN WORDSWORTH [1]

" 1876.

" . . . Thank you for your kindness in sending me your beautiful translation of Pindar.[2] It quite comes up to the great expectations which I had formed of it. . . . I need scarcely say that the book has a special charm for me as a tangible memorial of your Winchester lessons which we used to enjoy. . . . I was sorry not to have the pleasure of speaking to you as well as seeing you at Copleston's consecration.[3] Robert perhaps told you that we went over the ship together. . . . I am glad he has gone both for his own sake and Copleston's, and am inclined to envy him."

From REV. E. C. WICKHAM [4]

" WELLINGTON COLLEGE, 1876.

" . . . I could not help reading the first Pythian at once. . . . I have always grieved over having

---

[1] Afterwards Bishop of Salisbury.
[2] Bishop Moberly had his translation of Pindar printed in 1876.
[3] Bishop of Colombo, afterwards Bishop of Calcutta, Metropolitan of India.
[4] Afterwards Headmaster of Wellington College and Dean of Lincoln.

George Moberly.
Bishop of Salisbury

lost an old school Pindar which had notes of translation from your lessons in pencil all down its sides.
My Thucydides with the same adornment still
does good service. . . . You will be just parting
with Bob for his interesting six months with that
splendid fellow Copleston. . . ."

From REV. J. T. BRAMSTON

"CULVER'S CLOSE, WINCHESTER, 1876.

". . . I cannot tell you how pleased I was when,
in opening a volume from Wells to-day, my eye
fell on a certain passage, 'As when men range their
file of pillared gold,' which with the following lines
you once wrote on the back of a continent roll and
gave me, and which I still have. I at once looked
for another passage—the birth of Iamus—and
found my old friend in print. Having read both
the Pythian and Olympian odes twice through
with you, I had quite caught your love for Pindar,
and the translations will be delightful reminders of
those dear old days. When I was at Wellington,
the only time I seriously disagreed with my
Head Master, Benson, was when he asserted that
Pindar was the most artificial and manneristic of
the classic poets, while I had always felt under
your teaching that he was the most completely
free and natural.

"It was so refreshing to hear your voice again
in Chapel last night ; the boys appreciated it fully,
and to me it was a very delightful return to old
feelings and thoughts. . . ."

HOME LETTERS

"*April* 1876.

"The Synod is just over. The debates were
extremely lively and the attendance larger than
ever. One discussion was on the formation of a

Diocesan Evangelisation Society. It was proposed that a company of missioners should be created, under strict organisation, of clergy and laity which could be applied to by any clergyman for help in preaching in the open air or in any other way, urging people to go to church and Communion. All would have to be trained (an immense difficulty) and commissioned."

" The ' daisy wedding ' was on the 20th of April. With Sir John and Lady Awdry and eleven or twelve of the Awdry brothers and sisters, besides all our own family, we were a large party. The bride's white-robed company looked charming as it wended its way through the garden over the daisied lawn and through the cloisters to the Cathedral door. Here it was met by the clergy and choir, and, singing a hymn, all passed through the south aisle to their places in the Lady Chapel. Every one wore bunches of daisies, and, though Miss Yonge was present, we were careful not to offer her a daisy chain. Daisies were scattered in front of Maggie as she stepped out of the cloisters into the garden sunshine."

" On April 25th (Mr. Keble's birthday) a good many of us went to the opening of Keble College chapel. This was the more interesting to us as the Warden of Keble and Mrs. Talbot had been staying with us at Salisbury when he received the offer of money for building the chapel, and we had all rejoiced together.

" Dr. Pusey preached, but owing to the bad acoustic arrangements of the chapel some could not hear him at all. We sat for an hour through what appeared to be an animated discourse, for we *saw* the preacher's agitation, and saw him drink water at intervals, but as far as we were concerned, we did not even hear the sound of his voice. It was most truly funny.

"As before, we found ourselves in a gathering of old Hursley friends : the Heathcotes, Robert Wilsons, Peter Youngs, Frewen Moores, Mr. and Mrs. Cooke Trench, and others. The thought of our having been present at the foundation and opening of one of Oxford's colleges was thrilling ; but more so the realisation of the honour done to the author of 'The Christian Year' by the erection of a college on such a scale, coupled with the remembrance of Mr. Keble as we used to hear him preaching, summer after summer, at Hursley ; or as we were accustomed to see him, on each anniversary of his wedding day, in Winchester Cathedral, listening with rapt attention to the service, but almost wholly unknown and unrecognised."

GEORGE MOBERLY'S JOURNAL

"*April* 30.—The last fortnight has been wonderfully full of interest. The wedding, the visit to Oxford, and, lastly, the Synod. I do not know how to talk of Oxford—so grand, so exalting, so fatiguing. I was lodged at Charsley's Hall, taken for the occasion by Lord Beauchamp, and saw scores and scores of old friends. I greatly admired the interior (not the exterior) of the chapel.

"In Synod, I fear I distressed many : in regard to the 'Evangelists' especially. High and low joined in the proposal.

"*May.*—Convocation, and the debate on Lord Granville's Burial Resolutions. My 'Infant Baptism and Confirmation' sermons are in the press. The subject has been much on my mind.

"*Sept.*—Terrible tales from Bulgaria. . . . I trouble about the Colombo business. Bishop

17

Copleston has telegraphed for Bob, who is now in India. I hope they will adopt wise and prudent counsels.

" *Oct.* 5.—Bob is in England. His mind about Ceylon is much the same as mine and Bishop Mylne's.

" A great new affair is George Ridding's engagement to Miss Palmer. We sincerely rejoice.

" *Nov.* 6.—The opening of the Choir is over. It is unfinished, of course, but still full of loveliness and grace. The procession included near four hundred clergy ; the communicants, morning and midday, about a thousand, and the collections near £500. I preached in the morning; Bishop Woodford, nobly, in the afternoon ; the Bishops of Oxford and St. Andrews yesterday. The crowds were enormous.

" George Ridding's marriage is over, honeymoon and all, and they are at home again. If we were not going to be out to-morrow, they would have come over here.

" *Dec.* 12.—On the 1st I went to Winchester and confirmed 81 boys in the College Chapel, and celebrated and preached there on Advent Sunday. It was—it could not fail to be—deeply interesting and touching to me. Alice and Edith were with me, and we had a very pleasant visit to George and Laura in the altered household. Nothing could have been kinder or more loving."

HOME LETTER

" *November* 1876.

" George Ridding has identified himself with us too long for us to be anything but entirely sympathetic. Any agitation felt at his marriage has been chiefly due to the excitement of a great change ; for change it will be for us ; but knowing to the full the gain a wife will be to him and to

Winchester, we are really happy about it. We have thoroughly realised his increasing loneliness ; for as our home duties have become larger, and the home party smaller, it has become impossible for us to be with him in Winchester as much as he desired and needed. Laura Palmer is the eldest daughter of the Wykehamist we have revered from our earliest years as Sir Roundell Palmer,[1] who became last year Chairman of the Governing Body at Winchester. The marriage is eminently suitable, and it is truly delightful to see George so happy. The wedding took place on October 26th, in the course of the school half-year. A week's honeymoon in the New Forest was secured by making use of a week including two saints' days and a ' whole remedy.' Alice and Edith went to the wedding, and Walter was the best man ! "

George Moberly's Journal

" *Feb.*—I am thinking of taking a twelvemonth's lodging in London for the Revision work ; possibly chumming with my dear Walter, who went to London yesterday to begin work at St. George's, Hanover Square, as Mr. Capel Cure's curate, after two years in Dorsetshire."

From Mary Anne Moberly

" Feb. 1877.

" I send you on the letter from Walter. You will see he is unhappy about his first sermon at St. George's. I have a letter from General Wilbraham to-day, written on purpose to say how much he liked it. He says, ' I cannot resist telling you how very much pleased I was with my godson's sermon last evening. My opinion is not

[1] Baron Selborne 1872 ; Earl of Selborne 1883 ; Lord Chancellor 1872-4, 1880-4.

worth much, but after service I walked home
with Mr. Capel Cure, and he spoke of it in terms
which would have gratified the Bishop and yourself.
" There was so much thought in it," he said.' . . ."

GEORGE MOBERLY'S JOURNAL

" *May* 1877, *Salisbury.*—We have just parted
with Lord and Lady Selborne. It has been a very
pleasant visit. He is as friendly as of old, and we
have chatted and argued continuously. Yesterday
Cardwell and his wife dined with us. . . . The
Ridsdale judgment is given, and the Church Association is jubilant. It seems to me very unsatisfactory in many ways. But I must study it more
carefully. I begin to understand Lord Selborne's
view, which seemed at first to me very unnatural.
. . . I spoke a few words in the Committee of the
Lords on the Burials Bill. . . .

" *June.*—They are going to hold their first
Conference in the Winchester diocese this month.
G. Ridding, Fearon, and Jack are members of it.
. . . Maggie's dear little son is greatly grown.[1] . . .

" *Oct.*—I have just had a laborious week of
confirmations, and look forward to another. I
was at Exeter for the opening of the Cathedral,
and preached one of four sermons. Sir William
Heathcote is much bent on bringing the Winchester Conference to something like my model. . . .

" *Jan.* 8, 1878.—We have had five sons, five
daughters, two sons-in-law, six grandchildren, and
Scott Holland all in the house together : a merry
Christmas party. . . . George not strong, and
Robert established here as my resident chaplain ;
Johnnie, Edward, and Walter as happy as school-
boys, and full of music. . . .

" The dioceses of St. Albans, Chester, and Norwich are attracted by our Synod. . . ."

[1] Charles Selwyn Awdry.

From Dean Stanley

"Westminster, *Nov.* 1877.

" My dear Lord Bishop,

"When at Constance this year, standing on the grave of Robert Hallum, Bishop of Salisbury, I thought you might like to have the engraving (made by order of the Grand-Duke of Baden) of the brass that covers his remains. He seems to have been worthy of his successor ; but I trust that the present occupant of his See will take warning by his fate and not run the risk of attending a General Council. Pray accept this slight remembrance from a grateful pupil, who is yours faithfully and respectfully,

"A. P. Stanley."

Extracts from Conversations

G. Moberly.—" I think that we ought to have some means of showing fraternity and sympathy with some of those Churches with which we are not in full communion—for instance, the Moravians, Old Catholics, Spanish Mexicans—without making light of the grave differences between us ; to open our churches more to those who profess the Nicene Creed, that those who are baptised men and agree in the fundamental truths should feel our willingness that they should hear our preaching and fraternise as far as is consistent without admitting them to the holiest of all our services. . . . We are too apt to bind every one to the Thirty-nine Articles and Canterbury, and to recognise no one till he becomes a pure Anglican."

Bishop of ——.—" Bishop Patteson fought against the idea of making the islanders Anglicans."

G. Moberly.—" The Anglican Church ought to have a wonderful future in its capacity of uniting opposed Churches. The Romans would have to relinquish their doctrine of the Papacy, and the Greeks must become more spiritually religious."

Bishop of ———.—" Certainly, if there is to be a future reunion, one cannot imagine that it would not be on the Anglican basis."

On the Question of making an Order of Evangelists

Bishop of ———.—" You would have set on foot in some quarters a taste for Methodist talk instead of the serene and quiet teaching of the clergyman."

G. Moberly.—" Don't you think that there are a great many men of religious zeal who might have been saved to the Church by a minor order ? We lose men of deep zeal who must speak, and from being without an outlet are not only lost to us, but run into opposition."

Bishop of ———.—" There may be such in your country."

G. Moberly. — " Ah, your Church-people in America only join from conviction ; but we have an immense residuum."

Bishop of ———.—" Take the case of a layman with little knowledge of theology : he will speak with animation, but what will he teach ? "

G. Moberly.—" I do not think so much of their teaching as of their exhorting ; reiterating again and again the simple truths ; dwelling on the sinfulness of sin, the coming to Christ in penitence ; urging affectionately and earnestly the coming to Holy Communion ; bringing children to be baptised and confirmed. Fervour and enthusiasm have an effect that no expounding of a book of Scripture has. Laymen already become readers and preachers in some districts ; why not send them to other places where they are more needed ? "

Bishop of ——.—" And how would such preaching reflect upon the clergyman ? "

G. Moberly.—" I grant you that the moonlight might seem mild after the comet had been blazing away."

G. Moberly.—" I have lately been thinking with great interest of the story of Apollos. He was a learned man (wrongly translated *eloquent*) ; he knew the Scriptures *accurately* (meaning the Old Testament), also the prophecies ; he was perfectly acquainted with the history of our Lord's life ; he knew the prophecies relating to His Birth, His Cross, His Ascension ; he was baptised with John's baptism : he must have known all that John the Baptist knew ; he had much faith ; he was able to teach and convince men of the truth of Christianity; what then did he *not* know ? He knew to the end of St. Luke's Gospel, but he did *not* know the Acts of the Apostles ; he did not know of the subsequent edifice of the Church, of the orderly and ordered channels through which grace should flow and the Holy Spirit be given. No doubt he was re-baptised, for we know that in the case of certain disciples St. Paul had them rebaptised (Acts xix. 5). He was baptised and confirmed, and taught the doctrine of the Church.—It strikes me that in these times we find the counterpart of Apollos' case so very often. . . ."

G. Moberly.—" Dean Stanley seems to think that we have got beyond the need of Creeds and Sacraments : that they were all very well in ancient days, but that we have got beyond them and are living and discovering the spiritual meaning of life in them : that we must expect them to expire, and that they *are* expiring. But the human nature that required the help of Creeds and Sacraments is ours still in all its imperfectness. We still need the checks and rules to prevent us from wandering into all kinds of wrong and fictitious imaginations. Our nature is the same,—the vine still needs the pole to train it up in all orderly and true methods of thought in religion. In the mouth of Dean Stanley these words are compatible with a great deal of earnestness and devoutness ; but not so in the mouth of the *Pall Mall* and other newspapers, which applaud and are delighted."

EXTRACTS FROM CONVERSATIONS

Robert.—" Do you remember that story in Keble's life, how he preached a very effective sermon somewhere and heard it much praised ? When his friends went with great expectations to hear him again, they were greatly disappointed to hear a simple, commonplace sermon, which he confessed had been purposely done, as he considered it a reproach to have been thought to preach an *original effective* sermon. It seems difficult to apply such to oneself. It is strange that it should not be best to be as effective as possible : would it not be sacrificing the congregation to your own moral good ? "

G. Moberly.—" I think there are two views : one of them is the individual man doing his best in his generation, working *himself* out as it were ; and the other deeply conscious of the whole working for good, and sinking himself in entire modesty in the mass and weight of moral good in the world, which has and will have such immense power. And there is no doubt which is most effective in the end,"

Robert.—" It is difficult to carry out, and to feel it really best and the higher course."

G. Moberly.—" I think Keble would have said: 'The other is a high and grand thing, but it is not for me; it is not for me—it would be bad for me, and I am not capable of it without harm '—and in his tranquil, modest way this would tell most in the long run."

Robert.—" Then you would consider it the———"

G. Moberly.—" If you would be a Keble; but there are many men who will do their best in a different way; it will be very rare to find another acting so. His sermons at Hursley were not *effective.*"

Robert.—" I only know one of his volumes well—the Lenten one—and they are very quiet and gentle: but after all there is nothing like them. The indignation and impetuousness and eloquence he did not give way to."

G. Moberly.—" And yet no want of strength in speaking the truth: only he refrained from much that must have been in his mind."

Robert.—" No, certainly there was no want of strength; but—Mr. Keble could not have conducted a mission."

G. Moberly.—" No; and that is a striking saying, my son, capable of conclusions and inferences; for if a man like Keble could not have conducted a mission, it is probable that there is much that is mistaken and harmful in the way of conducting missions."

Robert.—" But St. Paul could."

G. Moberly (laughing).—" Well, that is certainly true; St. Paul could conduct missions, and *did.* . . ."

G. Moberly.—" How one would like to know more of the details of St. Paul's acts and sayings in his mission work, if it had so pleased God!

For instance, he spent three weeks at Thessalonica :
what a great deal must have happened there ! If
each night St. Luke had sat up and written as a
faithful secretary all that his Apostle had said and
done during the day, what a thing it would have
been for us ! We do not know what he taught.
It is a mistake to think the Epistle to the Thes-
salonians a mere repetition of what he said to
them. He wrote for two reasons—to correct a mis-
understanding concerning an interpretation, and to
comfort them because persecutions had begun."

Robert.—" I suppose that the sermon at Antioch
in Pisidia was probably the type of all his teaching
to the Jews."

G. Moberly.—" That sermon was a repetition of
St. Stephen's, showing how *that* sermon was burnt
into his memory."

Robert.—" Yes, in the second place ; but surely
the three sermons at Antioch, Lystra, and Athens
are the types of his way of teaching the Jews, the
uneducated heathen, and the philosophical world ;
and that is the reason why we are not given
more, for his teaching (as St. Stephen's was) must
necessarily have been on the historical basis."

G. Moberly.—" Yes, the expressions used are
such as—reasoning with them out of the Scriptures,
opening and alleging that Jesus is Christ. And of
course his epistles are to those who believed, and
so he does not go over the same ground again."

On Vows

G. Moberly.—" The theory of the vow of poverty
in the Church took its rise very much from the
history of Ananias and Sapphira. That story had
a deeper meaning than being a mere lie—it was
sacrilege. There was a profession of charity to
the Church not kept ; an attempt to cheat the Holy
Spirit that was in the Church, by vowing more

than they meant to perform. St. Peter accepted the vow, but examined them on its sincerity."

Walter.—" A contemporary writer says that there was no vow of poverty before the time of Benedict, though there were numbers of hermits, monks, and monasteries."

G. Moberly.—" A vow is such a very sacred thing that the Church must make the necessary rules and laws, with a possible dispensation from them in some cases, before any one is allowed to make them. No individual bishop or lay person can do so, as it were in a corner ; but when it is a thing recognised and sanctioned by the Church (as the marriage vow) I would willingly hear any woman of mature age and judgment profess the vow of poverty in my cathedral."

Walter.—" People seem to have differed about the proper age : some say ten, or fifteen, or seventeen ; and even felt a vow made by another person for an infant to be binding."

G. Moberly.—" Yes ; there is the case of Hannah, vowing that her son should be a Nazarite. Of course wherever there is a vow to do wrong, it is equally wicked to keep it. King Herod was bound to break his. . . ."

On the Revision of the New Testament

Mr. —— " Are you one of those that like the change of ' evil ' into ' evil one ' ? "

G. Moberly.—" I am not really in a position to judge. I have not read enough. Dr. Lightfoot's arguments seem to me to be unanswerable ; but I find one or two, whom I trust, think it might have been wiser to have left it as it was.

" What a wonderful light has been thrown upon those last verses of 1 John v. by the revised version ! There are two realms indicated—the realm of the wicked one, and the world of goodness. ' The whole world lieth in the wicked one '; in that place it is undoubtedly masculine. ' We know that whosoever is begotten of God, sinneth not '; then, in the preterperfect, ' but He that *was begotten* of God keepeth him, and the evil one toucheth him not.' Such a bright light has been cast upon an obscure passage, owing to the change of ἑαυτόν to αὐτόν.

" ' Resist not the evil man '; if this were not in the masculine, it would indeed need a great deal of interpretation ; it would sound like a denial of all one's ideas of the Christian battle.

" There is one alteration not made which, I think, would have been a gain, in Acts viii. 23. St. Peter says, ' I see with prophetic eyes that thou art in '—the word is not *in*, but *set for* (only I would bar any idea of destiny)—' that thou art in the way of being a gall *root* of bitterness, which will have terrible consequences ; thou wilt be the root of all gnosticism and many kinds of evil in the time to come.' And then Simon Magus exclaims, ' Pray to the Lord that none of these come upon me '; showing that St. Peter had spoken of things to come upon him in the future."

Mr. —— .—" How do you interpret the words ' Sleep on now, and take your rest. . . . Rise ! let us be going ' ? "

" I think it is that twice He had come and warned them against sleeping when they ought to have been watching ; but the third time there was no need of warning on that ground—the time was over : ' Sleep on now '; no need to trouble themselves on that ground. In respect of warning— sleep ; but in respect of imminent danger—rise."

AFTER EXCHANGING GHOST STORIES

Dean G.—" Do you think you could bear to see a ghost ? I do not think that my nerves would bear it, and yet people are seldom dreadfully frightened; they seem to be wonderfully supported."

G. Moberly.—" I do not know : I fancy I could."

Dean G.—" There was a very good article in the *Church Quarterly* some months ago on the subject, which said that the stories of people appearing to their friends at the moment of dying are so numerous and so well attested, that it is impossible to disbelieve them."

G. Moberly.—" I entirely believe in the possibility of such appearances; but when I am asked whether I believe in this or that particular ghost story, I say no, because it is not proved in such a way that I am bound to believe in it. . . . People trouble themselves to find special reasons for each story they are inclined to believe. No doubt one reason of occasional appearances and the great mass of consequent stories, is that they keep alive in our hearts a great consciousness of a mysterious and supernatural world, which is very near us and with which we have a great deal to do. That is reason enough, without finding a special object in each particular case. People so often say, ' Oh, but I don't see any reason or use in that appearance.' Well, I should say that the reason is, that it keeps up the sense in individual minds of God's mighty unseen world.

" I have never seen anything, but I will keep my heart open should it be God's will that I should; anyhow I will not close it by irrational incredulity to the possibility of such an appearance being made to me."

Dean G.—" No, no, certainly not; I entirely agree with you."

HOME LETTERS

" The present great subject of interest concerns the recently-formed Central Church Council in London. Our Bishop has always hoped that some day there would be such a Council, called together by the Archbishops and Bishops, consisting of clerical and lay representatives from every Diocesan Council, when each shall be organised on the representative system.

" He considers that the Salisbury Synod alone has at this time the organisation which makes it entirely representative ; all other Conferences having a large number of *ex-officio* members which, in his opinion, make the numbers of clerical and lay members disproportionate, and who are not in any way representative, being (in the case of the rural deans) nominees of the Bishop.

" The Central Council formed now seems to him altogether unreal and anomalous ; the members of it are elected by Conferences, only partially representative of the whole body of communicants in each Diocese, and there is a layman at the head of it. He speaks of the mistake made in trying to put a roof to a house before building the walls.[1]

---

[1] " I feel it to be important that the relation to be borne by any such Central Conference to the Houses of Convocation should be clearly apprehended and distinctly laid down. *There* is the place where reform ought to begin, and the very first thing to be done is to readjust the representation of the Clergy in the Lower House of Convocation. This ancient institution is first of all to be guarded, improved where necessary, and loyally preserved.

" But, when it is so improved and perfected it is but the *Synod of the Clergy*. . . . Alongside of this the separate Diocesan organisations of Clergy and Laity may be growing up gradually and with continually increasing uniformity of constitution, until the day comes when they can, by a still further development of the principles of representation, produce by a sort of natural growth a *Synod of the Church*, in which by double and triple process of representation every Parishioner of every Parish is represented first by his communicant Parochial representative, then by his communicant Diocesan Synodsman, and lastly by his

" He dissents from the opinion that such an assembly, though imperfectly organised, can do no harm and may fill up a want. He thinks it may be tempted to call itself, and be gradually looked upon as, the ' voice of the Church ' when it is not really so. Also, that it may gain the allegiance of many, who will have forgotten its imperfect origin, and may object to being superseded by the time that a perfect Central Council can be brought into existence, and in these ways be an obstacle to such a scheme. . . ." [1]

" The home party is now so broken up that we do not often meet. Walter is now the home brother, minor canon of the Cathedral, and clerical secretary to the Synod. After Mr. Daubeny's resignation in May 1878, Robert became Principal of the Theological College here, but since his engagement to Alice Sidney Hamilton (the late Bishop's second daughter), he has been hoping for a living, and has now gone to Great Budworth, in Cheshire. The marriage took place this summer. Last autumn, William Awdry

communicant representative to the Central Synod. And every member of each of these bodies, whether clerical or lay, holds his place by equal, personal right, as elected by those whose duty it was to elect ; not as ex officio, not by invitation or permission, but by right.

" I shall probably be told that I am sketching a constitution unknown to the Primitive ages and inconsistent with the principles and practice of the early Church. As far as regards the ' practice ' of the early Church, I acknowledge the truth of the allegation, but I venture to say that it is otherwise with their ' principles,' as I have endeavoured before to show. And I further venture to say that the gradual usurpation by the clergy of the entire government of the Church, going on and becoming complete in the proclamation of the Infallibility of the Pope, has been the early germ and the gradually developed perfection of the corruption of the Church. We cannot go back to mediæval times and principles. We must look to the future. . . . The *Synod of the Church* must recognise both portions of the Spirit-bearing flock."— *Extract from G. Moberly's note-book.*

[1] See Charge for 1882.

succeeded Canon Ashwell as Principal of the Chichester Theological College, and now we hear that George has been appointed Principal of the Lichfield Theological College. We cannot help questioning how far his physical powers will allow him to cope with the work.

"We have heard of the death of Mrs. Eden, and my mother keenly feels the loss of her early friend, who made the first trial of England and English clerical life sweet to her. The annual visits of the Bishop and Mrs. Eden have left a great tradition of happiness and merriment behind them."

From BISHOP EDEN

"MY DEAR MARY,

". . . It was real pleasure to me to have been allowed such a happy interview with you and the Bishop yesterday. How my darling wife would have enjoyed it, for she did so love you! And it may be indeed one of those good things which God has prepared for those who love Him, their reunion in His Presence, where tears will be wiped from all eyes. If it be His blessed will, may we yet be permitted to meet again here. Believe me, my dear Mary, your affectionate cousin—yes! I like to feel that I may, through her, claim you as such—

"ROBERT,
"*Bishop of Moray and Ross, Primus of Scotland.*"

GEORGE MOBERLY'S JOURNAL

"*Aug.* 1881.—We have lost my old schoolfellow, friend, and landlord, Sir William Heathcote; and with him dies another element of our old Hursley circle of close friends. What an exemplary life his has been! A pattern schoolboy and undergraduate, a first-class man, Fellow of All Souls, M.P. for the University of Oxford.

" *Oct.*—It is now twelve years.   I came without experience.   They were anxious times, and circumstances threatened a strong disunion of theological feeling.   I had theorised, and got the opportunity of action : representation : practical action.   These are, I am convinced, the real principles which will ultimately set right the Church of England, established or disestablished.

"Mutual confidence.   More widely spread information.   Suggestion of local wants.   Direct effects few, beyond them very valuable ones.   As time went on the Synod began to possess records of the parishes ; maps ; finance board ; Church house ; itinerant mission ; scale of fees ; nurses ; deaconesses ; cottage homes ; ladies' associations ; boards of Missions.

" I have entered into my 79th year, and the birth of Robert's little son [1] at Great Budworth has given me 27 grandchildren."

[1] Walter Hamilton Moberly.

CHAPTER IX

LAST YEARS AT SALISBURY

As a fond mother, when the day is o'er,
Leads by the hand her little child to bed,
Half willing, half reluctant to be led,
And leave his broken playthings on the floor,
Still gazing at them through the open door;
　Not wholly reassured and comforted
　By promises of others in their stead,
Which, though more splendid, may not please him more:
So Nature deals with us, and takes away
Our playthings one by one, and by the hand
Leads us to rest so gently, that we go
Scarce knowing if we wish to go or stay—
Being too full of sleep to understand
How far th' unknown transcends the what we know.

LONGFELLOW.

HOME LETTERS

"SALISBURY.

"We occasionally make expeditions to Hursley on summer afternoons. The other day Mrs. Walter Hamilton and all her party joined us, and we went to Chandler's Ford station, intending to walk the three miles to Hursley, wandering about on the way in our own farm woods. But we had hardly gone a mile when we were caught in a heavy thunderstorm. The rain was so tremendous that we had to look for shelter, and ran to a thatched cottage, quite unknown to us, standing alone at

the back of a little common.   An old man in a
smock-frock made us welcome, but asked us, as
we trooped into the little kitchen, to be very
quiet, as his 'old woman' was upstairs dying.   We
were kept there nearly an hour.   We asked him
in whispers whether he remembered Mr. Keble,
and he volunteered that his wife had, years ago,
worked at Fieldhouse.   He inquired, 'Be you Dr.
Moberly's long family, then?' and said, after a
pause, 'Yesterday my old woman kept on saying,
"The company is coming to-morrow: the company is coming to-morrow."   We did not know
what she meant, but,' he added, with a twinkle
of fun, 'I know now.'   After some time a pleasant,
middle-aged woman came downstairs, saying that
her mother had awakened out of a deep sleep and
had insisted on her going down; 'for,' she said,
'the company has come.'   As soon as the heavy
rain became somewhat less, we quietly left the
cottage and went back to Salisbury.   Two days
later, on a glorious afternoon, we went again, carrying a hamper of good things for our hosts.   The
old labourer was leaning over his gate, and seemed
quite to expect us, and told us that his wife had
died the day before.

"After a long rambling walk through the woods,
we reached Hursley; we showed the church and
churchyard to the Hamiltons, ventured up into the
vicarage garden, had tea at the King's Head, and
then wandered back to Chandler's Ford, through
the Grotto wood and over Halsted common, in all
the stages of sunset light, and reached Salisbury in
summer darkness.

"A year or two ago, when Kitty was with us,
Miss Yonge asked us to let her know when we
were coming, in order that she might 'renew
old times' with us in the woods.   She met us
at Chandler's Ford station and walked with us to

' Cuckoo Bushes ' and the ' steep stony hill ' ; but distances were rather long for her, and after a good rest and chat amongst the ferns and the heather, she found her way back to Otterbourne across Cranbury Park."

" Last year my father and mother distinctly went down in strength. A long illness of Walter's made them anxious, but the Bishop's wonderful elasticity of mind enabled him to go on with his work, though he has had to share his confirmations with Bishop Abraham ; my mother, herself over seventy, became less able to go about, and is now completely laid aside on her sofa, scarcely ever leaving her sitting-room. Much has fallen upon Alice, both outside and inside the house.

" My father is eighty years old this year, but often when he dreads the fatigue of confirmations beforehand he finds himself the better for going. He has gradually had to drop some of his extra diocesan duties ; he left the Revision company after going twice through the New Testament, and so, to his sorrow, missed the third and final revision. His journeys to Town are fewer, and are only undertaken when some important division comes on. He has had to give up going to the early Celebrations in Cathedral, and this year he has not been able to administer at the Altar-rail, being unable to trust his feet on the slippery tiles : this has been a great loss to us, for regularly every Sunday for years his sons and daughters have felt his hand rest on their heads at the solemn moment of administration. But he is as bright as ever, interesting himself in everything and reading every book that comes to the house. He comes briskly out of his study, calling out in his bright voice, ' Is there any Christian here to speak to ? ' and then walking up and down between Alice at her bureau at one end of the drawing-room working

for the ' Friendless Girls ' and Edith at her ' office '
deep in G.F.S. correspondence at the other end
(to such has the family come), discusses whatever
topic is in his mind, before going back to his sermon
or letters.

. " Our Bishop is longing to resign, but is stopped
by two things. First, a letter from the Archbishop prevents him from going forward; and
secondly, an unpleasant and lingering diocesan
lawsuit is in hand, and the Bishop does not think
it right to pass on the difficulty and the cruel
expense of it to another. It will not be settled
until next year, and may very probably entail the
loss of a thousand pounds."

From ARCHBISHOP BENSON

" LAMBETH PALACE, *Feb.* 29, 1884.

" MY DEAR AND REVERED LORD,
        " . . . I will only say that while the whole
Church and your loving friends sympathise with
every word you say, and feel that the overtaxing
of your strength is a sorrow to them, and that
your desire to lay down a burden which *humeri
non animus recusat* cannot but fret you, they still
desire that your withdrawal from an office, which
you so adorn as that we all share your honour,
may be for all our sakes postponed as long as it
properly and rightly can be. Aἱ πολιαί teach as
well as tongues.

" From London, of course, you are more than
excused.

" I look to George Ridding to organise both
simply and powerfully. And to affect the tone
of Nottingham very importantly with its strong
lay life.

" I have just had a most kind and gentle-hearted

letter from Walter, telling me of his engagement. We all hope it will be full of happiness to him. He does not say how he is. I trust he gets strong."

Home Letter

"George Ridding's appointment as Bishop of Southwell has been a great pleasure. He has been Headmaster for eighteen years, and his reign has been glorious. Both the external changes and internal reforms at Winchester have been very complete, and yet he has effected them with such loyalty to old traditions as only a lifelong Wyke-hamist could safely do. We, at least, realise how unusual it was for such a work to have been done from the midst of his predecessor's home without the smallest strain upon the most sensitive feelings. Though we know that Wykehamists will look upon all the years that went before him as dark ages, yet he is to us the brother who adopted our home as his own for seventeen years, and who has always trusted us absolutely to sympathise in all his doings at Winchester.

"He has undertaken a difficult task—a new diocese cut out of two older ones. We know partly what that means. The diocese of Salisbury had lost one county and gained a new one two episcopates before the present one, yet when my father came to the diocese the two counties of Dorsetshire and Wiltshire had not wholly coalesced.

"The consecration was on St. Philip and St. James' Day, at St. Paul's Cathedral, and, to every one's disappointment, our Bishop felt that he could not face the fatigue of being present."

From THE FATHER OF A WINCHESTER BOY

" DEAR DR. RIDDING,

"I am sure my best wishes and prayers will go with you to your exalted sphere of labour, where I hope your usefulness will be as great and as marked as it was at Winchester. It may be just a remote encouragement if I cite my own experience as to the power which a high and sacred position may exercise over those with whom its occupant is brought into relation and communion. For thirteen years I have been a member of the Salisbury Synod, and the periodical contact with the highly-cultured and well trained and disciplined mind of your predecessor has been of the most beneficial value to me. I feel I am morally better and intellectually wiser; far more ready to *weigh evidence* and to test conclusions, less rash and impulsive in discussion, than I was thirteen years ago. I have, literally, sat at the feet of our excellent Bishop and watched every movement and listened to every word, just as an earnest schoolboy would do to a loved and venerated teacher, and am ' a world the better for it.' "

From MISS YONGE

"OTTERBOURNE, 1884.

" . . . How little I thought when I met dear Joanna Patteson in your drawing-room that it was the last time I should see her! Fanny Patteson had come back, and is sure Joan knew and was thinking for others to the last. . . . I hope you are profiting by the splendid summer weather. I never knew a year of sweeter smells: the sheets of wild honeysuckle are quite amazing. . . ."

Another from MISS YONGE

" Many, many thanks for the beautiful little miniature of a holy life. I do think the last half-century must have been a period of saints, when we think of the many blessed ones we have known. Nothing so causes me to realise the ten thousand times ten thousand in the Revelation than the ' Bollandist Lives of Saints' in about 150 years, having got no further than C, and those only canonised Roman Catholic saints with their names recorded."

December 22, 1884, was the Golden Wedding-day—a bright, beautiful winter's day. When our mother came to breakfast in her sitting-room she found her wedding-dress laid out over the sofa upon which she was to lie all day. The dark green silk poplin in which she went away after her marriage and the old sable muff, still in perfect order, were hung up in her sight. These dresses had been put to most profane uses, and the younger members of the family chiefly knew them as the material of Henry VIII.'s best doublet and as clothing for Sir Walter Raleigh and others.

Flowers from friends poured in all day, until the house was as sweet as at a real wedding.

As she lay on her sofa, looking flushed and a little tearful, letters and presents came showering upon her, and the Bishop, taking his wife's hand, said, in his arch way, " Mary, will you marry me ? " She laughed merrily, but answered, " I am afraid I

have no choice." We gave them a standing gold
Iona cross, and the designer, being greatly interested by the commission, sent a congratulatory
letter himself. My father's letters included some
from friends of every date : Cardinal Manning
represented old Balliol days, and recalled " the
music and metaphysics with which my undergraduate wits were quickened." Bishop Charles
Wordsworth sent congratulatory Latin verses.
The Headmaster of Winchester (Dr. Fearon) and
Wykehamists of all dates, as well as diocesan
friends, etc., remembered the day.

Fearing lest there should be any anxiety about
preparations, we said nothing beforehand as to a
family gathering for the occasion. Kitty and
Henry Barter were staying with us, and by noon
George, Esther, and Georgie Keble, Emily and
Willy Awdry, and Johnnie and Carrie had walked
in. During luncheon Dora and Charles Martin
and Walter arrived, and the parents' pleasure was
complete when, later in the afternoon, the door
opened and Maggie and Charles Awdry and
Robert appeared. My mother then revealed what
her suspicions had been, and said to us quietly,
" I was wondering where you were going to put
them all."

At tea-time the drawing-room was arranged
for a reception, and Dean Boyle and other friends
came in. A wedding-cake, with the initials and
dates 1834-1884, stood on the table, and the bride,
obedient to orders, put the knife into it, and then

deputed a son to finish cutting it.   All the servants
of the house and grounds, and every old servant
who was within reach, came and shook hands with
the parents and joined our party, whilst the
Cathedral choristers, clustering round the piano,
sang " Auld lang syne " ; then, not wishing any
one to break down, we told the choristers to sing
Christmas carols.

The evening was very quiet, but charming.
The brothers and sisters were so glad to meet one
another ; some had not met for years.   Groups
of threes or fours carried on separate conversations,
with occasional outbursts of general merriment.
It was so hopeless when the mothers took to com-
paring notes about their children, each believing
her own to be the most beautiful and perfect, but
too polite to confess it honestly.   In the absence
of the children, the fathers and mothers found
themselves relegated to their old places in the
family, and were chaffed in the manner of twenty
or thirty years before.   My mother, who had not
been into Chapel for some time, was well wrapped
up and almost carried up the stairs for evening
prayers, which were offered by a very large congregation.   The Bishop was clearly enjoying the
service greatly, and delighting in hearing the full
chorus of his children again in the hymn " The
King of Love my Shepherd is."   He was singing
the tenor part himself, gazing meanwhile with
his dim eyes at the dark east window opposite
him.

"We had a glorious meeting of all the brothers and sisters ; they kept coming in by various trains all day. The Dean was in the room when the last party arrived. He was very much impressed by the numbers, and said he would not have missed the gathering for anything. In one way it was good that you were abroad and not here ; for when Papa grew agitated over the meeting, we said, ' But we are not *all* together, for Edward is away.'"

"*Dec. 29, 1884.*

" Emily and Willy Awdry have been here to say a long goodbye,—for seven months. Who can say where we shall be then ? They sail on Thursday for Gibraltar and Bombay. Edith and Annie, Johnnie and Carrie, have gone to Bitton for Walter's wedding to-morrow. I trust they will get through the day without snow. Alice starts to join them at 6 a.m. to-morrow. I suppose you have heard what a wonderful day we had on the 22nd ; besides the immense pleasure of having eleven of our children and six sons and daughters in law with us, we were quite taken by surprise and almost overpowered by the numbers of letters and gifts from so many unexpected quarters. Amongst others, the Mayor of Winchester sent a handsome four-faced clock, with a pretty letter. . . ."

From G. MOBERLY

" *May 3, 1885*

"My DEAREST GEORGE,

" . . . . I sit down to write to you on Sunday, while I wait for Annie to take me to church for Holy Communion, wishing to speak a few loving words at the present critical time of my life, which

is probably the beginning of the last stage of a long
and varied prosperity, now drawing very near, but
how near I cannot tell, to the end.   For I have
made up my mind to resign my Bishopric, and
several reasons unite to fix upon the last days of
June in the present year as the days on one of
which I propose to take the step of writing to the
Archbishop.

" My life has been very long and prosperous ;
from one step of undeserved promotion to another
it has carried me from one resignation to another,
till none remains except to go home and be no more
seen upon the earth. . . . .

" I do not wish to be flatteringly spoken of when
I am gone. . . . . I desire nothing but the tears
and sorrow of my own people, and the acceptance
in Christ my Lord. . . .

" I have resigned my Fellowship of Balliol, my
Headmastership, my Fellowship of Winchester, my
Canonry (of Chester), and now I am about to
resign my Bishopric, and then my body to the
earth, and my soul to Him Who gave it.

" Lord Jesus ! give me Faith, Hope, and Love,
and cleanse me of all my sins.   God bless you all,
my boys and girls, and bring us all together to the
Invisible Home for Christ's sake.

" Your loving Father,
" GEORGE SARUM."

ANNIE'S STORY

" During the spring of 1885 my father was
perfectly well, but very feeble.   He did his business
at home, only glad of our help in talking when
he felt too tired to carry on conversations with
strangers ; anything with the sound of an argument
in it wearied him at once ; yet at times he would
talk eagerly.   I remember that one of the last

Sunday afternoons Sir George Grove came in full of the interest excited by one of the psalms sung in Cathedral ; talking, in his bright way, he began criticising the Revised Version rather fiercely. The Bishop reminded him that he had been one of the Revision company ; and, sending for his Greek Testament, dilated with great earnestness on some of the important and most interesting improvements. It was a long and first-rate discussion on both sides ; and afterwards Sir George said to us, ' What a magnificent mind it is : how clear and keen ! ' And, to a friend, later on, Sir George said, ' I never saw a greater combination of dignity and fatherliness ; had I been alone, I should have knelt down and asked for his blessing.'

" On Sundays I came out of church to wheel him to the Cathedral for the Communion Service. Leaving the chair in the cloister and supporting him on my arm, I took him to a seat close to the Bishop's throne. At last he had to be helped up and down from his knees ; though he had to hold my hand for support, he always stood for the Gloria in Excelsis.

" My room was near his dressing-room ; and opening my door in some alarm on hearing a loud voice, I have heard him repeat (evidently in prayer), the name of each of his children, grandchildren, and servants, down to the smallest kitchen-maid. As he became unable to hear all the conversation at meals, he became very silent ; but when any old friend, or son, or chaplain came, he enjoyed a good conversation on any subject— political, historical, literary, or theological ; and to the last there was a delicate raciness about his words, or the way in which he turned his sentences, which was all his own.

" The newspapers had constant announcements of his resignation during the last two or three years, giving the impression that he as often changed his mind.   It was not so : he told Bishop Kelly that he should be glad of his help until 'the end of June ' : he told his butler that he would not be required after June 30th.   As it happened, he never heard the cost of the law-suit, which was the event for which he was waiting.

" At the Trinity ordination the Bishop saw the candidates separately, as usual.   Afterwards he said to us, ' I have not been able to speak to them as I wished, but they have been very kind and have sat by me, and have talked so gently to *me*.'   One of these young clergymen told us that it had been most impressive to sit by the side of the old Bishop, visibly fading away, and that such words as he had said then could never be forgotten.

" A few weeks before the end Canon Warburton from Winchester came to tea, and had a long chat about that Cathedral.   My father spoke of all the corners and different beautiful little pieces of carving in detail, and told old stories of the people he remembered, such as Dean Rennell, Dr. Nott, and others.   He broke out with delight at the recollection of the statue of Bishop North in the Lady Chapel—the kneeling attitude, and the delicacy of the work—' so that you can see the old fingers trembling with age as he holds them together in prayer '; and as he spoke he put his own hands together and was unconscious that they too were evidently held there with difficulty.

" On Sunday, June 28th, my father became a little confused in his words, and was not able to go to church.   The moment the afternoon service was over, Edith came to his study and said that the anthem had been Martin's ' Whosoever dwelleth under the defence of the Most High.'   The Bishop caught up the words and repeated them again and

again, and made us say them to him. That was
the keynote of the last week. Later, that afternoon, Alice and Edward went out for a walk, and
Edith left us in order to read to the choristers in the
garden, so I sat with our invalid in the window,
where he felt the air on his head. The choristers
were running about the field, and every now and
then a boy's merry laugh was heard. My father
smiled and said, ' The laughing of boys is a very
familiar sound to me.' After a long silence he said,
as to himself, with a sigh, ' I bless my children, but
I wish for their blessing. I need it very much.' I
answered, ' We do bless you, for our happy home,
and for the heavenly things that you have taught
us.' He started at the sound of my voice, but
turned and gave me a sweet look as though
listening to unexpected words.

June 30th was to be the day of resignation ; but
it was obvious that there was no need for such
an effort to be made, and no one mentioned it.
Whether he remembered it or not, we never knew,
for on this day he broke down entirely. He was
very restless, constantly asking us to put him on
his knees, where he prayed aloud at my mother's
knee like a little child, saying earnestly to each
person coming into the room, ' He will defend us
under His wings.' The doctor, arriving in a hurry,
had him put to bed. The rest revived him, and the
next day he refused to stay in bed, declaring that
it would be waste of time, and when he came down
he was ready to talk over all the usual subjects of
interest, and asked for political news.

" On July 2nd there was no further question
about getting up, for he was weak and confused,
and we sent for all the brothers and sisters (in
England), who arrived in the course of the next
two days. In the intervals of consciousness our
father was delighted to recognise one and another.

We heard prayers, psalms, collects, creeds, rapidly repeated, and long recitations of Greek poetry, which we tried to identify as Pindar ; but there was no time for even the shortest celebration of the Holy Communion, for his waking moments only lasted long enough for him to open his eyes, look round to see who was with him, smile brightly, murmuring a few words, of which the most constant were, ' Preserve thy body and soul—everlasting life,' coupled with one of our names, and then fall into deep sleep again.

" There being no specific illness, and the hot weather allowing all the windows and doors to stand open, we could all go freely in and out of the room, and no one liked to lose the chance of a greeting. His jewelled prayer-book (given him by an old Wykehamist) lay open on the bed, and whenever he began to struggle for the words of a psalm, whichever son or daughter happened to be nearest at the moment immediately read it aloud to him. Bishop Kelly came in and blessed him, but it was during a period of sleep. Dr. Phillips Brooks and a party of Americans called ; and remembering our father's interest in his American visitors, George and I showed them the gallery of bishops' portraits in the drawing-room and told them the present circumstances of the family.

" On Sunday morning he looked ill and we were all called ; but there was another revival, and as the pulse grew stronger many of us ventured to the early Celebration in the Cathedral. When we returned he said quite strongly, ' I should like some prayers,' but sleep overtook him before more than a psalm could be said. The joyful songs seemed to be uppermost in his mind, he murmured ' Sing unto the Lord,' Edward, O be joyful in the Lord.' About 2 p.m. he looked up and round, recognised my mother, then, resting his eye on Robert, he exclaimed with great joy, ' Robert ! ' He immediately closed his eyes, and never opened them or spoke again.

" We watched in silence. When the bell rang for service, the ' Bishop's chorister ' came as usual to fetch him to Cathedral, passing under the open window with careful step to avoid making any sound on the gravel walk. From the room we heard the organ accompanying all the services, the chanting, the hymns, his favourite anthem (Stainer's ' Lead, kindly light ') with its cry at the end :

> ' And with the morn those angel faces smile
> Which I have loved long since and lost awhile.'

" The great fugue of Bach's, played as a voluntary, pealed out and came floating into the silent room ; he lay in calm, untroubled stillness, his brow becoming more and more placid and the expression loftier and grander every moment—only the dear mouth open with panting. The air was full of the scent of roses from the garden. The servants, one after another, crept in, gazed for a few minutes and then stole softly away.

" The lovely summer night came on again. Those of us who had ventured to go and rest for a time had joined the watching company by 4 a.m. I remember the look of the dawn breaking, and the sky gradually brightening behind the spire into full daylight, and the feeling of the fresh morning air. What a glorious summer morning it was ! The birds in full chorus, the sweet flowers, the colour of the blue sky ! The morning psalms were ' Heaviness may endure for a night, but joy cometh in the morning.' At 8 a.m. my mother was called ; she greeted the messenger with, ' Oh, I am so glad.' When the last, almost impercep-

19

tible, sigh came, Robert led the 'Nunc Dimittis'; this was the signal for the entire household to enter the room and join in the 'Te Deum,' at the end of which George pronounced the Blessing. So he went forth with the blessing of all his children, which he had asked for just a week before.

"Every member of the family went in turn and kissed his hand and forehead, and Edith placed a 'Souvenir d'un ami' rose on his shoulder."

From DEAN CHURCH

"THE DEANERY, ST. PAUL'S, *July* 7, 1885.

"MY DEAR GEORGE,

"Thank you for writing to me. Yes, the shock is greater than I expected, now it is come. He has been so long a part, and a large part, of my world that the world seems different without him. No one knows, no one knew, not even he, how much all that I am, and can do, and can hope for, I owe to him. You know something ; but he was the person who opened my dull eyes, and put a high reality of character and purpose before them, and made me feel the difference between narrowness and manliness, between the mere shell and letter of religion and its living truth.

"You will give my love, and all our loves, to your mother. Of course I hope to be at Salisbury on Friday."

MISS YONGE'S STORY

"I always said that Mrs. Moberly was like Early English architecture, and thus it seemed in the perfect fitness of things to see her under the shadow of Salisbury Cathedral. The glorious spire, grey yet sunshiny, against blue sky and clouds ; the

falcons swooping round it, and beneath the fresh
green of the garden, and especially of the delicate
weeping birch, are pictures to live in one's mind.
And the cloister, with its lights and shades, and
the quiet resting-place in the midst is a lovely
thing ! And yet the Cathedral could only be a
second love to old Winchester. One gets through
it so much sooner, as we found when we tried to
go round it, than we used when we went round the
massive old edifice, the growth of ages, whereas
Salisbury always seems to me as if it might be a
sort of petrified iceberg grown up in a night. At
the first arrival of the family the Cathedral was in
a state of restoration, so there was all the interest
of progress.

" The Palace is a strange house of broad stairs
and long passages, the great drawing-room a huge
place, with three doors and three enormous windows, but charming ones—one looking on the spire,
one over the garden, one across the paddock and
pond to the green hill ; not an atom of town to
be seen. The north and west ones always full of
choice plants, among which may specially be remembered the delicate iris.

" Dusty and fusty was that big room at first,
but it must be confessed that the shading of the
dust in the corner of the ceiling, totally undis-
turbed, was so softly graduated that if one had
not known it to be sheer dirt one would have
called it admirable. And there hung all the
Bishops, each generation apparently requiring a
larger portrait than the last — Seth Ward, and
Brian Duppa, and self-complacent Burnet, and he
of whom it is averred that he killed three wives
by never contradicting them, and the two Church
champions, Denison and Hamilton. Over the fire-
place was the peculiarly hideous portrait of poor
good George III. in the robes of the Garter. But

his red bluff face and white feathers recall many a delightful association! The room became thoroughly home-like and characteristic with all the dear old properties — the emu's egg set in silver, the piano, the well-known chairs, and the tables loaded with all the books one wanted to read, and the special corners for conversation by the fireside—one delightfully situated between the hearth and the Bishop's arm-chair, a nook for a daughter to nestle in and be caressed. The easy-chair on the other side was a place for all sorts of discussions, from the Revision to the last joke! Metaphorically, one sat at his feet, really in an easy-chair by his side. The times for the Revision talk were chiefly after Prayers in the Chapel, when the Lesson was read from the copy printed in anticipation. He would explain the reasons of alteration, answer moans over the alterations of familiar expressions, and dwell on the new lights cast by the criticism. I am grieved not to re-collect more of the details of these talks, much as I valued them.

"Mrs. Moberly's chair was on the other side, and there were many delightful conversations with her. The *good* times were the lingering after break-fast, sometimes a space before and after the early dinner, the five-o'clock tea, and the evening. The Bishop would discuss any kind of subject, with special appreciation of anything humorous, such as the case of the semi-cracked individual who sowed an opprobrious attack on his curate in mustard and cress. The noon meal and the twilight one were much resorted to by clergy, deaconesses, and visitors on all sorts of errands.

"There were state dinner-parties, of course, from time to time, and in the summer a very large garden-party. 'You cannot think how we all look forward to this' said a little old lady to me at one which had been threatened by a thunderstorm and was given under difficulties.

" Alice and Edith soon had their hands full of work. West Harnham and chorister boys were Edith's vocation, also G.F.S. ; whilst Alice was principal helper and nurse to her mother, and busy as to Friendless Girls. Annie was deep in books, played the piano, and unconsciously prepared herself for her future work. Maggie flitted about in silence, filled up gaps, found whatever was wanting, quotation or reference, and was a dignified little household fairy.

" The diminished numbers at home made the old habits of fun, games, and habitual merriment gradually die out, though animation and playfulness never ceased for a moment. Selwyn's death brought a certain twilight, taking away the element of boyhood, and Maggie's marriage removed the most youthful member of the party remaining. Yet the general characteristics were untouched— full of interest in everything, tender kindness, cheerfulness, keen bright wit as brilliant as ever, but more guarded and less incisive, and always, as ever, the devotion which had been lifelong.

" Peace and devotion grew with the increasing feebleness of the outward man, and, so gently that the stages do not mark themselves, were the bonds loosed till the good white head was laid low, and one of the most precious of friendships closed for this life."

CHAPTER X

MARY ANNE MOBERLY

In la sua volontade è nostra pace :
Ella è quel mare al qual tutto si muove.
Paradiso, Cant. vii.

Life ! we've been long together
Through pleasant and through cloudy weather ;
'Tis hard to part when friends are dear—
Perhaps 'twill cost a sigh, a tear ;
Then steal away, give little warning,
    Choose thine own time ;
Say not Good Night,—but in some brighter clime
    Bid me Good Morning.

MRS. BARBAULD.

AFTER Count Campello had first seen my mother in 1886, he exclaimed with enthusiasm, "È bellissima, nobilissima, santissima," adding "Ha il paradiso nel viso." This description did not seem to us greatly exaggerated.

As a girl she had been called "The Beauty of Naples," and until she was quite old few people saw her for the first time without speaking of her beauty. She was near seventy when Prof. William Richmond came to Salisbury to paint my father's portrait. He was much interested in seeing *his* father's picture of my mother, and desired very much to see her ; but she was ill and he had to wait. One day he came into the drawing-room just as she, in a fit of shyness, was hurrying out of another door ; unfortunately for her, she dropped her ball of knitting-wool, and he, guessing who it must be, raced across the room to pick it up, and said to us, " Yes, she is lovely." Mrs. Cooke Trench wrote, " She will always be to me a sort of vision of grace and beauty ; I can never remember not thinking her the most beautiful person I ever knew." The strong religious life which softened her natural grave severity of character and raised her delight in beautiful things to the level of worship, so that her very appearance was as a temple adorned for the honour and glory of God, gave her a queenliness which was unique. A friend writes : " It grieves me to think that I shall not meet her again until the next world, and how beautiful she will be ! There are some people who seem so fitted for that world—as beautiful and noble ladies at court—and she was one. Some have so much to learn first, but she was so very gracious and full of good and true thoughts and deeds." Highly nervous and easily fidgeted as she was at little occurrences, such as the dropping of crumbs on the carpet, the blowing out candles, or carrying the ink to unsafe resting-places, etc., yet no one was more proof against real trouble and sorrow ; such things lifted her at once into the world of spiritual realities ; silent and almost tearless she was then as strong as a rock.

So it was when her widowhood came to her, and Mary Moberly had to leave the Palace and its grounds for a house in a dull street. We saw her countenance change when she first realised that she would never see moonlight again unmixed with gas, but she said not a word. She spent her days lying on the sofa, too infirm to move about the house; and the dust and glare from the street, the perpetual passing of heavy omnibuses, and the screaming of street children playing for hours together under her window, were a far heavier trial to her than they would have been to a less sensitive person. At the Palace the large trees full of rooks, the roses and French honeysuckle round her windows, and the constant rippling of the fountain, reminding her of the Palazzo in Genoa, seemed the more natural setting for her.

During those four and a half years of bodily pain her life was as busy as ever; neither sight nor hearing failed her; if she was not busy with her fingers, working or writing, she was reading. She studied the newspapers carefully, taking the warmest interest in political and Church matters. This activity of mind made her most interesting to talk to. She did not intend to be behind the times where she could at all sympathise with modern thought; and when a daughter had to do with the Higher Education of Women at Oxford, she inquired into all the details of the life and work in order to judge the question fairly.

This readiness to be converted to fresh opinions,

always difficult to old people, was seen in her increasing interest in schemes for helping friendless girls. Perhaps no living person had ever been more averse to approaching such a subject. Sensitive in the highest degree to the hatefulness of women knowing enough of the subject to be able to carry out organised help, and keenly distressed to think that in order to lessen the terrible evil an association would have to be formed involving talk about it, yet in her old age the whole force of her religious reality rose above her almost overwhelming prejudice—prejudice which, in her, amounted to a passion for such exaggeration of refinement, as would have made her prefer to live in an unreal world rather than hear of what was unlovely and unedifying. In 1881 my mother was informing herself as to the needs of Salisbury in respect to the subject, and she called together a committee of ladies to consult as to ways and means, with the result that St. Michael's Home in Salisbury was started as a shelter to which girls could be taken on the moment, either from the streets or from unsafe surroundings. The experience gained by this means showed that the work to be effective should be more widely spread ; and the Synod, taking up the subject, asked her, as head of the local committee, to create a Diocesan Association for the care of Friendless Girls. This was done in 1882, and the report of its work was made biennially to the Synod. In 1886 she wrote an address to

be read at the local committee, expressing her
thankfulness that God had raised up helpers in the
great work " which *only* pure-minded women could
do," with words of encouragement and practical
counsel.   A lady in the diocese, who afterwards
took a leading part in the work, wrote :

" You told me of your mother's ardent wish that
something should be organised to shelter and save
poor friendless girls.   There she was, so calm and
lovely in countenance, so anxious for the work, so
clear as to details of what must and what must not
be done, all so thought out in her clear quiet head,
and that impression of pure quiet power has always
been renewed whenever I have seen her."

Her friends at a distance perhaps knew her
best ; for she could pour herself out in a letter as
she could not do in their presence.   When her
children went out into life, they seemed to discover
her from her long letters, which were made as perfect as everything else about her.   It was touching
to see how, as she grew older, the former difficulty
of showing demonstrative affection passed away.
She made it her business to know all the interests
of her 21 sons and daughters and 35 grandchildren.
She expected the mothers of the different families
to keep her informed of all that was going on.   She
reminded us of Caroline Perthes, who liked her
daughters to " fill their letters with turnips and
cabbages," that she might follow them in their
daily lives.   Thus her interests became those of
the second and third generations ; and she knew at

what stage each grandchild had arrived, and what would be the appropriate book or ornament to send them. She was very anxious that they should all think a great deal of cultivation of mind, and she used to save up her money to supply them at Christmas with such books as would be helpful and yet prove attractive. In this way she became a very real presence in the hearts of the said grandchildren; and it was no wonder that her married daughters and daughters-in-law loved to come and receive her hearty sympathy in their anxieties.

The first great sorrow of her widowed life was the sudden death, from pleurisy, of Walter's wife, two months after her confinement. A week before, Walter and Mary had been staying at Salisbury, and he brought the baby straight back to our mother. How her whole heart went out to Walter and his little motherless girl![1]

Bishop John Wordsworth helped my mother to keep up her interest in external things by coming in on Sunday afternoons and telling her Diocesan and Convocation news. He sometimes made use of her knowledge of Italian by getting her to translate letters from persons connected with the Italian Church Reform movement, and bringing them to visit her. By this means she made several interesting new acquaintances, who corresponded with her from Italy, and told her of foreign Church affairs.

But her greatest interest was in our own Church

[1] Mildred Agnes Moberly.

work abroad : she had large personal acquaintance with the workers in all parts of the world, for many missionaries and American churchmen had haunted Hursley vicarage, and she had entertained many, year after year, at the Palace.   At the Pan-Anglican Synod of 1888 a large number of bishops were staying with Bishop and Mrs. Wordsworth, and many came to call upon her.   Very much surprised were they at her intimate knowledge of their dioceses ;   several of them compared notes in our drawing-room when they came out of her sitting-room.   " It is astonishing to me," said one, " that Mrs. Moberly knows all my stations and the names of all my workers."   " It was just the same with me," added another from a different quarter of the globe ;   " she knows all about *my* diocese."   We knew that as long as we could remember, she had diligently read her missionary magazines on a Sunday evening.   She had never omitted this little bit of duty, with the result that she could be turned to, as to an old friend, for encouragement and sympathy.

On coming back from the Mission Festival in 1888, we found her radiant, for in our absence the Bishop of Minnesota (Whipple), " the Apostle of the Indians," looking like an Indian himself, with his hawk-like face and long straight black hair, had come in to see her.   He did not know her before, but said that he could not leave Salisbury without telling her that " The Great Forty Days " had been a turning-point in his religious life at a very critical time. He did not stay a minute, as he was on his way to the station ; but, she said, "he just flew in like a great bird and blessed me, and then flew out again."

Many old friends passed away during these waiting years, but the news seldom came as sorrow. Bishop Eden of Moray and Ross, the friend of her girlhood, was one, and Mr. Robert Wilson of Rownhams, for so many years curate to Mr. Keble, was another. From him she received earnest words of farewell, "to you, who before all others made me feel that in College Street and at the Palace I had a sort of home."

At this time these family records were sent to Miss Yonge to read, and she returned them with the following words :

"I am exceedingly enjoying those dear old times. It is such a living over again of the dear golden age of our lives. I have made a few notes in pencil. . . . I quite dreaded the first wedding. I keep it for my last hour before going to bed. I think I must put in when all the children were found on the landing killing Oliver Cromwell ; and Alice mourning for the *beauty* of the old Hursley church. It was strange to be reading it just at the passing of almost the last of the friends of those good old times. I wonder if I shall see any of your people at Rownhams to-morrow ? There is the earthly farewell to a very long precious friendship. I was a growing girl when Mr. Wilson was Hursley curate, all fun and brightness, and my father was so fond of him. Did you know that when he accepted the curacy at Hursley he was told that he must make up his mind to its being the prevention of all promotion ? and you see that the canonry of Salisbury was all he ever had. . . ."

From ALICE

" Oct. 1888.

". . . Yes, I went to Rownhams yesterday— Mrs. Sidney Lear and I. There had been an early Celebration in the church, so that we went to church without any fuss : they said that all the village came to the early service, and it was like an Easter Communion. There was no such crowding of flowers as to feel artificial, and the church was very full when we went in. I found Emily there, and Harry, and Johnnie and Carrie had walked over from Basset : Miss Yonge joined us. Afterwards our own special party lingered together in the churchyard, joined by Lady Heathcote, Charlie, Ellie, and Be. Heathcote. It did feel strange—just the remnants of that noble party which we knew so well in old days ; but it was so gentle and so quietly cheerful—a grey afternoon with lovely gleams of sunshine and a golden line of light over the dark blue distant woods. Nothing could have been more fitting. . . ."

During the last summer of her life my mother had the pleasure of almost daily visits from her old friend, Mrs. George Augustus Selwyn,[1] who had taken lodgings in Salisbury. Many happy and merry chats they had over days too old for our recollection, and helping one another to remember things that had happened before either were married, when Mrs. Selwyn was Miss Sarah Richardson, living in Russell Square and going in

---

[1] Widow of Bishop Selwyn, of New Zealand and Lichfield.

and out of Judge Park's house. How merrily my mother laughed at being told that, after a famous archery party at Stourhead, to which she (fresh from Italy) was taken by Mrs. Bennett, accompanied by her brother, Mr. Moberly, old Mrs. Hobhouse, on driving home, had said to her daughters and to Miss Richardson, " Now, girls, mark my words, that's a match! " And then Mrs. Selwyn reminded her of her having thought them all "*so* plain in England, and the gentlemen *so* rude! "

Mrs. Selwyn wrote to us six months later:

" I am not sure that I did not see your dear mother at Leghorn in her childhood ; that is misty, but not so my remembrance of her in her beautiful girlhood both in London and in Somersetshire. My lifetime in New Zealand made a suspension, but not a severance, of many friendships. I am more glad than I can say to have seen her again in her as beautiful old age, and to have enjoyed so much sweet and profitable intercourse with her. I followed you all on Saturday to that perfect resting-place where her mortal part awaits the Resurrection : it must have been so lovely and all so entirely in keeping in its holiness, in 'its quiet, and in its beauty, with her and with the occasion. . . ."

Miss Yonge came constantly to see her; and her visits were much looked forward to, with the eager, cheery discussions on all subjects, from high concerns of Church and State to ghosts : for my mother's Scotch nature responded to such a subject, and both laid by any specially interesting story with which to regale the other. Mr. Frederick Myers had been one of our many visitors in Winchester days, and he had caused her to become a member of the Society for Psychical Research in its early days; but, owing to my father's intense dislike of what he called "the ghost society," she relinquished it, and did not take in any of its writings. I am bound to say such ghostly talks as my mother and Miss Yonge indulged in more often ended in fun than in seriousness. Miss Yonge wrote:

"One can only thank God for the beautiful, holy vision that your 'sweet mamma' has been to me all these fifty years or so—the looking-up friendship which was so precious. There has been no presence for a long time more sweet and blessed to me; and that last summer I specially enjoyed, when it had come to be almost the *bien-être* of relationship, and all redolent of old times. . . . Well, I don't think there can be much to alter in her on the other side of the door of Paradise. How blessed to have two such lives to dwell upon! . . ."

So passed the years of waiting; the long days often weary with wearing pain, yet full of the interests which her own diligent sympathy had created for her. After thirty years of racket in the midst of public school cares, and sixteen in the centre of diocesan work; having seen fifteen children grow up, constantly devoting herself to their necessities,—she rested. Placed a little on one side, where she could still enjoy much, she never allowed herself to stagnate or be out of touch with her surroundings. Neither blind nor deaf, she still ruled the house. Often she would ring her handbell and call one of us: " I wanted you just to look at that beautiful light on the spire "; or, " What have you been doing this afternoon, and what are you reading now ? "

Her room was a bower of ferns and flowers, the golden wedding-cross was on her table with the jewelled prayer-book beside it, and a little silver box of potpourri was at hand to smell from time to time. The walls were covered with modern sketches of Genoa and Naples, of the homes of her sons and daughters, and with photographs of children and grandchildren in all stages of existence. Truly she was still the queen bee of a large household. Whenever we returned home from distant visits, we realised afresh that our mother had surrounded herself, almost unconsciously, with an atmosphere of spiritual fragrance that we never found elsewhere in the same degree. " I felt," said Lady ——, " on going into her room as one does on entering a beautiful church—as if all the rush and worry of daily life could never come near that calm, patient saint." But it was a great mistake to suppose that the calmness was the result of ignorance of cares and worries. She heard of and shared in them all ; the secret was that she turned everything into prayer and high communing with God.

20

She was delighted with " Crossing the Bar," which Miss Fanny Wilbraham, the dear friend and correspondent of forty years, had copied for her with her blind eyes.   In return mamma sent a long letter of thanks for

" the truly lovely lines which could hardly be read for tears, and yet so beautiful and comforting in their depth of meaning, for one especially who has to the margin come and waits her call to rest.   I too hope to learn them by heart and to add them to my store of treasures for a possible time when I may be unable to read, and yet able to think and remember."

The letter touched on family interests, the anxieties of George Ridding " and his Laura " about the distressing poverty of too many of the North Derbyshire clergy, the position of Spanish and Portuguese affairs, the deaths of Dr. Döllinger, Robert Browning, and Bishop Lightfoot, showing the range of her thoughts and daily interests at that time.

For some reason, Miss Wilbraham sent this letter to Lord Tennyson.   Mr. Hallam Tennyson, in returning it, wrote, " He was greatly touched by the letter and the account of Mrs. Moberly that you sent.   It quite broke him down as I read about her.   He is thankful that his lines were a comfort to her on her death-bed."   A few days later Lord Tennyson asked for a copy of her words, which was sent to him.

When she was known to be ill, her table became more crowded with flowers than ever—so much so that the doctor remarked that she must have had a birthday ; and two funny little notes of condolence arrived, enclosing violets, from two small grandsons at their first schools.[1]   Highly characteristic was the independence of mind which declined to look forward to sending for any clergyman should no son be at hand.   " I have thought so much and prayed so much, it would be unreal to me.   I am always praying, and should feel him outside of my prayers."   She asked to be prayed for in Cathedral, saying, " I don't like that sort of thing," meaning the publicity of it, " but think it is right."   Her last Celebration, a few days before, was at Walter's hands ; she liked to remember that she had last seen him with his hand raised in blessing.

The influenza, so much dreaded for her, came with bronchitis to complicate it.   It was not an acute attack, and her children had not been summoned.   But the vitality was gone which could have resisted it, and on February 6th, 1890, when she was thought to be better, she suddenly sank and died before the absent sons and daughters could reach home.

Her last effort had been to take a long look at my father's picture, which she always did when roused to take her food.   She had been repeating to herself the Good Friday hymn, beginning :

" And now, belovèd Lord, Thy Soul resigning
Into Thy Father's arms with conscious will,
Calmly, with reverend grace, Thy Head inclining,
The throbbing Brow, and labouring Breast grow still."

[1] Captain Bertrand Richard Moberly ; Rev. William Keble Martin.

Her last words were to George, who offered to say some prayers ; something she said of which the words " dear boy " alone were audible. She followed the first prayer, and then, so quietly that at first no one could say whether she was gone or not, she had flown away.

As a beautiful bride she lay through those days, covered with her wedding dress of nearly sixty years before, its old tawny whiteness contrasting with the snowdrops and lilies of the valley that were scattered on it. " Truly," as her friend wrote, " from the first time I saw her, nearly fifty years ago, with her baby on her knee, to my last look, there was no blemish of any kind ; and now, the fine Gold has received its final purification, and reflects perfectly the image of the Refiner."

INDEX

093330011

Printed by Hazell, Watson & Viney, Ld., London and Aylesbury.

ImTheStory.com

CPSIA information can be obtained at www.ICGtesting.com
Printed in the USA
BVOW05s1111060514

352713BV00022B/1358/P